n nn finden das [illegible] in die-

Ansicht, lieber [illegible]

auch wir [illegible] ein gutes geseg-

vielmals, Misse Liesel, [illegible]

eln tausendmal [illegible]

[illegible]

Tante

e lieben Wünsche

l. Clärli beglückt – ein

immer recht trübseelig –

Nachricht hat uns

stimmte Gefühl, dass

mein Enkelkinderl

amm gehalten hat

rat, ob es ein Bub

Falls Ihr Augen mal

[illegible] hätte, [illegible]

Barbara Borowiak

A Thousand Kisses

Mamina (Henriette Pollatschek), c. 1939

A Thousand Kisses

A GRANDMOTHER'S HOLOCAUST LETTERS

Translated and Edited by

Renata Polt

THE UNIVERSITY OF ALABAMA PRESS

Tuscaloosa and London

∞
The paper on which this book is printed meets the minimum requirements of American National Standard for Information Science–Permanence of Paper for Printed Library Materials, ANSI Z39.48-1984.

Library of Congress Cataloging-in-Publication Data

Pollatschek, Henriette, b. 1870.
A thousand kisses : a grandmother's Holocaust letters / translated and edited by Renata Polt.
p. cm. — (Judaic studies series)
Includes bibliographical references (p. 207).
ISBN 0-8173-0930-6
1. Pollatschek, Henriette, b. 1870—Correspondence. 2. Jews—Persecutions—Czech Republic. 3. Holocaust, Jewish (1939-1945)—Czech Republic—Personal narratives. 4. Czech Republic—Ethnic relations. I. Polt, Renata, 1932- II. Title. III. Series: Judaic studies series (unnumbered)
DS135.C95 P65 1999
940.53'18'094371—ddc21
98-9066

British Library Cataloguing-in-Publication Data available

JUDAIC STUDIES SERIES

Leon J. Weinberger, *General Editor*

To my mother,
and to the memory of
my grandmother
and my father

You have always been in others and you will remain in others. And what does it matter to you if later on that is called your memory? This will be you—the you that enters the future and becomes a part of it.

—Boris Pasternak, *Dr. Zhivago*

Contents

Illustrations

Acknowledgments

Many people helped bring *A Thousand Kisses* into being. My deepest thanks go to the following:

My mother, Elizabeth Polt, who kept the letters safe after my father's death and shared her memories of specific events and people, without which my task would have been immeasurably harder;

My husband and in-house computer guru, Fred Schmitt, who never failed to encourage me in my task while also providing the essential technical expertise;

My brother, John Polt, who remembered facts and looked up those he didn't remember and got library books and made contacts with other helpful people;

The members of my writing group—Sue Brown, Naomi Cavalier, Alice Wirth Gray, Mary Kent, Ellen McKaskle, Mollie Poupeney, Jane Strong, and Dorothy Stroup—who listened to portions of the manuscript week after week, lending their suggestions and encouragement;

My friends Nola Perla and Elizabeth and Peter Ryan, who read the manuscript through from top to bottom and urged me on with their enthusiasm;

My cousin Patricia Millward and her husband Richard, who read and commented and provided data;

And the folks at The University of Alabama Press: Curtis L. Clark, who recognized the manuscript's merits and put everything in motion for publication; Suzette Griffith, meticulous and thoughtful copyeditor; and the staff of the Editorial, Production, and Marketing Departments for their hard work throughout the publication process.

Introduction

"Mamina" was my family's name for my grandmother, Henriette Pollatschek, whose letters tell the story of this book. The accent is on the first syllable, and the vowels are all short; the name is a Czech nickname for "Mamma." It was a name she herself probably chose, as she was the only one of us who spoke Czech fluently.

Photographs reveal her to be a small, rather frail woman with high cheekbones and pronounced features. Since I was only six when I last saw her, my memories of her are childish ones: I remember her writing poems that she read or recited to me and her showing me the resemblance of fuchsia blossoms to twirling dancers. I have been told that Mamina was artistic, poetic, and good with her hands. She had, they said, "temperament." To me she seemed imaginative, playful, and yet somehow mysterious and slightly reserved.

Whereas Mamina was small, her daughter, my Tante (Aunt) Lene Fürth, was large-boned and tall. Though not conventionally pretty, she was renowned as a fashionable dresser and a captivating personality: When she entered a room, my mother said, people stopped talking and took notice. She, too, was known to be artistic; but since we did not often get to the Fürth home in nearby Nestersitz, Lene remains for me more a name than a person.

Both of my parents were born in Aussig, an industrial city in northern Bohemia whose population in 1930 was around forty-four thousand. My father was an attorney. We lived in comfort, if not luxury: skiing vacations in the winter, trips to the mountains in the summer, the usual number of domestic servants for people of the upper middle class at that time and place. Mamina, as mentioned, spoke Czech, as, to a lesser extent, did my father; my mother spoke a few words only, and at home, my parents, my brother and I spoke German.

From about the twelfth century, Germans as well as Czechs had lived in the border provinces of Bohemia. Aussig (in Czech, Ústí nad Labem

[Ústí on the Elbe]), had been predominantly German from at least the seventeenth century. The 1930 census showed the area around Aussig to be 80 to 90 percent German.

A much smaller, yet economically and culturally significant group, were the Jews, comprising, at an estimated three hundred thousand people, about 3 percent of Czechoslovakia's 1939 population. The earliest medieval Jewish communities in Czechoslovakia were formed in the Czech-speaking areas. In the second half of the nineteenth century, large numbers of Jews migrated to the industrial German-speaking areas. Since German was the primary language of the Austro-Hungarian Empire, of which until 1918, Czechoslovakia was a part, many of the new settlers saw learning the language as essential to economic success, while the Czech language and culture came to appear more limited and parochial. Therefore, despite the prevalence of anti-Semitism in the German-speaking lands, many Czechoslovakian Jews of Henriette Pollatschek's generation came to consider themselves Germans: In the census of 1930, 31 percent of Jews in Bohemia declared themselves to be German "by nationality" (some 46 percent declared Czech nationality, while about 20 percent claimed Jewish nationality), and German schools comprised 20 percent of the total. In 1930 Czechoslovakia, sixty-three daily newspapers were published in German (compared to fifty-three in Czech).

The Czechs had never been notably anti-Semitic, and when the Czechoslovak Republic was formed in 1918, religious and political liberty were guaranteed to all citizens. No significant organized political anti-Semitism existed until the rise of the pro-Nazi Sudeten German Party, and such anti-Semitism as there was, was directed mainly at the pro-German allegiances of many Jews. Yet these allegiances were not as clear-cut as some Czechs thought them: Franz Kafka is probably the most widely known German-speaking Czech Jew whose allegiance was both German and Czech, and whose Jewishness posed an identity problem that he never succeeded in resolving. In this complex self-identification, Kafka was by no means unique in Bohemia.

Still, on the whole, Jews, Czechs, and Germans lived peaceably together. Intermarriage between Jews and Gentiles was not uncommon (in 1931, for example, 32 percent of Bohemian Jewish men married Gentile women; a lesser number of Jewish women married Gentile men), and being Jewish was not considered a major handicap. But in the 1930s, the events in Germany and the rise of the Sudeten German Party forced Czech Jews to reconsider their position and to realize that to be German was not in their best interests. It was their fortune that the Czechs by and large forgave them their "Germanness"; that the Germans did not forgive them their Jewishness, however marginal, was their catastrophe.

In 1870, Henriette Heller was born into this fairly benign atmosphere of Austria-Hungary. She was the second of eight children of a substantial farmer and sugar-beet refiner in Hořice, a village in eastern Bohemia. In 1890 she married Hermann Pollatschek, director of the I. Petschek coal works in Aussig, and in 1898 they built the large house on Kroitzschgasse (Kroitzsch Street) in Aussig that was to become the family home for the next thirty-six years. Two sons, Hans and Willi, died during World War I—Hans in battle, Willi in the 1918 influenza epidemic. Daughter Helene (Lene), born in 1893, married Eugen Fürth, a paper manufacturer, and moved to nearby Nestersitz.

Son Friedrich, born in 1896, married Elisabeth (Liesel) Lederer in 1927; her father, a Jew, had converted to Lutheranism on marrying her mother, a Gentile. After Hermann Pollatschek's death in 1926, Friedrich and Liesel moved into the Kroitzschgasse house, which was remodeled to include a downstairs apartment for Henriette. In 1929 Friedrich and Liesel's son, Hans, was born, and in 1932 a daughter, Renate (this writer).

To all intents, my family was Protestant. My father, raised in some nominally Jewish way, had broken with religion altogether when he was about eighteen (because of a falling-out with the rabbi, he once told me, without elaborating). My brother and I were baptized Lutheran, though I can scarcely remember attending church. The fact is that nobody in the family took religion, of whatever denomination, seriously, with the exception of Mamina's brother, known as Onkel Fritz, who was an ardent convert to Catholicism. Lene and her family had also converted, but the change had apparently had little effect on their lives. So far as I know, Mamina had no special allegiance to Judaism: she converted to Catholicism in 1939, but her letters thereafter reveal that her Catholicism was also nominal. Of the family's friends, many were Jewish, some were not; none that I know of made any fuss about religion, their own or that of others. The Christian holidays—Christmas, Easter, and so forth—were routinely celebrated.

On May 22, 1938, my parents, my brother, and I went to Switzerland on vacation. After our return to Aussig on July 30, my parents became increasingly concerned with the rising Nazism both outside and inside the borders. Like all educated Czechoslovakians, they had been aware of the rise of Hitler's Nazi (National Socialist) party during the 1920s and 1930s. Nineteen thirty-eight saw the acceleration of the menace: The *Anschluss* (annexation) of Austria took place on March 13, and the following months saw an increase of anti-Semitic measures in Germany and Austria, such as the requirement for identity cards for Jews, the obligatory adoption by Jews of the "Jewish" names Sara or Israel as middle names, and the exclusion of Jews from the practice of medicine and law.

In Czechoslovakia, imitating their German mentors, the Nazi-leaning Sudeten German Party staged boycotts of Jewish stores, persuaded Gentiles to stop patronizing Jewish doctors, and agitated for a "return to the Reich"—annexation by Germany. In our own family, some of my mother's Gentile relatives suddenly stopped speaking to her because she was married to a Jew. My father knew that if the Germans invaded, they would immediately arrest him—first for being Jewish, and second for his affiliation with his law partner Eugen Mahler, a socialist.

So with increasing seriousness, my parents considered leaving the country, at least temporarily. As a start, they rented an apartment in Prague, away from Nazi-influenced northern Bohemia, which the Germans were to refer to as the "Sudetenland." While they were trying to make this decision, my mother's brother, Willi Lederer, returning from a business trip to Germany, saw the gigantic buildup of military strength at the border. The news was decisive: On September 11th, taking minimal luggage and leaving business affairs unfinished, the family left for Switzerland on "vacation," as my parents told everyone. Eighteen days later, on September 29, the Munich Agreement ceded the Sudetenland to Hitler.

Before that, family and friends thought my father crazy—literally so, in some cases. Mamina, normally an intelligent and perceptive person, had told my mother the previous summer that, though she hated to say it of her own son, she thought he was having delusions and should be hospitalized. Later in the fall, after Munich, Mamina and Lene, together with about twenty thousand other Jews, fled from the German-held area to Prague. Lene's husband, Eugen (nicknamed Putz), had gone to France to be with his ailing parents. Mamina moved into the apartment that Friedrich and Liesel had rented, and to which their furniture had been shipped. Their safety there was to be short-lived.

In February 1939 Mamina came to visit us for a few weeks in Lucerne, Switzerland. My father had already procured visas and ship tickets for all of us for Cuba. But though he begged Mamina to accompany us, she refused and returned to Prague. On March 15, the Germans marched into Prague. On April 5, we left Lucerne for Havana.

Why did Mamina refuse to accompany my parents to Cuba in 1939, and why did she later hesitate to leave Prague until it was too late? These questions and their answers again raise the specter that has haunted students of the Holocaust for decades: Did the Jews suffer from a "ghetto mentality"? Why did they go "like lambs to the slaughter," as some writers have claimed? Perhaps the realities of Mamina's life can shed some new light on the problem.

Mamina and Lene were not among those Jews lacking the money to emigrate or the connections abroad to get them the required affidavits of financial support. Such persons were often aided by Jewish and other organizations. Rather, as members of the upper middle class, the two women were, ironically, in a worse position, having more to lose. Their possessions—the objects they were familiar with and all they had left of their home—had both a real and a symbolic value for them.

If they emigrated, most women and retired people stood to lose the nonexportable incomes that gave them independence. Their pride in this independence was both admirable and, as it turned out, fatal, because even those who, like Mamina, had relatives abroad who would have supported them, were reluctant to "become a burden." This was true especially of younger persons such as Lene (who was forty-six in 1939); an old person might be expected to be dependent, but a younger woman—according to that code of behavior—could accept support only from a husband. Lene, whose husband was unable to support her, could not allow her brother to do so. And, though she was willing to work, she lacked any sort of job training. Thus the thought of a future abroad was filled with uncertainties.

Family ties played an equally significant role. Mamina did not want to leave Lene. Lene did not want to leave for the United States, Cuba, or any other possible refuge country, partly because she clung to her possessions but also because she wanted to join her husband Eugen in France; however, she had no way of getting to France and staying there. Thus, another essentially admirable trait—family loyalty—became a cause of fatal immobility.

For any person already hesitant because of economic fears or family ties, the incredible formalities put in the way of potential emigrants posed a further barrier. That Jews applying for emigration were made to fill out at least sixteen individual forms, supply certificates of health, good conduct, property, tax payments, and so forth, ad infinitum, by a government whose declared policy was the *encouragement* of Jewish emigration, is one of the ironies of the period.

If they succeeded in overcoming the Nazi regulations, potential refugees still had to deal with those of the governments of potential refuge countries, which were in constant flux, as were those of countries that refugees had to pass through. Finally, even those people who had (seemingly) successfully scaled these hurdles frequently ran into difficulties, as we shall see in Mamina's accounts of the journeys or attempted journeys of Fritz Bischitzky, Hilde Goldmann, Harry Lentner, and others.

Adding to the difficulty in deciding to emigrate was the confusion and ignorance in which the Nazis forced the Jews to live. As early as October 1939, all Prague Jews were ordered to give up their radios. Needless to say, foreign newspapers were unavailable, and later, even German ones—which printed almost exclusively propaganda anyway—were forbidden them, with the exception of the *Jüdisches Nachrichtenblatt* (*Jewish Newsletter*). This periodical printed primarily the latest regulations and restrictions pertaining to Jews; what little "news" there *was,* was often contradictory. For the rest, the Jews had to depend for their information on gossip and hearsay and on the often unreliable (and censored) mail from abroad.

All of these real hindrances contributed to fostering the comfortable illusion that the remaining Jews would continue to "live completely unmolested" and to giving them the "certainty that it [would] all pass and that [they would] see each other again," as Mamina wrote in September 1939. The "boundless optimism" that she and other writers of the period displayed can be seen as the gallows optimism of those who, having lost their positions, their property, and their power (if any), had, after all, nothing else to lose. How could their situation go anywhere but up? How could they imagine a Holocaust?

A Note on the Translation

This book does not include all the letters written by Mamina and Lene during the years 1939–42; entire letters, as well as parts of letters, have been omitted. The omissions are mostly from letters by Mamina; Lene wrote relatively rarely. For the most part, the sections and letters that I have omitted repeat information included in other letters or deal with matters of peripheral interest. For purposes of readability, I have omitted ellipses, added paragraph breaks, which were often missing, and, in most cases, standardized spellings and punctuation. In a few instances I retained some of the original punctuation and spelling to give a sense of the prose.

All material was originally written in German, except where noted. I have left some words in the original German; I have italicized these and defined them in the footnotes.

I have adopted the device of referring to myself (Renate; later Harriet, now Renata) in the third person in the explanatory notes.

A family tree follows this introduction, explanatory notes precede or follow some of the letters, and footnotes contain briefer explanations and identifications of people and places mentioned. A glossary of names, places, and organizations follows the postscript.

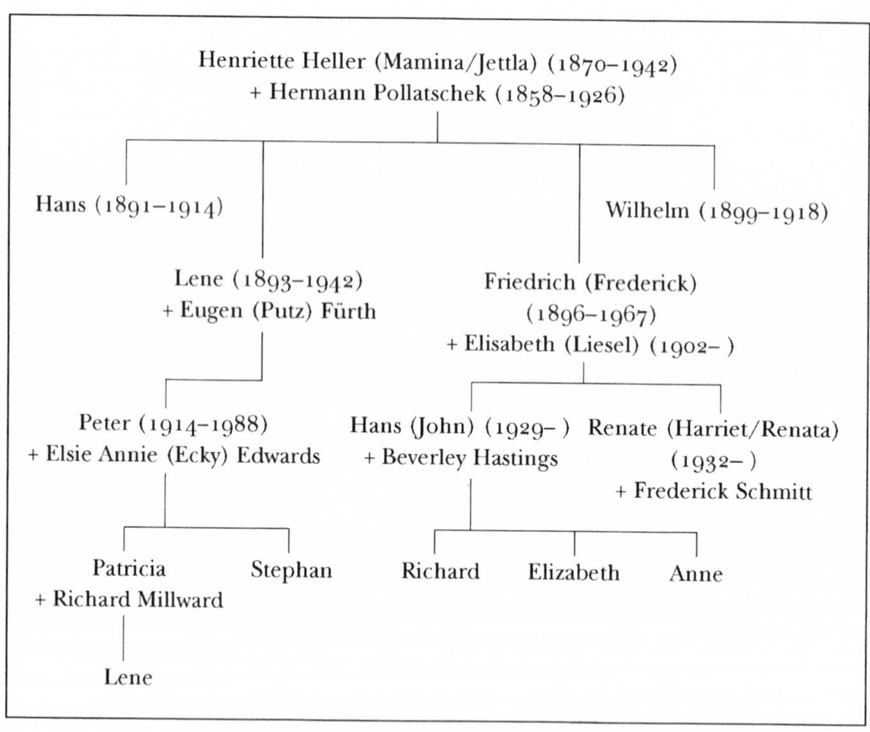

Mamina and Her Descendants

German-Controlled Area of Central Europe, 1940–42

A Thousand Kisses

1939

▶ Friedrich and Liesel Pollatschek and their children, Hans and Renate, had fled Czechoslovakia on September 11, 1938, eighteen days before the Munich Agreement ceded the Sudentenland—the largely German-speaking part of Czechoslovakia where the Pollatscheks lived—to Hitler. They settled temporarily in Lucerne, Switzerland, but their ultimate destination was the United States. On April 5, 1939, the family left Lucerne, traveling via Paris to La Rochelle, where, on April 8, they embarked on the Pacific Line's *Reina del Pacifico* for Cuba, which was to be their next temporary home. This and many letters to follow were written to them in Havana.

April 7

My beloved children,

These lines are meant to be your first greeting in your new and better home. May God grant that they find you in the best of health after a good voyage. Now of course I will be a long time without news of you, but in my thoughts I am always with you.

Since yesterday I have been waiting in vain for word from František,[1] but I am sure the agencies[2] are overfilled now before the holidays. I wrote asking him to call me tomorrow, Saturday, and then perhaps I can still add a few lines to this letter. The problem now is just the tax confirmation,[3] which is causing such difficulties.

1. Mamina's attorney
2. Travel bureaus? Police offices?
3. One of the many documents required for emigration

But after all, there has been some good news today: Fritz[4] has returned from his involuntary excursion, and Tante Tonscha, who was here with Lene till 10 at night, called up a few minutes ago. She was overjoyed, and so Easter won't be quite so dismal after all. Sunday noon the two of them and Lene will be here with me, and we will drink a bottle of Liesel's Rhine wine to our and your health. I hope that you will have something to enjoy also. I can imagine the eyes of the children, the little world travelers, astonished at all the new and wonderful things that they will now be seeing.

April 8

I asked Ernst Skutsch[5] on the phone whether he had seen František here in the past two or three days, but he hadn't. During these days before Easter it is more difficult than ever to get anything done; you cannot imagine how complicated every little thing is now, with new decrees every day, and nobody knows what the next day will bring. So apparently our new advisor, Dr. M.,[6] whom František has put to work, has not yet done anything about the transfer business.[7] Whether I should do something of the sort for myself also, must still be discussed with Dr. M.; but for the moment one can't even think of that.

I must also find out whether František has made out my tax form; you wanted to give him the copies that we made out together in Lucerne, didn't you? This year—that is, since I have been here in Prague—I have not yet received any request for tax payment, and so I am sure I still have much to pay. After that there is still the surcharge, etc., so one has to have much patience before one can even think of taking a journey. For now I would just be happy if I could send off the lift[8]—everything depends on the missing document.

If I decide on a rather large lift, I will also put in the most neces-

4. The only son of Mamina's sister Antonie, known as Tante (Aunt) Tonscha. His "involuntary excursion" was imprisonment by the Nazis, March to April 1939.

5. A cousin

6. Josef Morák, an attorney, also referred to as Dr. M

7. This refers to attempts to transfer some of Friedrich's funds abroad, where he could have access to them.

8. A lift was a huge wooden crate large enough to contain a whole roomful of furniture.

sary things for myself: silver, rugs; as for linens, I already sent my good things in the other shipment; a simple, practical, lightweight bed, mattress, bedding. I've sold your bedroom furniture with the heavy beds but will send you the children's brass beds, which are very light, and your beautiful newly covered mattresses and whatever else by way of small, practical furniture there is room for. I'll keep the rest of your furniture for now; I will sell only my dining room furniture and let the other things wait until the time comes.

Now I will count the days until Pepi[9] notifies me that you have arrived safely. We recently had a few beautiful warm spring days—if you can call it spring this year—but today it is once again cold and unfriendly.

I kiss you all a thousand times. Do write often and happy things.

Your Mamina

Easter Monday, April 10

My dear children,

Your letters of the 6th and 7th came this morning. Your dear, good words of farewell—my heart was so heavy as I read them, but you are right, we must not lose hope for a better future and a reunion. Lene is a good, brave person and a great support for me; we will endure, whatever may still come. It is a great comfort to me to know that the children are so good and make everything easier for you. Today is a beautiful spring day, and you will be lying in the sun and, I hope, enjoying yourselves.

This morning after I had read your letters, I went to the Botanical Garden. Because of the early hour, it was still very quiet, and I consoled myself with the thought that if this springtime miracle has taken place, despite everything that has happened to us here, then finally another miracle will come too, for which we must all wait and hope.

You should both first of all really recover your strength and take care of yourselves until you are accustomed to the climate and plunge into your work; it would do you much good to stay a while in a hotel where Liesel, especially, could get some rest.

9. Josefine Lederer, Liesel Pollatschek's mother, Friedrich's mother-in-law

Yesterday noon, Tante Tonscha, Fritz and Lene were here. We enjoyed a good roast lamb; the male guest in particular developed a fabulous appetite. This afternoon we will be at Lene's. Tomorrow our everyday life begins again, and I will put František to work, so that we finally start making some progress.

A thousand greetings to you and the children,
Your Mama

April 14

My dearest children,

How often by day and by night I think of you, whether you are well, whether you are feeding the sea gulls—that must be very distressing for little Renate, as she doesn't care for those impudent birds and was always so outraged in Lucerne when they snatched the bird feed away from the ducklings. So I hope that she holds on to the feed, and that you are all well.

Here at least the weather is sunny, almost too hot. Yesterday I even sat a while on my dirty kitchen balcony among the brooms and buckets with the view of the sooty facades. The difference between then and now is about like the difference between sitting on my blessed veranda and on this balcony. Nonetheless, there are much worse fates than mine; above all, up to now I have suffered no deprivation, and then too I know you to be in safety—that means so much in our explosive times.

In order to distract myself a bit, I am equipping myself with everything I need by way of dresses, underwear, and shoes, so as to be set for a long time in that respect at least, and not to have to buy anything else. Presumably they plan to wheedle the money out of us anyway with various assessments, etc., so then I would at least have something to wear.

I also keep looking around for some practical furniture that I could put into the lift, if I live to see the day it is sent off. Probably the best and most durable is steel furniture, which I generally am not too fond of. I am thinking not of living room furniture, but one can get, for example, very attractive beds, night tables, and dressing tables, completely unadorned, needing no upkeep and work, and one can certainly always get rid of them if one doesn't need them.

A floor lamp would be practical too, since here there is only a gigantic, heavy wooden one with a monstrous shade. This is hard to pack and to carry around.

I hope they have built-in closets there; then we would need primarily chairs, small or larger tables, and other small things. I would like to know the voltage in America because of the vacuum cleaner, as I have a choice of yours or Lene's in different voltages; also irons, etc.

Lene too would like to take along a lift with the most necessary furniture. She wants to sell the dining room furniture, and to give away many other things. How sad to have to part from all these possessions that have become so dear!

Today František was here, and I read him everything in your letters that would be of interest to him. For the past three days he has been working on this and that. The transfer affair is still not quite completed, but he is doing whatever is possible. He has also applied for me; I have given him the latest bank statement, a list of deposits, and other such data. Tomorrow evening he will report to me again, and he sends his greetings, as do Lene, Tante Tonscha, and Ella.[10] The latter writes diligently. It must be hard for them to part so involuntarily from everything here, but there is nothing else to be done.

Now I am very excited to hear how your new life will develop. I am looking forward more than I can say to the first letter from all of you. Moreover, I discovered the little white toy chest here, with all sorts of toy animals and other stuff, and it will get a place of honor in the lift.

I kiss you all many times,
Your Mamina

▶ The question of *what to take along,* which so absorbed Mamina and Lene (especially, as we will see further on, the latter) and which, with the benefit of hindsight, appears now so futile and indeed destructive, was an understandable preoccupation of would-be emigrants. It is quite possible that the ladies and their friends had read Joseph Wechsberg's *Visum für Amerika* (*Visa to America*), a book

10. One of Mamina's sisters who, with her husband Emil, had gone to London to visit their daughter and son-in-law a week before Hitler's invasion of Prague in March.

of advice for potential emigrants. On the question of what to take along, Wechsberg counsels as follows:

> Every careful immigrant will outfit himself for at least two years. It will take that long before he will be able to buy himself suits or underwear without wiping out his carefully constructed budget. He will have along a sufficient quantity of clothing, underwear, shoes—but also accessories, such as ties, colorful shirts and scarves. . . . Bring only the finest of the fine! If necessary, one can always buy cheap articles, but expensive ones are out of reach when one has to calculate in dollars. . . . Bring along nothing that is un-American and useless. Almost all apartments have built-in closets; therefore it would be costly and pointless to bring wardrobes. All furniture should be small: small tables, small couches, small rugs. (113–15) (my translation)

April 17

Dear children,

I just received an answer from Pepi to my last letter. She writes that she is hard at work at giving up her household. I would be happy if I were already at that stage; instead, I keep on sitting in this dreary apartment, guarding the furniture and other things. However, I asked the shipper to come here so that I can reach a decision with him. If possible I will have everything that is to go into the lift appraised and packed, and then move, take everything along and deposit it in one room for the time being, and as soon as possible, ship it from there. Then at least something would have been accomplished, and I could get out of here and find an apartment into which the sun shines.

Now Lene is also very concerned about her furniture; she is sending some of it to Putz's[11] address, which causes great difficulties be-

11. Eugen Fürth, Lene's husband (nicknamed Putz), had gone to France to look after his ailing parents. His and Lene's son Peter was there also. The situation for refugees in France was difficult: though France was the largest immigrant country in Europe (and, next to the United States, in the world), the chances for finding work were poor. Each refugee had to apply for a *Carte d'identité* (residence permit) within eight days of arrival. These were granted only to refugees with valid passports, which in turn were often impossible for refugees to obtain. A refugee who wanted to work had to apply for a worker's identity card, which was usually given only to an alien with five to fifteen years' residence in France and possessing a certificate from an employer requiring his services.

cause he still has no residence permit. I don't know whether I wrote you that he as well as Peter wants to move to some little town in the provinces, where life is cheaper and where they would have a better chance to see that wish fulfilled; it would be only then that they could find work. Also, Peter would have a better chance of learning the language there than in the bosom of the family in Paris, where they always speak German.

From Moravia I received the pleasant news that Hanne[12] is engaged; three weeks ago she met a young Scotsman, a reporter for some English newspapers, who instantly fell in love with her, and the wedding is already scheduled for May. This is all the more joyful for her parents, as they have already sold their property and are thus without any living, the leases having been canceled too; now they hope that this will make it possible for Mädi[13] to get to England. They are both very hardworking girls and are especially talented in languages. Our little ones would do well now to build up their linguistic talents too—that shouldn't be so difficult. I am terribly excited to hear how they behaved on the trip and how your new home impresses them and you.

My neighbor, Mrs. Friedländer,[14] is all alone now; Willi and his wife, who went to England and have stayed there, got Paul in too before the door was closed, as now there are no more possibilities for emigration. I hope that will soon change.

Now good-bye for today, many kisses,
Your Mama

April 20

My dearest children,

I hope that the tornado which, as we read in the newspapers, rages so terribly, has not influenced your journey and caused any delay, because by today you should have solid ground under your feet, and your cable might arrive. You can imagine how I yearn for it.

12. Hanne Goldmann, a cousin
13. Hanne's sister
14. A former neighbor from Aussig. Willi and Paul were her sons.

As for the lift, the complications continue; in fact, they are multiplying as the permitted articles are further and further restricted. Thus, for example, a family can take along not more than fifteen kilos of silver, naturally after paying the fee. How little that fifteen kilos is you can barely imagine. The dinnerware alone, the sterling (nickel silver is unrestricted), weighs over nine kilos; the two trays with the coffee pot and the tea pot, almost four kilos; the candelabra 1.80. Everything else, the bowls too, would have to remain behind, or instead of sending them, I would have to get some smaller, lighter ones.

Now I hope that the tax declaration is finally ready; up to now, not a single transfer has been made just because of this difficulty, and the question of the lift stands or falls by this also.

At any rate, next week I'll have the things packed, sealed by the customs department, and will move with all the stuff to Veverková Street. Until you hear further, write to my old address; the mailman, that is, the post office, will be notified.

▶ The tornado to which Mamina refers did not delay the Pollatscheks' voyage, though it caused considerable seasickness, especially to Liesel and Hans. They arrived in Havana on April 19. There, they initially stayed in a hotel, where they found life anything but pleasant. The heat and the strangeness of everything were not conducive to relaxation. Thus Mamina's fantasy of her family "sitting under breadfruit trees or cedars, eating . . . Havana lunch of bananas and pineapples" was a bit idealized (letter of April 21). The children found the strange new foods, a combination of Cuban and American, foreign and inedible, and Renate in particular refused to eat.

Renate remembers the narrow hotel room—high-ceilinged, tile-floored, with a small, high window—and the irrational fear it caused her. Worst of all, she slipped one day on the freshly washed steps to the hotel veranda, splitting her chin, which, in the mode of the day, was stitched up without benefit of anesthetic. (Mamina refers to the accident in her letter of May 20.)

Friedrich and Liesel spent their days trying to find a house to rent; they moved into one later in the month. Between that activity and worrying about events in Europe and the elusive visa to America, they had little leisure to relish tropical pleasures.

April 21

Right at noon your first telegram arrived via Pepi, and I am overjoyed, will go right down and phone Lene so that she can share my joy. There are, after all, some pleasures in life, even if rarely. Now I imagine to myself how you must be sitting under breadfruit trees or cedars, eating your Havana lunch of bananas and pineapples and ice cream or other things, and then resting and resting some more. The children of course will not rest for long, but will go exploring, marveling at the Negroes and Chinese and this whole foreign world. Now I look forward to your letters, which I hope will arrive regularly and tell me much of yourselves and your journey.

Lene had a long letter from Peter from Saint Malô, on the coast of Brittany not far from Cherbourg. He is very happy there and hopes to reach his goal much sooner—that is, to get a work permit.

I hope you are well and have a good place to stay, and I kiss you all many times.

Your Mamina

April 25

My dear children,

I keep trying to figure out when your first letter might arrive—I suppose around the middle of May. That will be a holiday, and from then on I will again be able to depend on regular mail; the days are so empty without any signs of life from you.

However, since the day before yesterday and for the next six weeks I have a change of pace three times a week in the form of an hour of devotion at the Cloister of Emmaus with Father Heinrich, a good friend of Onkel Fritz's and his regular visitor in earlier times. Toncha goes too, as well as ten others, gentlemen and mostly ladies. The old Father tells stories from the Bible in a very wise and totally natural manner, also general doctrine, partly on a philosophical basis. Each person studies the catechism by himself at his own discretion, and after the prescribed time has passed, I hope to be found worthy of adding a new page to my collection of documents.

The most important thing now would be something stamped in my passport, as a beginning and "point of departure"—in the literal sense—but I can't think of that right now. When that is going to change only heaven knows, also what more the future has saved up for us.

A thousand greetings,
Mama

▶ The "change of pace" culminated in the "ceremony" described in Mamina's letter of June 29—baptism into the Catholic church. Raul Hilberg, in *Perpetrators Victims Bystanders* (1992), writes: "Notwithstanding the emphasis on descent in the [Nazi] decrees [on who is a Jew], thousands of Jews, driven by panic, adopted Christianity as a talisman. They did so especially in countries where churches were believed to have some political strength" (151).

Mamina obviously was one who thought that the "something stamped in her passport," a document of conversion or a statement that she was a Catholic, would make emigration and other daily problems easier for her. It is clear from later letters, however, that she was also drawn to the aesthetic and spiritual aspects of Catholicism, if not to the religion per se.

That the Czechs, among them Catholic priests, were of great help to the Jews is a well-documented fact. In 1940, a Prague priest was arrested for baptizing 454 Jews and pre-dating the baptismal certificates so that the new converts could get permission to immigrate to South America.

Of course religion played no part in the Nazis' determination of "race"; thus conversions, at whatever date, saved few of the Jews from their fate.

April 30

My dear children,

If you mailed a letter at your last landfall before Cuba, as I hope, then I might soon be hearing from you. The time that I have been without news seems endless to me; it isn't actually so long, but time crawls along so joylessly.

We are all in good health except that I have caught my annual cough, the first since I've been in Prague, but just for that it is all the more tenacious. Of course it is almost always cold, windy, and dusty, but that's something one can't change.

Tomorrow is the first of May. Where you are, it must be good and warm by now. I am eager to know whether you have met some of our countrymen yet; I have heard of whole masses of people who are there already or want to go.

I hope to move in a week or two[15]: Prague VII, Veverková 9. But keep on writing to the old address for now; I will notify the post office.

Fritz B.[16] is getting his visa to the USA on Wednesday. Then the fight for the Gestapo permit begins, without which any passport is invalid but which, on the other hand, is not given to non-Aryans—a difficult situation, on which our emigration, too, runs aground. I had a card from Tine[17] yesterday, saying that they were about to go to the Riviera, where they have been invited by friends in Monte Carlo. What they will do after that they don't know yet—whether there will be a reunion with you or whether they will remain in France.

What do you hear from Pepi? Someone here said that she was accompanying Willi and his family to Germany,[18] but what people say isn't always true. Still, I would be happy to hear that Willi has found something to do again. That kind of news would be good news from Eugen and Peter also, but it isn't the case yet. Now I just hope that you, dear Friedrich, are happy, and Liesel too; I kiss you a thousand times,

Your Mamina

May 4

My dear children,

Your first letter, dated the 23d, is a bit of a disappointment, for you write nothing about the journey, so I assume that another letter, sent earlier, has not yet arrived.

15. The new apartment was smaller; the purpose of the move was evidently to save money.

16. Fritz Bischitzky, son of Mamina's sister Tonscha. The Gestapo permit was the permit to leave the country. Between the end of March and the establishment in July of the Center for Jewish Emigration (*Zentralstelle für die Jüdische Auswanderung*), none of these permits were issued.

17. Wife of Mamina's brother Fritz Heller (Onkel Fritz)

18. Willi, Liesel's brother, who was half Jewish and married to a Gentile, lost his job as a chemical engineer in Aussig. He was offered a partnership in a firm in Görlitz, Germany, by another half-Jew, and he and his family moved there. Pepi, however, did not accompany them.

I can imagine that everything is different and strange, and I just hope that you will give yourselves time to probe everything before reaching any conclusions. The best thing would be to go to the beach during the hottest time instead of starting off right away with housekeeping, which I am sure will be quite complicated until Liesel has penetrated the secrets of the cuisine, etc. The language and many other things too will cause you problems at first, especially the strange foods, but I hope the children will become accustomed to it and regain their appetites. I will try to send these lines by the quickest possible route in order to have an answer soon; up to now I have simply written via New York, since there is no air mail service from here, and everything goes via Berlin.

Ella writes from London that she has never in her life been so cold as since the beginning of their involuntary stay; the weather is constantly cold and stormy. They are quite unhappy, with no money at all, staying with their children, who are themselves hard-put, and with no possibility of work for Emil. Life is really a series of problems, and only the minority of them have solutions.

Tomorrow, if nothing else comes up, we will conclude the transfer. The conditions are as miserable as you can imagine, but there is no alternative.

A thousand kisses,
Mama

May 5

My dear children,

Today I was rich in mail; after receiving Liesel's letters from the ship from Pepi yesterday, the air mail letter of the 20th arrived this morning, via Aussig, and at noon Friedrich's cable. I read your letters so often that I know them by heart, as Pepi wants them all back and of course I'll send them to her, hard as that is for me. After all, it's my only contact with you. That poor Liesel and our good boy suffered so much from sea-sickness makes me very sad; but I hope everything has been forgotten by now and that you are really well. Homesickness, from which Liesel apparently suffers the most, is certainly an illness that only time and distraction can heal—not work only, but also occupations of a pleasanter sort, for which I hope you will have the opportunity as soon as you are really acclimated.

I am happy to see from Friedrich's cable that he already has my visa; that is by far not all, but at least a beginning for my coming journey to you. Such a thing is not to be carried out so rapidly—I also want to wait until you yourselves are settled in and sure that you want me; there are still many things to be put in order here. The formalities are difficult and endless; you will understand that most easily when I tell you that we still have no tax declaration, thus no permission to send off the lift, and the transfer has not been completed either. One makes no progress with anything and drives oneself mad with all the difficulties. Just a while ago František was here and assured me that on Tuesday the transfer affair would be settled. Of course I have heard this story many times, but I hope this time it will be true. That way the other question, regarding the lift, would also be brought closer to being settled.

I kiss you all a thousand times and wait for good news of you.

Your Mamina

May 8

My dear Friedrich,

I do not know whether this letter will arrive in time to bring you my birthday wishes, but whenever it may arrive, whether too late or too early, it is full of love and wishes for your present and future life. That all eight of us should once again be reunited is of course the dearest of my wishes, but I fear it will never be fulfilled, since a reunion with you would inevitably mean a parting from Lene and her people, and so my heart is torn apart between the things I want most in the world. For the moment there is no chance of getting out of here, and we can do nothing but wait; I would now just be happy to hear that you are halfway settled and recovered from the worst of the homesickness, for a total recovery is something that never comes to anyone who has lost his homeland.

I was going to move this week, but the shipper asked for a postponement so that he might perhaps still be able to get your things ready to send off; that would make our work much easier. The shipper says that he has often sent electric ranges in the lifts—that of course is the only way to keep house in that climate.[19] Perhaps we can rearrange things so that we can find room for some more furniture, possibly even a Miss America kitchen cabinet[20] and a collapsible wardrobe, if we can get it in—perhaps your big white one that comes apart, or the other big white one. Some of the crates could be sent separately, which would make more room for other things.

How are the darling children? Are they still so good? And have they started to eat again? Kiss them a thousand times, and a loving embrace from your

Mama

May 14

My dear children,

Yesterday your letter of May 1 came from Pepi, and I am very happy about it. You can't imagine how happy I would be to move into your little flower-surrounded house; but now it seems that, according to the latest J.[21] laws, the matter of emigration too will be somehow regulated, since it really cannot continue as it has. I will of course inquire at the ship company and do everything possible; also, the day before yesterday I spoke with František about my tax form and yours; he is continuing his efforts but has to keep prodding the Aussig lawyer.

I regularly receive my pension, that is, the state one of 539 Crowns monthly; from the company I received, as I once wrote you, a payment for 17 months as a settlement. The employees, I believe, received only one year's salary.

Tomorrow I'll renew your subscription to the *Prager Tagblatt*, now called *Der Neue Tag*. I never read it and would be very happy to have a good newspaper to read, but unfortunately there is none. I get a Czech one—not too satisfying either—and if I'm lucky I get

19. The Pollatscheks' Havana house, like most Cuban houses, had a charcoal-burning stove.

20. Friedrich penciled "new?" here.

21. "J" always refers to "Jewish." Mamina here probably refers to establishment of the Center for Emigration in Prague.

my hands on an English paper now and then, and that helps keep my linguistic skills alive.

How lovely if Lene and Eugen would have the chance of living with us in Havana, but I doubt that this dream will ever see fulfillment; perhaps Eugen can find some work in Paris, but Europe is no resting place, and who knows how long they will be able to stay in France. Lene is especially worried about Peter, in case something were to happen. I wish she could get a Ba'ta[22] agency in Havana; she is very clever, much more energetic than Eugen, and I'm sure she would be able to manage anywhere; but unfortunately their means are so modest.

Stay well, a thousand greetings from your
Mamina

▶ Later in 1939, the state pensions to which Mamina refers were to be revoked in the case of Jews, on the grounds that Jews were to be put into "protective custody" anyway. Private pensions were also confiscated, except that companies were allowed to make a lump sum payment, as did the Petschek firm in Aussig, for which Hermann Pollatschek, Mamina's late husband, had worked. By the end of 1939, most businesses had been "Aryanized"—that is, confiscated and turned over to Gentiles. By April 26, 1940, Jews had been excluded from the liberal professions, government employment, journalism, the arts, the theater, and so forth.

The *Prager Tagblatt* was a German-language newspaper (Max Brod, Franz Kafka's friend and editor, had at one time been its theater critic). On March 16, 1939, its name was changed to *Der Neue Tag (The New Day)*, and it took a pro-Nazi line. Friedrich probably did not know this fact, but it no doubt explains why Mamina no longer read the paper. A "good" newspaper thus must mean a non- or anti-Nazi one.

May 17

Dear Friedrich, dear Liesel,

I wrote you a long epistle about the lift, on the assumption that the arrangements for payment could be made in Czech Crowns; yesterday the shipper told me that this had not worked out

22. A large shoe manufacturer with world-wide exports

and is at any rate only possible for Reich Germans.[23] We have to pay the ocean freight in hard currency, as well as the insurance, so the shipper advised me that if I didn't make an immediate decision, he couldn't assure me that any shipment would be possible at all. It's impossible to await your decision, I must simply decide by myself or else get rid of everything that might be valuable for you and dispose of it for nothing. So I will take the responsibility on my already bowed shoulders. Since naturally only one lift is now possible, I will restrict myself to choosing only those things of most value to you: silver, rugs, glass, china, etc.; pictures and furniture only as far as there is room for them. If I should have mail from you regarding this within the next few days, I will of course do as you wish; but otherwise please be satisfied with what I am doing. If, one day, I am able to tell you everything, you will understand a thing or two; it's not possible to write it all.

God, how beautiful it would be if I were already with you and able to rest from all these difficulties; sometimes I am so tired that I think I can't go on any more. Yesterday Ernst Skutsch was here; he is dying to travel with me, together with his wife Mimi, of course, and that would be wonderful; but what might still happen before that day! At any rate, it would be a big help to me.

Pepi sent me Liesel's letter of the 25th, heavy with homesickness but fortunately now out of date. I understand her very well, but you mustn't believe that we are happy here. Nobody, without exception, can do anything but envy you. That the children are often bored is something I can understand; they miss school, but now you have your house and your garden, and everything will surely get better. Do you go to the beach? I am so eager to hear how everything is in your household; do write in as much detail as possible.

My most heartfelt kisses for you all,
Your Mamina

May 20

My dear son,

Today unfortunately I must tell you of something highly disagreeable that happened to a good old friend—her grandchildren call

23. Germans from Germany proper

her "Mamina"—and her daughter. Because they were afraid, living alone, to keep cash in their apartment, they entrusted this cash, in fact a substantial amount, to a good friend, who, because of his background, family, etc. was totally reliable. Unfortunately, there occurred an event which I cannot describe more fully, and the poor women have little hope of getting the money back. Thank God they both have enough to live on, but the imminent tax surcharge makes them anxious, and the old lady in particular can't sleep because of her worry about the future. The money belonged to her son—he knows how attached she is to him—and was meant to cover various costs, such as for lawyers (these costs will be quite substantial), the shipment of his furniture, etc.; now she worries about how she is going to take care of all this. This son does have a friend and well-wisher[24] who might be in a position to help, but only if it were absolutely necessary; but she doesn't have the courage to ask him; she will sell her jewelry if necessary—but would that be enough?

It is so terribly difficult to make an estimate of costs as we could have done before, because one never knows what the next day will bring; therefore the worry. Life is really difficult and full of complications.

Now as to us. I received your dear long letter on the 18th. I will inform myself about my journey at the various travel agencies; but since the Gestapo permit makes any voyage impossible, the question is not too pressing. You can be sure that I will do everything possible, despite Onkel Fritz's admonition against going to Havana; the only decisive thing for me is what you write about the matter, the climate, etc.; not to mention the fact that I am convinced that it will be autumn before things reach that point, and then I will have until the next summer to acclimate myself.

As to the lift, it is a great disappointment for me not to be able to ship it; for weeks now I have been busy with it, preparing everything for you. The costs, too, would have been colossal for me; you know my financial situation. Payment of the ocean freight charges and insurance in Czech Crowns is impossible—if anyone tells you

24. Franz Petschek was the son of Hermann Pollatschek's (Friedrich's father's) former employer and a second cousin of Friedrich. At the time he was living in Switzerland. Mamina often refers to him in code as "your friend and well-wisher," "your well-wisher," "Franz Conrad" (Conrad was his middle name), "Konrad," "F. K.," or "F. C."

the contrary he must be a Reich German or else he has German Marks in a blocked account; with that one can pay the ocean freight and a ship ticket. Do you have any such? Your German securities, as well as the others for the transfer, have been released for sale, and the business has already been concluded.

This week I am finally going to move—write your next letter to Prague VII, Vererková 9. For now I will leave behind the furniture that is to be sold but will of course take your things with me.

With a heavy heart, I today began unpacking the already packed crates of glass and porcelain and selling all the magnificent things. We have lost so much, and still I am sorry about all these beautiful things, for which one gets practically nothing. But I've heard repeatedly that they almost all arrive broken, and that would be an even greater pain. After all, these things are not so important for you as they have seemed to us heretofore. The shipper will tell me in the next few days what the costs will be for the individual packages; I'll write it to you immediately and wait for your answer.

I am very happy that you seem to be happy in your new home and have found such good friends. I am very sorry about Renate's accident[25] and the scare you had; I hope everything has long since healed and the children doing well, eating again, and bathing in the sea.

Herbert[26] is at home; he will come to me in a week, and I will fatten him up. I cannot do more for him, much as I would like to, since I have to live very economically now.

I am going to give up the apartment on July 1, as will Lene, and if we are still here on October 1, which I don't hope, we will sell the rest of the furniture and move to a furnished room.

I sometimes feel so miserable because of all these difficulties; my nerves can't hold out any more.

I kiss you all a thousand times.

Mama

P.S. I still receive the national pension, but it is impossible to transfer it abroad.

25. Renate's fall on the hotel steps
26. Son of Mamina's brother Karl

▶ What happened to the money, and who the "friend" was, is a mystery. In some cases people entrusted money to those about to emigrate and were betrayed by them. In other cases, Jews entrusted property to Gentiles, who in turn were found out by the Gestapo. What the "imminent tax surcharge" was is not clear either: in the Reich, a special income tax was levied on Jews in 1936, and a 15 percent surcharge was added on August 5, 1940. Similar regulations must have applied in the "Protectorate." It is also possible that the surcharge was only a rumor. Hard news was difficult for Jews to obtain, and rumor was often the only source of "information."

Regulations applying to Jews in Germany sometimes differed from those applied to Jews in the "Protectorate," though in most cases Reich regulations were sooner or later adopted by the "Protectorate" government. Sometimes two sets of anti-Jewish regulations obtained in the "Protectorate": those proclaimed by the "Protector" in the name of the Reich, and those passed by the puppet Czech (Hácha) government, usually having to do with local matters.

Whitsunday [May 28]

My dearest children,

I reproach myself for having written you about that dreadful money business, dear Friedrich. You will just worry about it, and really it isn't so bad. With Otto's[27] help, I have been able to sell almost all of my securities, even if at a poor price—especially the treasury bills, etc., sold at only 40 to 50%. But I can draw 1,500 Crowns weekly out of the blocked account, at least until further notice, and thus put away a fund for my future needs. So you need have no worries about me; I even hope to be able to help Lene. I would have to turn to you for help only if some unforeseen situation were to arise. Unfortunately it's now said that emigration to Cuba has been stopped, as Onkel Fritz writes also, but I'm sure you have more information about that. Emigration from here is impossible at the moment for everyone and to everywhere, so there is nothing to do but wait.

Since yesterday I have been in my new apartment, and with Lene's and Tonscha's help I've already fairly well fixed it up. Two

27. Otto Grüner, a cousin of Eugen Fürth who had worked in the Fürth paper company

rooms are pretty much habitable and very pleasant, the whole apartment is sunny and friendly, the location very pleasant and convenient. The third room again is a furniture warehouse, despite the fact that I have already sold a great part of the things and have left others to be sold in the old apartment. Now by and by I will get rid of more, and not sell it so cheaply. Naturally, here too I have the feeling of temporariness; but then, who has a real home on this earth today?

Herbert, who was supposed to come to me this week, writes that he can't get a passport unless he commits himself never to return and now asks himself if he will be able to remain here and how long I will be here, because he has nobody except me who could take him in. Now I would love to be rich; how many there are to be helped!

A thousand greetings to you all,
Your Mama

▶ Early in May, the Cuban government, alarmed by the large number of Jewish refugees, issued a new decree requiring all immigrants to post a $500 cash bond, and all consuls to refuse visas without the approval of the Cuban Departments of State, Labor, and Treasury. Later in the month there occurred the notorious episode in which Cuba refused entry to over nine hundred refugees traveling on the *St. Louis,* because their landing permits had been issued before the new regulations had gone into effect. Thereafter, Cuba again began admitting refugees, becoming one of the largest transit countries in the world.

June 1

Dear children,

I heard today that poor Eugen Mahler[28] is in an Austrian sanitarium, but I wasn't able to find out anything more definite. All our other acquaintances are without exception poorly off, eating up what little money they have; not one has succeeded in getting away

28. One of Friedrich's law partners. "Sanitarium" was evidently a euphemism for "prison," as is later the case with Lene. Eugen Mahler was a socialist, which probably in part accounts for his imprisonment.

from here to make a living, with the exception of Franz B.,[29] who with Else has been in Milan for several weeks now, has traveled to Sweden and lately to France for his company, and will now move to Paris to go into business with a Frenchman.

Putz is in Amiens, but most of the time he spends in Paris, as his father is very ill. Peter wrote today that he is with a British firm, working as a chauffeur on a trip through Brittany. He is delighted that he's earning 50 Francs a day. Fritz B. is still sitting here.

You simply are not at all informed about our circumstances. One can have a visa and everything imaginable in order, but without the Gestapo stamp there is no emigration, and this nobody receives, at least for the present time.

June 2

Well, *finally*—with the help of two assistants of Dr. Normann, clerk of Dr. M., and František, the transfer has been brought safely home. Yesterday and today, from 8:30 in the morning to 1 in the afternoon, together with one or two gentlemen, I traipsed back and forth from the bank to the Ministry of Finance, waiting for hours everywhere, while Dr. Normann, a hard-working and very pleasant person, negotiated back and forth with various gentlemen, and all I had to do was sign; and at last the matter is finished.

A thousand greetings and kisses,
Mama

June 8

My dear children,

Yesterday I received your dear, good letter of the 26th, Friedrich, and just now Ernst brought me the enclosure of the 28th. First of all, thank you for your and Liesel's cheerful and generous offer to take care of me; it helps me to bear a great deal to hear that.

29. Franz Bischitzky, son of Mamina's sister Olga. Elsa was his wife. Two of Mamina's sisters married brothers, and another sister married one of their cousins; hence the prevalence of the name Bischitzky among the relatives.

Your suggestion that I go to France with Lene for possibly quite a long time will probably be frustrated above all by the fact that I would not be able to get a residence permit. Eugen himself has to remain in Amiens because he was not allowed to stay in Paris, and he waits impatiently for the *carte d'identité*. Furthermore, everything with them is still so uncertain that I can't possibly count on anything.

Above all, I have only one wish: I still do not have the emigration permit—it will probably come tomorrow, and then I just have to wait until they start issuing the Gestapo stamp again. At any rate, I will speak with František; he knows that he has to make out my tax declaration, which should create no difficulties; I have all the other required documents, except for one which I will get in the very near future.[30]

Getting a visa for the USA, however, is more difficult: I would first have to have an affidavit, which they admit takes several months; then for a long time nothing happens, then the visa and then a two- to three-year wait before one gets the quota number. After that, the stamp from the Gestapo.

Fritz B. has been waiting for a year now and his turn has still not come, despite the fact that he has received all sorts of help from an American Catholic organization. At any rate, I will ask him to inquire at the consulate, where they are very unwilling to meet one halfway. You would have to try to accomplish something from there, or at least support me here, for, as I said, it could take years.

I always thought that I would come along with you, or soon after. If on the other hand I have to live alone in Cuba for years, and on top of everything at your expense, that changes it all. Can I venture toward a goal that has suddenly grown so distant? But what should I do here after my little fortune dwindles away? It is a difficult problem.

Lene and I have tried to imagine various alternatives, but everything goes awry, and that is the reason that my optimism has totally left me. It is a world of complications, and perhaps the best thing is to stay here so long as money and nerves hold out. For now I will make no plans at all and just wait to see what happens with you; af-

30. No doubt the certificate of baptism

ter all, nothing else makes any sense. Just today I met Grüner, who thinks that I would have to wait four years to come from here to the USA if I started working on it now. So let's hope for the Messiah, who will change everything.

As for my health, don't worry; although I only weigh 51 kilos, there is surely no physical reason for that, only, as with us all here, my nerves leave something to be desired, especially with regard to sleep; there's no help for that. One simply never gets any rest, and everything we see and hear around us constantly works us up. But everything will be better once I'm away from here.

Yesterday I found your blue gardening apron, Friedrich; I'll tuck it in the top of one of the crates. I always see you before me in the garden, with the children and Liesel bustling about; I think of you all the time and am so unboundedly happy that you are all well. The children will be busy now too, with school and with other children; they will surely like it, even if it is hard at first, but they will learn the language most quickly that way.

Pepi recently sent six beautiful, almost new sheets for you, and another six are on their way. For now you have enough, though. Whether I can get light-weight blankets, however, is very questionable; there are many things that are not available, especially in this line—for instance, no dust cloths, cotton flannel and other fabrics, no twine. On the other hand, plenty to eat, but everything very expensive compared to what it was. Fruit—cherries, and strawberries—but since these things are displayed in front of the stores here instead of inside them, they are so covered with dust and dirt that I can't bring myself to eat them.

I kiss you all a thousand times,
Your Mama

P.S. Ask the little ones to write me a line sometime.

▸ An affidavit (or affidavit of support) was required by every would-be immigrant to the United States, with the exception of persons of means, who could come in on a "capitalist" visa (later this category was eliminated). The affidavit consisted of a notarized statement by an American individual (not an organization) and contained information about that person's salary, bank accounts, length and type of employment, and so forth. It had no prescribed form, however. We will hear more about affidavits later on.

The quota for immigration into the United States for persons of each European nationality was established according to the following formula:

yearly quota of admissible persons born in a given country	=	population of the U.S. in 1920 whose national origin was traced to that country
150,000		total population of European descent in the U.S. in 1920

Quotas were determined by the fiscal, not the calendar, year. The Czech quota in fiscal year July 1, 1938, to June 30, 1939, was 2,874.

The shortages Mamina mentions were probably caused by the fact that during the months following the invasion, the Germans "bought" textiles—that is, confiscated or acquired them in devaluated Czech Crowns—and shipped them to Germany. Other materials in short supply were hides, leather, soap, fats, and high-quality meats.

June 11

Dear Friedrich,

I wish that I had a typewriter and knew how to type; how much simpler our correspondence would be then, and cheaper. Perhaps I will still learn. Above all, I am happy that you have such a pleasant neighborhood and the children have a little playmate with lovely toys. Now they will surely soon learn both of the languages.

It's an odd link in the chain of these tragic times that you sent the permit[31] off just on that memorable day, May 21st. May it be the beginning of the fulfillment of my heart's wish—to come soon to you. I hope that the Employment Office[32] won't cause any difficulties, because God knows that there's no one there except for Liesel whose employment I want to take away. How things will work out for a further trip for me to the USA is a different question and one that only you will be able to solve over there, because from here, as

31. Probably the Cuban landing permit

32. A Cuban agency whose concern was that immigrants not take up salaried positions

I wrote you in my last letter, there is no way that it can be done in anything less than three or four years.

Now I am looking forward to the promised photograph of the children, and I am happy that you, as well as Liesel and the children, have gained some weight. Moreover, yesterday I ascertained that my own weight loss has stopped too—in fact, I have gained a little. Don't worry about me—I am not any worse off than any of us here.

It is not so bad with the work I have to do for you either, and I am happy to do it. Nobody can help its being difficult and complicated, and once I am with you, everything will be all right again. Naturally, if it is at all possible, I would like to travel via France in order to see Eugen and Peter once more; it would no doubt be a farewell forever. In exchange for that I would have you again. It just seems these days that we have to pay for every happiness.

The two books are for Renate's birthday.[33] Now this lovely day too has been celebrated without Mamina. How beautiful these little parties were in our garden. I never stop missing the garden; I always feel as if I'm in prison, despite the fact that the apartment is very pretty. In the evenings I often go to see Lene and sit on her or Ilse's[34] balcony. Ilse lives on the sixth floor with a large balcony, a lovely view of the river and the city. Tonscha often comes too, and once or twice a week we meet in the evening at the Belvedere[35] and drink a glass of beer, the famous old Czech beer. But most evenings I sit alone in this hot room.

A thousand kisses to you,
Your Mama

▶ The languages that the children would learn were Spanish and English. The "little playmate," Charley, was not much help in the former, as he was the son of a Swedish family and spoke no Spanish himself. The children communicated with him in English. Hans and Renate attended Miss Phillips School, an American school in which instruction was in English in the mornings and in Spanish in the

33. June 4. Renate was eight.
34. Ilse Krebs was a friend of Lene.
35. The Belvedere was a Prague park.

afternoons. Renate attended only the English sessions, but Hans, aged nearly ten, attended both.

The significance of May 21 might be as follows: on May 21, 1938, the Czech forces mobilized against German troops massed on the border. This maneuver kept the Germans out for a few months and seems to have taken on a larger significance at the time than it has for us now.

June 15

My dear, good son,

Yesterday I received your letter of June 5—in just nine days—a letter about which I was beginning to feel somewhat anxious—the answer to my Job-like letter—and I am very sorry that you are so worried on my account. I wish I could have kept the whole thing from you, but that just couldn't be done; Lene, too, wavered for a long time but finally confessed to Peter. He, like you, took it calmly, as an occurrence of a time in which such and similar things can happen. Meanwhile I have repeatedly assured you that there is no occasion for worry, and that I will certainly get by without outside assistance.

František was here today; of course he is completely informed about everything and is convinced that everything can be arranged, and even, depending on how things go, that he might be able to arrange a small transfer for me. He tells me that your transfer will not be sent off any more this month, but definitely in the first half of July.

Herbert did not come. His father-in-law is employing him as a farmhand, and he plans to stay as long as he can. I sent him the clothing that you donated and will pay his dental bills. Because of a gum infection he lost five front teeth, others are in danger, and of course they have no money for that. For now, so long as I don't have to support him here, I want to do at least that for him; unfortunately nobody in the whole family has anything to spare.

Brother Fritz, whom I asked for support for Herbert, writes that he unfortunately can do nothing for him, since he has no cash here and securities are not salable. Regarding the latter observation, I could inform him more accurately, but then he always was a sensitive soul and will most likely remain so. It's characteristic that he doesn't even answer your letters, just as he never asks about anyone of the family here nor writes what his plans are.

Last evening I was at Paula's, Otto's sister. The conversation dealt exclusively with emigration and confirmed the depressing fact that a departure for the USA from here would involve a delay of from three to four years. It all depends on the country of one's birth, regardless of whether one emigrates from here, Cuba, France, etc. If that is correct, then you too would have to wait that long.[36] If I were with you, I would gladly wait much longer, but alone it would be quite impossible, and so the dream of joining you in Havana is postponed into the endless distance. But let us wait and see; one can't do anything else.

Excuse the dreadful paper: this is the first time I have used it, and I see that it runs like mad when it feels ink. You will have to place it on a white backing in order to read it.

I kiss you fondly, and once again, don't worry.

Mama

June 20

My dearest children,

At the end of October we will give notice on our apartments, but until then we will both stay where we are; I need a little peace right now and would like to enjoy this pretty apartment for at least three months, since I have to pay for it anyway. Then I will try to find a studio apartment in Lene's building. Ilse will keep her own apartment in the same building, and Lene will rent a room from her. They will keep house together; I will share their cleaning woman and cook for myself whatever and whenever I choose, or not at all if that's my pleasure. Diversion of that sort might be quite good for me, and I would be able to live very cheaply that way and exactly to my own taste and yet not have to be alone if I don't want to be.

36. It was correct: A person's position on the quota depended on his or her birthplace, not place of residence. By the spring of 1939, enough Czechoslovakians and Germans had applied for U.S. visas to fill the quotas for the next four to six years. The reason why the Pollatscheks did not have to wait that long will become clear later.

Of course what I would still rather do is to go to France with Lene before coming to join you; but I doubt very much that this can be done. All the countries are locking their doors against us poor emigrants, and one finds welcome nowhere. I thank God every day that you have found a sanctuary, and such a beautiful one at that.

Tonscha is bracing herself for her move. She found a studio apartment in the *Weinberge,*[37] very far from me, unfortunately, but nothing else suitable was available, because everything was too expensive for her. She, like Emil's family, lost most of her money, and moreover she still has her son with her. Now they will have to share one room, and she will have to cook for him too on the gas cooker. With his appetite he is always a tangible burden for his mother, and he can't get away; Mimi[38] was here for a few days about her visa but is now back in her native city, Vienna—she wants to go to the USA with him, but nobody knows when that will come about.

Like you, dear Liesel, I cannot understand heaven's dispensations.

Stay well, I kiss you a thousand times,
Your Mamina

June 25

Dear children,

You should have no illusions about an influx of funds from Aussig. František of course immediately inquired after the appearance of that regulation, but as usual received no answer. Now we have engaged a J. lawyer there whom František will contact, just as he has been doing everything at all possible. He doesn't yet know whether it will be possible to sell the remaining securities: the new laws may put an end to the matter, also to the contents of the crates that are to be sent. We lost a great deal of time because of the change in plans, and therefore our chances have become worse. But I no longer worry any more than necessary about these things, since I have come to recognize that nothing is achieved by it, and one's nerves are totally destroyed.

37. An area in western Prague (*Vinohrady* in Czech)
38. Fritz's wife

It is a great solace to me to know that you tolerate the climate so well and that you are healthy and happy—everything else is unimportant compared to that. If the day that reunites us should ever really arrive, then all the calamities that have broken in upon us will be forgotten.

Renate's adorable little letter made me very happy. Mamma shouldn't judge her spelling so harshly—how could the poor child have learned to write properly in her few hours of school?[39] It's enough that she manages as she does. English will give them both difficulties in the first year, but that will pass.

Within the year I hope to get a little piece of birthday cake; that will taste better than the most splendid delicacies that one can get in Prague. In fact, whatever one might wish by way of food is available here in great quantities.

I often go for walks again now; today, Sunday morning, Lene and I went to the Botanical Garden despite rain in order to admire the splendor of the roses. It made Lene think of hers in Nestersitz[40]—poor thing; of us all, she has lost the most, for practically nothing is left them, and she bears it all with admirable calmness.

Mostly in the evenings, if I have no guests, I go walking alone in the Belvedere for at least an hour; it is barely five minutes from my apartment. The air is very refreshing, especially in the evenings, and the view of the illuminated city is magnificent. Poor Prague. We also often sit on Ilse's balcony; there are usually a few people there, and it's a distraction after the various efforts of our daily lives, even though the topic of conversation is always the same.

A thousand kisses to you and the little ones,

Your Mama

▶ On June 2, the Law on the status of Jewish Property was passed. According to this, Jews had to register all of their valuables by July 31 (see Mamina's letters of June 29 and August 1). As for goods to be shipped, the law ruled as follows: Goods acquired before September 1, 1939, could be exported duty-free in "nor-

39. Renate had had only one year of German-language schooling—a few weeks in Aussig before the Pollatscheks left, the remainder of the first grade in Lucerne. She entered the second grade in Havana, in an English-language school.

40. The Fürths' former home

mal" quantities, but all other property was taxed at 100 percent of its assessed valuation. Any gold or silver objects that had previously been exported were subject to a tax of 300 percent of assessed value. The authorities collected handling charges. Only after these fees and taxes were paid could the Jewish owners receive the permit required to have their property sent abroad; and this had to be done by an "Aryan" shipper, licensed by the Ministry of Finance.

June 29

My dearest children,

This week I was notified that I can keep my citizenship, and I am eager to know how that will work out with you. Thus I have a new document for my collection, and in a few days I will have a second one. Tomorrow morning at seven a little ceremony will take place—those invited are Tante Tonscha with Daisy's husband[41] representing her, and I with Maňka Ružičká.[42] I'll write you about it before I send this letter off.

Now I have a new worry with the registration of jewelry, silver, etc. Jewelry cannot be taken over the border, nor can it be sold here. Of the other things I am sure they will allow only very little to be taken out; what happens with the remainder nobody knows yet. So we have constant variety, but never anything joyful. I hope all of you over there continue to be well; that has to make up for the rest.

I should like to know why the photocopy of the permit is not legal and whether it might be contested in this form. I shall at any rate ask František to find out; it would be safer though to have a second legalized copy in one's possession; when one finally starts in with those bureaus, these documents are always just in the mail.

June 30

Well, this morning at 6:30 I picked up Maňka R. in a taxi, in order to make things convenient for her, and we met the other two in front of St. Emmaus. It was very beautiful and festive, in a splendid little chapel of this large church, quite an extraordinary feeling. Afterwards Father Heinrich invited the whole company to breakfast,

41. Daisy was Onkel Fritz's adopted daughter. Lolly was her husband.
42. Maňka was a friend of Lene.

since of course we had come without having eaten. He sat comfortably in the midst of his flock, enjoyed the food, and was graciousness personified. Now this phase[43] has been completed; once in a while something does work out after all.

Lene and I seem to have succeeded in getting some of our books, which we are very much attached to, into Putz's possession; then if I really got there, I would have pleasant reading-matter. Dear son, get Putz to tell you more about this.[44]

What you write in your two letters about the climate and what you report about your life makes me immensely happy, that the children are so good and adapt themselves to everything; finally, that you have gained weight so nicely—Renatchen's turn will surely come too.

One thing is sure: your wife and children are a treasure that no decree in the world can change. Liesel is excellence itself, and for you this means more now than all the silver baskets and valuables in china cabinets. Nor does it hurt me so much any more to see the contents of those two china cabinets of ours in the antique store windows in Národní Street, or our beloved bronze with the angel standing on its big toe in another window at the Café Steiner in Celetná Street. So I will also be able to separate myself from the rest of our belongings, to trade for them the happiness of being with you again.

Eugen is still trying to get a visa for there for both of us; up to now he hasn't succeeded, but of course we are keeping our eyes on this possibility. You are right, one should have two or more irons in the fire; I hope that someday one or the other of them will start to glow.

Yesterday I spoke with Erich Schneider[45] and his wife. They are still here, as is the eye and ear doctor. They are all very pathetic. But the other people aren't any better off—those who are looking for a livelihood, even if they belong to a different faith and nation.[46]

43. The "phase" was Mamina's and Lene's conversion to Catholicism.

44. Although mail was not officially censored at this time, Mamina sometimes wrote in code. "Dear son" and similar phrases within a letter usually signal that code is being used. The books "to which we are very much attached" are probably bank books.

45. A physician whose father was the Pollatscheks' family doctor

46. i.e., Gentile. Gentile Czechs as well as Jews were persecuted by the Germans; many lost their jobs.

So for example Lolly, the husband of my sponsor, can't find a job, despite the fact that he has two brothers in formerly very influential positions here.

Stay healthy and happy, I embrace you.

Your Mamina

Just now the daily afternoon thunderstorm is starting; at six o'clock it is so dark that I had to turn a light on in order to finish my letter. It is like where you are—every morning is sunny and hot, every afternoon or evening, a thunderstorm and torrents of rain.

July 13

My dearest children,

That the occurrences of our times are not peaceful, that nobody knows what is still in store, applies not only to us but to everyone else as well, and one must simply bear what is apportioned to him. Lene and I are helped in this by the certainty that the men and little children, as well as Emil, are in safety; surely nothing will happen here to us women.

Our mouths water when we read about your inexpensive fruit; here there is enough fruit, but very expensive and for the most part not fresh. What we lack now is of course the rich supplies of the Elbe Valley; the same applies to vegetables. On the other hand, the bakery and confectionery shops overflow with the most magnificent things, before which our "foreign guests"[47] stand amazed. The same is true of the butcher shops.

We now want to engage another shipper, since our present one claims that it is impossible to do anything right now. I am really not very hopeful, but I want to leave nothing untried in order to save at least something for you.

I will write more frequently now, so that you won't worry too much, and I send you a thousand kisses.

Your Mama

47. i.e., German invaders; possibly an official term. Produce from the Elbe Valley, in German-occupied Sudetenland, was evidently being channeled to the Reich.

July 14

Dear Liesel, dear Friedrich,

You probably have direct news from Eugen; the poor thing unfortunately has nothing else to do. Peter, on the other hand, always finds work and even earnings. At Whitsuntide he drove an English party through Brittany, and not only were these people touchingly kind to him, but they also recommended him to someone else, with the result that for the past two weeks he has been driving around France with the head of Lloyds of London. The man has brought his fabulous car with him, treats the boy like a friend, and on top of it all pays him 50 Francs per day. That is quite an accomplishment for Peter, and he is overjoyed. He was on the Riviera; our last news of him was from Grenoble. Unfortunately this lovely time is soon going to end, but I secretly hope that the man, who must have lots of connections, could also do something for Peter in the future. Cross your fingers!

Before this beautiful trip, however, our dear son had a less glamorous job. For three days he was a carrier-pigeon keeper! Yes, Hansi, there are such things! There were four wagons of English carrier pigeons, which he had to feed, water, and clean; he slept in one of the wagons with them, and as he assured me, they didn't exactly smell like roses! The pigeons came from England and were taken to Nantes, where they were set loose to fly home. The pigeons' owners are Englishmen who keep them for sport. I should have their worries!

For today, then, 1,000 fondest greetings and kisses for all four of you, from your

Lene,

Are the chives growing yet? Wouldn't you have a gardening job there for me?

July 23

My dear children,

I enclose a little letter for Hansl's birthday; I hope the English book and the others from Lene arrive on time. I will buy the saints' pictures[48] today at St. Vitus Cathedral, where I stopped this morning while taking a walk over Letná Hill, and heard mass. It was an experience; the splendor of the interior, the pomp of the ceremony, the cardinals on their thrones, and the splendid choir. Indeed I very often go into one of the countless Prague churches, one more beautiful than the last, whenever I go by one. I have become neither more pious nor more of a believer since I outwardly joined that faith; but to be removed from this godless world, at least for a while, has such a calming effect—why should one not have at least that?

This week a friend of my sister Emma's family visited me. Max's health is improved, but their future is still very unclear; at any rate they won't have much left. Willi's house, store, etc. have been confiscated; he is still in Paris.[49] Toscha's Fritz hopes to receive his permission to emigrate within the next few days; this at least has become simpler, and many people are leaving—the lucky ones—at least they think themselves so; afterwards most of them are disappointed. Fritz is going to inquire at the American Consulate as to how the quota stands now; since one generally doesn't get beyond the doorman, he probably won't find out much.

Is it still so hot there? Do stay well, all my dear ones.

My heartfelt kisses,
Your Mamina

My dear sweet boy,

I had always hoped that I would be able to wish you a happy birthday in Havana and naturally also get a piece of birthday cake; unfortunately it didn't work out that way, and so I must wish you happy birthday on this piece of paper and imagine the cake. But in a year, we'll make up for it by celebrating a wonderful feast day, with Japanese lanterns and fireworks, just like at home.

I am so terribly curious about Havana and about your house, the garden, the cats, and the bananas, but especially about you and Renate; I won't even recognize you any more, you've grown so big.

48. Some of the books, along with some saints' pictures, did arrive for Hans's 10th birthday, August 20.

49. Mamina's sister Emma was married to Max Grünberger. Willi was their son.

Sometime you'll have to send me a map of the garden and write down all the things that grow there; naturally that interests me very much. If I can send you your crates, I want to put in some seeds and Papa's garden apron; I found it, and it's all ready to go.

Earlier I wanted to send seeds in a small package, but small packages aren't allowed. I've also packed a whole lot of your little toys that I had here—the ping-pong set and books, and I think the Wonderboat[50] is among them too. Tante Lene also wants to include some of Peter's old children's books. You'll have to write me all about what you got for your birthday, and if Mummy found 10 candles and made a cake.

By now you must already know lots of English. I am studying English hard too, all by myself, but I'm sure you have long since overtaken me, and I'll take lessons from you. The best thing will be if we play school; Renate will teach me English, and you, Spanish; that will be a terrific babble! Like hors d'oeuvres, a little of everything.

Now I have to stop writing, my fingers are all stiff and it's 10:30 at night. So I'll wish you a happy birthday once again, my dear good boy, and kiss you and Renate, my dearest girl, a thousand times.

Your Mamina

July 27

Dear Friedrich, dear Liesel,

We have a new hobby now, namely the declaring of jewelry, silver, and the appraisal of foreign bonds, etc. I am taking care of the former two for you, the latter doesn't concern you since you no longer live here; František is taking care of all the documentation. This occupation creates lots of work and very little pleasure.

You can imagine that Lene and I would be all too happy if we were already on our way. Eugen keeps consoling us with the assurance that everything is going well, but until it's accomplished we can undertake nothing here. Everything is soon declared invalid, and then one has to start over again from the beginning and go through the whole odyssey again.

50. Probably a battery-operated toy boat

I recently spoke with Walter Skutsch[51] at the Petschek office where I had gone to see Ernst. He has liquidated his household, "given away" his furniture, as he was not allowed to sell it—he brought it here just a year ago from Vienna. I don't know his new address. For the moment he wants to go to California. His childhood sweetheart wants to buy a bar or something there, and at her request he is learning to cook. He is crazy as ever, but looks well.

Stay well and happy,
Your Mama

▶ The difficulties that emigration involved are attested to by all writers on the subject, though they differ on the number of questionnaires required, some saying that fifteen were required, some sixteen, others eighteen. Probably the number changed, as did other requirements. Up to the early part of 1939, Gestapo permits had been easily available, and valuables and personal effects could be exported. On June 23, 1939, regulations were tightened, with more and more forms required and more restrictions on what could be taken along.

On July 22, Adolf Eichmann, representing the Department for Jewish Affairs in the *Reichssicherheitshauptamt* (the Central Security Office of the Reich government), established the *Zentralstelle für die Jüdische Auswanderung* (Central Office for Jewish Emigration) in Prague. It was manned by Gestapo officers who made the would-be emigrants wait in long lines, forbade them to lean against walls or put their hands in their pockets, etc.

August 1

Dearest Liesel,

It has been a long time since anything has pained me as much as having to take every single piece of your beautiful silver to be declared. Even if we haven't yet had to deliver it, that will come any day now; and thus these witnesses of former, better days will vanish too. My moods are like yours, my good child: Sometimes I can still come to terms with things and believe that life is still bearable, despite all of the past and the future; then there are hours during which I am consumed by longing for you, and everything here disgusts me; then comes another good letter from Friedrich and cheers

51. Ernst Skutsch's cousin, and a cousin of the Pollatscheks

me up. Your letters of course interest me especially, because then I can construct your lives and have the illusion of taking part in them.

The question of our departure is still very nebulous. Eugen recently asked again if we had heard anything from the consulate, but that is not the case—and once that has come, that is just the start of the odyssey of departure. You simply cannot have any conception of what difficulties this entails. Fritz B., who has twice been right at the door of his goal, now has to start all over again for the third time. Everything—documents, appraisals, etc.—is invalid and has to be obtained again. What that costs by way of effort, time, and money is something only those who have done it can understand.

A thousand greetings,
Mama

August 12

Dear Friedrich,

Both František and Dr. M. are still working on the transfer; I hope that will someday come to a happy end. For the moment of course everything is uncertain. However, some things are beginning to be tight: butter, for example, milk and other things; at any rate, everything has become expensive.

Yesterday I agreed with my landlord to keep the apartment until January—by then we will see more clearly what will happen, and either we will have left to visit Eugen, or we will have to arrange things quite differently. It may also happen that I might someday have Madeleine[52] instead of the maid; her cousin, together with her sons, wants to go to France where her son Walter lives, and it will surely be very hard for the poor thing—who I estimate must be 60 years old—to find another position. At her cousin's she works harder than ever and gets no salary at all—in fact, she even has to pay for her room—isn't that unheard-of?

A thousand kisses,
Mama

Chicken is something that we can't afford now; goose giblets are the only poultry we can manage.

52. Madeleine Schick, a cousin from Aussig

August 17

My dearest children,

It's terrible how long the mail takes, despite the Clipper;[53] on July 19 I mailed a letter via Clipper—I got it in the mail on time—and today, nearly a month later, I still have no answer.

I doubt, unless the Messiah comes, that the crates will ever leave here; but at any rate I have to give a precise list of the contents in order even to make a request—every handkerchief, coin purse, etc.—and in any case I should like to include in the list everything that you might need, so that I can then buy what I want; one can pack less than is listed, but not more. All kinds of clothing are very cheap now at the end of the season, especially shoes and underwear.

To save money is pointless in our case; I have enough money, and if I get away from here they won't leave me anything anyway. Beyond the Reich Emigration Tax of 42% of one's estate, everything else goes into expenses, the journey, etc., and fees, on everything that I take, each stocking, etc. I can keep 10 Marks. If I'm in luck and the state treasury happens to have money (I'm registered there), then I'm allowed to buy 100 Pounds Sterling at the current rate of exchange—but that only when I have the visa and exit permit, that is, just a few days before I leave. But usually the treasury has no money, and then whatever I still owned would stay here in a blocked account.

Of course I will attempt to set aside the amount for a possible exchange into hard currency, but nevertheless, I can easily buy a few useful things for you without impoverishing myself. Moreover, I don't believe in any departure in the foreseeable future. Even if one has the visa, then the Road to Calvary that one still has to travel is so indescribable, that I doubt whether my nerves would endure it. So let's wait a while, perhaps it will still change.

Our main concern now is plum dumplings. Meat is sinfully expensive, and we live mostly on vegetables and dessert, the latter almost exclusively made with margarine, since butter is scarce. But aside from that, everything is still available, even though the prices have risen a great deal. Of fruit I hardly eat any except for apples; it isn't fresh, and most of it is rotten. That is probably due to all the

53. A transatlantic plane

rain this summer; hardly a day passes without rain, and there has been much trouble and expense with the harvest.

The other developments you no doubt know from the papers. They aren't of a very happy nature, but our demands are no longer great. Moreover, I myself do not feel particularly injured by them, since I never sought these distractions and thus won't miss them; but for others it will be painful.

My only diversion is the weekly Sunday morning walk with Lene, which reveals the beauties of Prague in constantly new lights. Mostly we wander over the Hradčany,[54] but this time we also went to the deer park and saw the bears. What would I have given to have our little rascals there! Whenever I see a long skinny girl, or a boy of Hansl's age, tears come to my eyes and longing overcomes me.

Today I sat a while at the Belvedere—the benches are still ours, except in restaurants—and amused myself with a chubby little boy who with his father was playing soccer with chestnuts. Now and then he threw one to me and I had to throw it back. Every old man who came by was "grandpa." People here, like for example his father, are almost without exception nice, if one speaks their language.

In four weeks it will be a year that I have been here, and as I think about it, neither Lene nor I have made one step of progress, not even in sending you your few possessions. Albeit at the beginning it was our own fault, because of our indecision whether to send a lift or not; now none at all are shipped any more, and the people who did send them earlier had to pay large fees afterwards, so after all it's a good thing that we hesitated. On the whole, though, whatever we do is wrong, and we always have to pay for it; that is something we already count on.

I understand very well that you can bear the loss of your possessions more easily than I: you have come into new surroundings, thank God, and your new life brings you into new thoughts. We here hang on to all these accustomed things because they are the last thing that connects us with the past and with our lost lives—we have not yet found a substitute. What one calls "life" here is continuous agitation and anxiety with no resting place. I hope it will soon be different and better.

54. The Prague site of the castle and St. Vitus Cathedral

Are the little ones all over the eczema and the bandages?[55] Poor Liesel! What a lot of work she has, and I could help with so much of it, even though I'm not worth much any more.

A thousand greetings and kisses to you and the children,

Mamina

▶ The lives of Prague Jews became subject to more and more restrictions. A decree issued on August 14 prohibited Jews from using public swimming pools, hospitals, theaters, cafes, and restaurants, except for a few set aside specifically for them. Later, Jews were allowed to ride streetcars only on the trailer cars or on the platforms.

An example of the sympathy that non-Jewish Czechs exhibited toward the Jews was the boycott of streetcars undertaken one Saturday. On that day, workmen living in the outskirts arose at 3 A.M. in order to be able to walk to work and avoid the streetcars. This sympathy was all the more remarkable because of the fact that most Jews regarded themselves as Germans.

August 26

Dearest children,

The day before yesterday I received your letter No. 2 with the children's letters; I would have answered immediately, but in the evening we had a farewell supper with Fritz B., who is today, just as I write this, in the process of traveling to P.,[56] where he will get together with Eugen; from there he goes to the port, and with Mimi, whom he is to meet in P., boards an English ship that will, we hope, bring him to the land of his wishes.[57]

Yesterday Tonscha and we were still with him and in constant anxiety that some roadblock might yet turn up in the last minute. At eight in the evening I still rode out to see them; Fritz had deposited his luggage, with the duty paid, and had his ticket and documents; he was able to buy 150 Pounds from the English fund, and so we hope that everything will go smoothly.

55. The skin problem from which the Pollatscheks, parents as well as children, suffered was in fact boils, not eczema. These were deep and painful boils which, before the age of antibiotics, left large scars. The cause might have been improper nutrition.

56. Paris

57. The United States

A great many people have left during the last few days, including Mimi Skutsch's first husband for the USA with little Harry,[58] to his mother's great sorrow. We are now living through sorrowful days; I know that your thoughts are with us more than ever, and the knowledge that you are safe there helps us bear many things.

I interrupted the letter in order to go to the office to talk to Dr. M., and when I came home Toncha was just arriving. She had accompanied Fritz to the station. I intentionally did not go so that the parting would not be even more emotional. I kept Toncha here for the rest of the day; tomorrow too she will be here for lunch, and then we will go to Lene's. It will be very lonely for her all alone in the little apartment, but she is very happy that the boy got away, even though the worry about his daily bread will begin for him now.

A thousand greetings to you all, also from Toncha and Lene.

Your Mama

September 2

Dearest children,

I am sending these lines to Tante Ella with the request that she send them on, as I do not know if you can get news from us any other way. Since the 26th of August, on which I received Friedrich's letter No. 6, I have received nothing from you, except for Liesel's letter that came from Pepi on the same day. But today I received mail from Tante Ella promptly; on the other hand, Lene hears nothing from her men, which is very sad, since up to now these threads at least remained intact.

That, despite everything, the horror has now come to pass,[59] and the ways in which everything connects—about these things you are probably better informed than we. Naturally our mood is depressed, and all our plans and hopes are postponed into the distant future.

Outwardly, life continues peacefully, but yet everything is changed, and we do not yet know how to arrange our lives. At any rate we will sooner or later move in together, Lene and I, to await

58. Harry was Mimi Skutsch's (Ernst's wife's) son by her first marriage.

59. On September 1, 1939, Germany invaded Poland. Two days later, the day after this letter was written, Britain and France declared war on Germany.

the coming days before reaching a decision. If only we could find a smaller apartment; Lene's is terribly expensive, and at the same time not roomy at all, so that I can't store anything at all and would have to part with everything that I might still somehow be able to use. One must not be in too much of a hurry, since we must now count on having to stay here for a very long time yet, and our means will have to carry us through.

We are of course together every day, but in the evening everyone has to remain at home, since the blackout of the city makes going out impossible.[60] The windows have black paper pasted on the inside, so that one can have the lights on in the apartments, but there is no visiting.

Just today Tante Ella wrote that Fritz B. sends word to his mother that he is sailing on Wednesday on a different ship than planned; in other words, he is already on his way—alone, of course, since Mimi missed the connection.

A thousand greetings, also from Lene, who is here.

Your Mama

September 10

My dearest children,

I am preparing to move to Lene's as soon as possible. We have not been able to find a cheaper apartment, but we are lucky to have Lene's; the building belongs to a foreign company, and that is very advantageous.[61] Within the next few days I will sell the dining room furniture and a few other things that I can't find room for at Lene's. The bedroom furniture I will probably be able to keep—my dear old bed—and then we will get ourselves settled very cozily, without a maid; perhaps we will have the cleaning woman for an hour each day. Work is the best remedy for getting over all sorts of things, and we will do things very simply; the menu these days is no longer so complex anyway.

I can imagine that your thoughts must often wander toward us.

60. There was a blackout; however, a curfew on Jews (8 P.M. to 6 A.M.) was also imposed a short time later.

61. The advantage, no doubt, was that the foreign company did not discriminate against Jewish tenants. By November 9, Jews were forbidden to live in "Aryan" buildings.

Just tell the children that they must be patient, Mamina will certainly come, she just doesn't yet know when.

I kiss you thousands and thousands of times, and think of you all the time.

Your Mamina

September 28

My dearest children,

Today, after more than a month, mail from you—your letter No. 3. I received news from you last on August 24, and how much has happened since then! I can't report much about it, or else this letter would never reach you at all.

One thing will calm you: we are all well and bear what we must with the certainty that it will all pass and we will see each other again. But nobody can say when; all our plans are now invalid, regardless of whether they apply to the crates full of your things or to ourselves. We will wait patiently until our turn comes.

The worst thing is that we have no news of you at all, except for yesterday's letter and one from Eugen dated September 5. Nor do we know whether you have news of us; we write and write, by all the various routes. You can see by the number; I hope something at least has arrived.

Yesterday I moved to Lene's and am very happy about it. Now at least I am secure. My apartment was immediately rented, so that I didn't have to pay up the rest of my lease. We share the rent here, and with Ilse we share the maid and the cooking at noon; the other meals are of no great importance. Tonitschka, the maid, cleans up both apartments, washes our linens (with as little soap as possible), and we take turns cooking, one week at Ilse's and two weeks here. There is still enough to eat, but one must economize, and certain things are short at times—*c'est la guerre.*

Above all else, I am happy to know you and the little ones are in safety. Tonscha's Fritz has also arrived at his desired goal.

I am very happy about what you write of the children, that they are so happy and cheerful, and about their progress and Hansl's achievements. Life is a good school for them. By the time I see them again they will be grown-up young people, and I a little old woman;

but that doesn't matter—it will still be the most beautiful moment of my life.

Now stay well, don't worry too much about us; we'll hold out.

A thousand kisses,
Your Mamina

▶ Both Mamina and Friedrich numbered their letters to help each other keep track of what got through and how fast. The "routes" were probably via New York and via Switzerland.

After the outbreak of war in Europe, emigration became much more difficult. All 1,500 permits for Czech Jews to any of the British lands became invalid; for the United States, the Czech quota was only 2,700, and during fiscal year 1940, it was only 69 percent in use. By November, foreign shipping lines refused to accept German currency; thus, American consuls demanded proof of paid passage before granting visas. Washington also imposed stronger affidavit requirements. Nevertheless, between March 15 and the end of the year, 19,016 Jews left the "Protectorate" (how many of this number left before September, however, is not known).

October 5

Dearest Liesel,

Once more I wait from one day to the next for mail; in this I share Lene's fate; she is in the same position. Since the letter of September 3 that came via Switzerland, she has had no news. She recently heard—though indirectly—that her two men and those with them were well.

That is the most difficult thing for us to bear now, since, aside from the daily miseries of life, we are quite well. I feel very well since I've been living here with Lene, except that she spoils me very much and doesn't let me do enough work. We cook for ourselves now, since the card system makes it better for each to cook alone.[62] So Ilse keeps house for herself and so do we, with the maid's help. In the mornings one goes shopping with quite a nice little library,[63]

62. Rationing was instituted October 1.

63. The "library" included ration cards for different types of groceries—meat, bread, milk, etc.

sometimes one finds something, and sometimes not; but we get along quite well. After all, one gets used to many things; for example, I would never have thought that a mixture of half coffee and half Perola (corn coffee) would taste very good. In the mornings we drink tea in order to preserve the accustomed coffee hour for the afternoons.

Lene has given me the bedroom and fixed up the former dining room for herself with a couch. Of the furniture, I brought along only the bed, cupboards, your old desk, your old dresser and the sitting room set. The room is comfortable—your floor lamp, on the desk all your photos, on the wall the picture of Friedrich as a boy painted by Gaiger, under that the miniatures that I used to keep on my desk—that is my little world, which I can always creep back into.

Lene often has company, but that is good; most of them are dear people, and one has a chance for diversion and to speak one's mind, even if the topic is always the same. Grüner comes often; he is a dear old friend who takes care of everything that we women can't do alone; also Fritz Kettner, our assistant advisor in legal matters. František is unfortunately sick—for some time now he has suffered from a muscle disease in his arms and is being treated in a sanitarium here; I am awfully sorry for the good man.

A thousand kisses to you all,
Your Mamina

October 12

My dearest children,

At last the connection with you has been reestablished. I hope you too now have mail from me and from Pepi. Yesterday, from Pepi, I got Liesel's letter No. 11 of September 22, and at the same time Friedrich's No. 7 of September 18. Friedrich's letters Nos. 4, 5, and 6 are still missing.

I am boundlessly happy about the good news of you and what you write about the children, that they are always in good spirits and that they do so well in school. Each letter lost is such a pity and each line that tells of you; each is an hour of joy lost for me.

But with us too, so far everything has been bearable. That all of us J. had to give up our radios is very sad. The supplying of food by ration cards makes life difficult, but so far the provisions have been adequate, so that we suffer no hardship and always have enough to eat. Other than that, one notices little here of the events about which you, Friedrich, are surely better informed than we are.

We have had cold, autumnal, nearly wintry weather and already have to wear warm coats. I am busily knitting woolen gloves from old wool remnants that I found in Liesel's suitcase, scarves too, and whatever else I can get out of them.

Lene got a letter yesterday from Peter and today from Eugen. The former has work as a laborer; Eugen unfortunately has nothing yet, but they and Eugen's family are well.

I will deliver your greetings to Walter Skutsch. He has learned to cook, and, most recently, to make artificial flowers. He makes marvelous ones, some quite crazy, always original, and has also been able to sell some. The times aren't favorable, but someday he should be able to do something with this skill.

I will close now, and kiss you and the children a thousand times, as does Lene, also Tonscha.

Your Mama

▶ On the Day of Atonement, September 23, 1939, Jews had been ordered by the Gestapo to give up their radios. On the 25th, the Jews brought the radios to the synagogues, from which trucks hauled them away.

Meanwhile, the Jewish community ambitiously attempted to prepare would-be emigrants for making a living abroad. Jewish Community Centers in various cities, as well as the WIZO (Women's International Zionist Organization) sponsored courses in such activities as dressmaking, baking, nursing, photography, agriculture, candy making, making of artificial flowers, and various other skills, as well as languages.

October 31

My dearest Liesel,

Recently you are the one who has supplied most of the correspondence—that is, Pepi always sends me your letters, which, even though pretty stale, are always a great joy to me. Today I received your letter No. 6 of August 30 by this route; Friedrich's September

10 letter came yesterday and a card, No. 5, of August 13. So the mail makes the craziest leaps. Meanwhile I wait eagerly for the Clipper letter announced by Mrs. Conrad[64] and write regularly once a week to F. C., since I assume that that is the quickest way. Today for a change I am taking the simple route; it will arrive someday, I suppose, I imagine around Christmas.

Can one even think that there will be a Christmas once more? Better not for the moment; it would be good to break oneself of that habit entirely. Our only happiness is thinking of you and of our two men in that foreign land, even if we hear little of the latter, except that they are well and that so far they have not been directly affected.

That the children do so well in school and are so happy is my pride and my greatest joy; with God's help they will come undamaged through the insanity of this world and into a better future.

We live very quietly, mostly we stay at home within our four walls; that is the most agreeable place. The weather is cold and unfriendly; in the mornings mostly 2°,[65] in other words, not tempting for taking walks, and otherwise too the city lacks attractions. I only go out once in a while to visit Tante Tonscha or Mrs. Friedländer. Sometimes I go to Ernst and Mimi's, and they are often here too; anyhow, we have many visitors. Otto officiates as financial advisor on Lene's tax questions; Ernst Skutsch has taken over the commercial sphere, Dr. Fritz Kettner the legal matters, and a friend of Ilse's provides us with the news in the political arena. Then there are still others; at any rate they help pass the time, and that is important, since for the moment one cannot say, "*Verweile doch, Du bist so schön.*"[66]

Just now Walter Skutsch was here. Last week Lene and I were at his place, in his garret bachelor apartment, for him to take our pictures. He brought the proofs, which are quite excellent; as soon as we have the finished pictures I will send you some right away—they will probably have to serve as Christmas presents, if they get there

64. Franz Petschek's wife. See note 24.
65. Temperatures are given in Celsius.
66. "Remain a while, you are so fair," an often-quoted line from Goethe's *Faust*

at all. I wrote you that he makes artificial flowers, lately of fur—they really are little works of art; it's a pity that he can't get a craftsman's license to make his talents pay off here.

This afternoon we had a modest little tea: Mrs. Friedländer, Mrs. Libitzky,[67] Tonscha—everyone sends regards. Dr. Hans Libitzky is in London; his children have been there in a children's home for several weeks, and he is near them now. He himself lives in a camp, fells trees and cuts wood, and waits until he can move on to the U.S. His wife is still here for the moment and cannot travel there now; Mimi is in the same situation in Vienna. Life is not easy, and happy is he who can live together with his own family, however modestly. Among all our acquaintances here there is hardly one family that has this joy; all are separated and "gone with the wind."

Stay well, all my loved ones, and keep up hope for a reunion.

A thousand kisses,
Your Mama

November 6

My dearest children,

I engaged Ernst Skutsch to take care of the transfer question in František's stead. He spoke repeatedly with František and Dr. M.; the latter yesterday let me know via Ernst that I myself should go to the Bebka[68] to speak to the gentleman there whose name he gave me. So this morning I went there and was greeted very cordially (there is a new German employee there—our old acquaintance is not there any more); I described your dilemma—in a foreign country with two small children—and told him that you urgently needed the sum for the necessities of life. He said the following: write to your son; the company that took over this transfer business is no longer able, because of the circumstances, to finish them because it is a matter

67. A friend of Mamina. Her son Hans was a physician who, with his children, immigrated to England. His wife stayed in Prague and went underground. They both survived the war. The camp Hans lived in was one of several such set up in England for refugees.

68. The Böhmische Escompte Bank, a formerly Jewish-owned bank that had been "Aryanized"—i.e., taken over by Germans and its Jewish employees replaced by Gentiles—in February 1939.

of blocked Pounds. However, we have already given instructions to have the commission taken away from this company and given to another one, which works with Swedish Crowns, which can easily be changed into dollars, and we hope that we will succeed in bringing this matter to a conclusion.

We are working on this with all our energy. I am supposed to come again in about two weeks to inquire; I hope it will finally work. At any rate I have the feeling that the bank is really serious about it.

Lene sends her regards. She added to my last letter to Liesel. I hope that that letter will reach you, because the fact that you do not receive my mail, while Pepi's arrives, is inexplicable to me. However, there are more such things on heaven and earth.

A thousand kisses to you, stay well and don't worry about us.

Your Mama

November 17

My dearest children,

This letter is intended as a Christmas letter. How odd this sounds today, such a long time off, and yet I don't know whether it will even reach you in time, the mail goes so slowly. Next year I hope to be able to celebrate Christmas with you. What more may we live through by then! One mustn't ponder too minutely, but just hold out to the happy ending, which nobody here doubts.

Lene has been racking her brain about how you would get a Christmas tree this year—if there are such things as pine trees there. She remembers one day in Nestersitz when you came with the children, and she hung little presents for them on the palm tree in the solarium; she imagines that a Christmas tree in Havana would be something like that. At that time we never thought that our little ones would be wandering beneath the palms.

Lene and I plan to buy ourselves a fatted goose as each other's Christmas present, mainly for the fat. Such tempting prospects help us pass the time.

Stay well and happy, all my dear ones; my fondest kisses,

Your Mamina

▶ On October 28, the Czechoslovakian independence day, serious anti-German rioting had broken out in Prague. Four persons were killed, many wounded, and thousands arrested. The following weeks brought further unrest and demonstrations, especially from November 16 to 19. A number of students charged with being ringleaders of the October 28 demonstrations were shot—reports vary from twelve to one hundred twenty-four. Reports on the number arrested also vary, from two thousand to eight thousand. The university was ordered closed for three years.

Mamina reports in a brief letter of November 18 that the events those days had not directly affected her and Lene, as they lived away from the center of the city.

The following letter is addressed to Franz Petschek.

December 5

Dear Mr. Petschek:

Today I received the following telegram from Friedrich: "Could probably get Cubavisa for you and Lene, wire if and when possible to leave, all are well."

You can imagine into what a dilemma this telegram has plunged us; on top of that we cannot telegraph abroad, so I am not able to give Friedrich the requested prompt answer, even if it were possible to make such a difficult decision so quickly.

For us a journey to Cuba is hardly possible, and I think too that Friedrich is not serious about this solution for now. My daughter of course has just one goal—to see her husband and son again soon; for now that is impossible, and what should she do in Cuba? I, on the other hand, much as I yearn to see Friedrich, Liesel and the children, can't make up my mind to travel there, because, as Friedrich wrote me some time ago, he is ahead of me in registering for the USA, and so I would have to sit alone in Cuba for a year or even longer after he had left. That, and the fear of my health not bearing up under the summer heat, gives me pause: the past year has left its mark on me.

I assume that Friedrich's purpose with the visa is to give us both the opportunity to get away from here, and to wait it out in another country until some decision for the future can be made. But what country could that be? I think that aside from Italy there can be no other, and there too I am not quite clear about a residence for this waiting time.

Only one thing is clear: Both of us, Lene and I, would have to leave behind everything that we still own; and we have no sources of income abroad that we could live from, even if we lived as modestly as ever possible.[69] Friedrich can't possibly support us both, nor can Lene's husband, who so far has not succeeded in finding any employment. Thus the question is whether we shouldn't just continue our lives here, which, though not all too pleasant, at least give us the possibility of living simply and economically, without being a burden to anyone, until the moment that makes a reunion with our loved ones possible.

Excuse this long epistle; I had to burden you with it in order to give you a picture of our situation, without which an answer to Friedrich would be too difficult to understand. Since I can only give him this answer in writing, I beg of you, dear Mr. Petschek, to cable him a few words that will inform him to such an extent that he will neither rush into anything nor miss anything, if that is possible, and that he should wait for my letter, which will go out in the next mail. If I knew that the charges for the visas were not too high, then I would not try to prevent Friedrich from getting them at any rate; on the other hand, I, and especially Lene, don't want to burden him too much.

I hope you can understand the difficulty into which we two poor women have fallen and will forgive the trouble we are putting you to; you owe that to your own kindness, by which you offered to put yourself at our disposal.

This week I received a Clipper letter from Friedrich from October 19, which arrived here on December 1; the mail from there to here functions very unreliably.

I thank you very heartily for your last card; I entrust everything

69. An arrangement between Italy and Czechoslovakia permitted refugees to take along a certain amount of money, which they could live on for up to six months. (In view of Mamina's statement that she would have to "leave everything behind," it's not clear whether she knew of this.) In addition, the Italian steamship lines charged lower fares than most; however, on their way to Italy, many refugees got stuck in Austria.

to your goodness, with which you have heretofore treated my children and me.

With my warmest greetings to you and yours,

Yours very faithfully,
H. Pollatschek

December 7

My dear boy,

Your telegram plunged us into a quite an uproar, and since it is unfortunately impossible to wire abroad from here, there remained only one way, that is to ask F. C., that good man, to give you an answer, so that you would know something as quickly as possible. In the meantime, we, Lene and I, have consulted with our friends here; above all we asked Erwin Ch.[70] to visit us, which he still did yesterday evening before I wrote to F. C., as, at the first moment, we didn't know what to do.

The thing is that up till now nothing at all has happened to us personally; we live completely unmolested and have our good livelihood and our friends, who stand by us always and in everything. The other things that take place are not always very pleasant, and what else might happen, nobody knows. It is clear, however, that the emigration of Jews is desired and actively promoted by the government, though almost the only possibility in fact is Palestine. All of this primarily concerns men with families, though no cut-off has yet been set. As to us single women, whose men are already abroad and who naturally wish to follow them as quickly as possible—they will surely give us time.

Now if you can obtain visas for us, it would be, as everyone advises us, an advantage, above all if these visas are valid for a long period of time. For the time being we would like to wait and see how various things work out. Lene doesn't want to go to Cuba in any case, since she hopes above all to get to her people, which for the moment is still not possible. For me, this possibility (going to Cuba) is still not a serious one since I would after all have to wait one and a half to two years there alone if you should in the meantime reach your desired goal.

70. Erwin Chobocky, a relative, who later emigrated to Palestine.

I doubt very much that I would be able to get through the summer there; the year has not gone by without leaving its traces, and 70 years is not something that you can wish away. You mustn't believe that I am sick: I am totally well; but the extreme, humid heat would do me no good. And at no price would I want to become a burden to you, that is, to know in advance that that would happen.

Now, if we can get these visas, if you want to make that sacrifice for us, then we would have the guarantee of being able to get away to someplace as soon as the need arose. *Where* is quite unclear to us, as is what to live on there; I don't know how well informed you are as to the conditions under which emigration can take place. Just one thing: one leaves with 10 Marks in one's pocket. But the idea that you should support not only me, but Lene too, for months or perhaps years, is not conceivable to me, far less to Lene. So please, get the visas for us if you want to make the sacrifice for us, and we will wait for further developments. After all, we are all united in our fate here, and must bear together whatever comes.

Just incidentally, Lene would love to save the furniture and whatever else remains for her people, as would I the few things that still remain; if we leave, everything is lost beyond hope. Actually, if one goes to Palestine, one can take even a lift, if one has enough money, and even a partial transfer; but we can't go there just because of that—what would we do there?

Now just one cheerful item: yesterday I was at the bank and spoke with Dr. H., who is working on your transfer affair, and he assured me that things looked very favorable, and payment would follow in the nearest future. I hope to God that it's all really true this time; he will call me on Monday and let me know whether everything is working out. Till then I'll cross all my fingers.

Now, a thousand kisses to you all,

Your Mama

Do send a picture of all of you sometime.

▶ If the problem of *emigration* was complicated—by the dozens of permits and papers required, not to mention the sacrifices of money, belongings, and friends left behind—the problem of *immigration* was no less so. The only completely accessible goal was Shanghai, which had no financial or other requirements. Some eighteen thousand Jews did choose to go there; but the fact that a woman of almost seventy would not consider Shanghai a serious possibility is not surprising.

Palestine was also relatively accessible, if one had money. The British White Paper of May 1939 restricted Jewish immigration to ten thousand per year for the next five years. However, an additional twenty-five thousand Jews could be admitted immediately if they were able to prove adequate funds. (These emigrants were officially labeled "capitalists.") The language problem, however, was a cause of hesitation among many German-speaking refugees. Culturally, too, the Germans were markedly different from the Eastern European Jews, who formed the larger part of the Palestinian immigration.

Mamina's hesitation about spending the summer in Cuba might have been influenced by the following passage from Joseph Wechsberg's *Visum für Amerika,* published in 1939:

> As for the tropics! Many Europeans are so desperate today, that they declare they would rather go to the Gran Chaco or to the feverish areas of Sumatra, than to have to stay in Europe. If one no longer has any choice, if remaining in Europe is made impossible for him, then he can't take his time in choosing; but whoever still has the chance not to have to take the worst thing, should not disregard too casually considerations of the climate and the possibilities for making a living. . . . Emigrants should not forget that tragedies do not exist only in Europe. Out there, too, in the paradisiacal lands where they would so gladly be, fate can overtake one. Against that, one can do nothing but be careful, make conscientious inquiries before going anywhere, and above all, inquire of people who can give reliable information. (17–18)

Just preceding this passage, Wechsberg tells the story of a couple who went into the interior of Brazil and perished there of disease and "the climate."

December 11

My dear Liesel,

We now unfortunately hear so little from you, and when we do the news is at least two months old; the mail functions so badly. That is surely because all letters now arrive censored.

Now it will soon be Christmas, and it will probably be Easter before I find out how you celebrated this holiday in such a changed milieu. Now that the first Christmas trees have been set up in the squares—miserable, bug-eaten, broomlike spruces, one doesn't see any nice fir trees—I think with sadness of past beautiful Christmases, even though I keep telling myself that one should not think back, only forward: it's hard to avoid it.

In the past few days the weather has been just as it should be at this season—thick snow is on the ground. Today, Sunday, Lene and I were again in the park, the first time in a long time. It was as wonderful as in the mountains: not even the fog was missing. The young people raced around with sleds; here and there one could even see skiers, and we wondered whether Friedrich misses this sport. You will surely be able to control yourself, and perhaps there in the eternal sunshine the thought doesn't even occur to you.

Here the weather is just about all that is Christmasy. The breathtaking shop windows and the lovely things of earlier days are of course gone, and at four it's pitch dark except for the street lights, and one is happy to stay in the warm room knitting, so far as one still has wool, or one does what Lene does and rips out the old things in order to knit new ones, as there is no wool to buy. I use all the little scraps for gloves, for which I always find takers.

It will comfort you to know that of our various friends and acquaintances who are still here, nothing has happened to anyone. If only we would hear from you more often, everything would be much easier. Meanwhile our little rascals will become big, sturdy children, and when, as I hope, we see each other again in the USA, I won't recognize them, and they won't recognize their little shriveled-up granny either. Normally it would still take at least two years for me, but today I heard from an acquaintance that mothers, that is, parents, can be brought over by their children if the latter have been living there for a year. I don't know whether it is true; these matters often change also.[71]

I enclose a letter that Grüner gave me for you. He looks quite poor without there being anything especially wrong with him, but his sister complains that he eats too little, in order—true to form—to get accustomed to it; in other words, he allows himself nothing, even though he still has everything that he might want, since we do not yet suffer any need, even though not everything is to be had

71. It was not true, just another rumor.

abundantly, as it once was. One simply does with what one gets; it is strictly a matter of money and accounting.

I have lots of mail from Pepi; we always exchange your letters, and when there are none, we write each other anyway. I would so love to see her, but unfortunately that isn't possible. I have no longing for our old home. The people here, without exception and in all walks of life, are so nice and make us feel so completely at home that it does one good and helps one bear up under other things. When I think of our dear former fellow-citizens,[72] I can't feel any homesickness for them, no matter how hard I try.

That you have such nice friends makes me especially glad; since you used to live there in such isolation, you will know how to appreciate associating with nice people. Will the new German friend come to visit the children again? And has Renate found a girlfriend other than Josephine? I can hardly imagine what the children look like now, and would so love to have another snapshot of them.

Now I must close. I kiss you a thousand times,

Your Mamina

▶ Since they barely knew either English or Spanish, the Pollatscheks' social life in Havana was understandably limited largely to other refugees and their families. One friend was Friedrich's secretary, Dr. Heinz Ekstein, whose mother Mamina was to meet in Prague later on.

Language and cultural differences made it hard for the children to make friends at school, and as a result they relied much on each other for company. One friend, however, was Wolfgang Scheider, son of a German refugee couple, who came occasionally to visit. They also played with Josephine, the daughter of the Pollatscheks' Jamaican maid Lilla. Josephine, who was a few years older than Renate, spent weekends at the Pollatschek house, where Lilla lived. Renate had no other girlfriends.

Hans and Renate also found companionship in Scheki and Blacky, the cats that had come with the house. The cats' names, assigned them by the children,

72. Many of the German-speaking Gentiles of the so-called Sudetenland belonged to the Sudeten German party, which sympathized with the Nazis and welcomed the German occupation.

reflect the degree to which the children were assimilating English into their vocabularies: *Scheki* is German for "Spotty," while *Blacky* is already an English name.

December 18

My dearest children,

On Monday of last week I went with Tonscha to visit Tante Emma;[73] it was my first trip since February of last year, and I think I would not have gone at all if I'd had to go alone. But everything went well; we left here in the morning, were there by noon, and by Wednesday afternoon we were home again.

Tante is much better; she had been looking forward so eagerly to our visit—we hadn't seen each other in more than two years. She has to be very careful, but her heart, the doctor assures us, is not damaged, it's just a severe nervous exhaustion.

Max looks very bad, the poor thing; he is sadly changed for the worse. So is everything else in the whole family there, except that they have finally had news from their son. The three girls are scattered to all corners of the world: the oldest is about to immigrate to Palestine, the young woman, not yet divorced, lives with her brother, and the youngest is a hairdresser's apprentice and is delighted when she receives a tip. I thank God every day that He has spared you the fate of having to separate from your children, as so many parents must nowadays, and that you can live in that paradise of a country.

I hope Santa Claus kept his word and brought you a little, long-due gift.[74] I was asked not to write much about it, dear son, nor you neither, it is to be a surprise. But I quietly hope that you will cable me if everything works out.

I wonder whether my photo has arrived, that is, two photos, one with Lene and Tonscha taken some time ago by Fritz B. in my apartment a few weeks before his departure, and a second made by Walter of me, as well as one of Lene by the same hand. Two books for the little ones, as well as two from Peter's collection should have arrived by now; they are poor little presents this year. I still bought a whole series of the new Protectorate stamps for Hansl, but for now I

73. Mamina's sister Emma, her husband Max, and the rest of the Grünberger family lived in Trebitsch, near Brünn (Brno), Moravia.

74. i.e., the money transfer

have to keep them since I am not allowed to send them in a letter. I am also saving all sorts of envelopes.

I am terribly excited to find out what a Cuban Christmas Eve is like at your friends'; do write me everything about it, even if it is a long time before I receive the letter. At any rate we will be with you in our thoughts, and with our other loved ones, and as merry as we can be under these circumstances.

Stay well, and may you have all that is good and beautiful, my beloved ones.

Your Mamina

Greetings from Lene, Tonscha, Otto, Ernst, Walter, etc.

December 22

My dearest Friedrich,

It is true, as you write, that there are still people who are leaving, but I also know that all of them without exception lose their nerves and all their earthly goods in doing so. The former frightens me almost more than the latter. Palestine is easier, but for us that is out of the question.

By the way, upstairs at Ilse's they are having a farewell party for Erwin Ch., who, very reluctantly, leaves Sunday for the Promised Land—as a Capitalist, moreover, thus with more favorable conditions. He is a marvelous fellow, and I wish him and Margit all the best. In the afternoon he sent us, as a farewell gift, a magnificent box containing all sorts of delicacies—turkey, bacon, sardines, gorgeous fruit, wine, liqueurs; from Fribourg[75] we received a package of cocoa and chocolate. So we'll be able to carouse at Christmastime.

But we'll always think of you celebrating Christmas in your airy summer clothing, whereas we had 4° this morning.

Many, many kisses to you and the children, not omitting Scheki and Blacky; they are enchanting animals, and I look forward to making their acquaintance. Greetings from Lene.

Your Mamina

75. Home of Onkel Fritz

1940

New Year's Day

Dearest Liesel,

Dr. Fritz Kettner and Otto came to wish me a happy New Year; then at ten they went with Lene up to Ilse's, where the usual party of 12 celebrated New Year's Eve with a buffet and punch. Earlier Lene and I manufactured 70 sandwiches, partly kosher ones, and she also prepared two cold platters, appropriate to the times but very appetizing. They said it was very pleasant, and Otto was unusually lively; at any rate, the guests did not depart until four in the morning.

In the meantime I slumbered through the night sweetly and undisturbed, as you usually do also. This morning I went to New Year's mass at the nearby church, St. Antoniček; it was very beautiful, wonderful singing; and then I went walking for a hour at the Belvedere in sun and snow. It was only 4°, as opposed to 15° and higher, as in the last few days, thus very agreeable. Now we all hope that our New Year's wish will be fulfilled and that we will all see one another again in the year 1940. I'll cut a piece of paper off today, since the air-mail lady found the last letter too heavy, though I have used the same paper for a long time.

So I must close. A thousand kisses to you all,

Your Mama

All the best from Lene.

1940

January 8

My dearest children,

Yesterday František visited me for the first time since he went to the sanitarium, and he sends his greetings; he too would like very much to know whether the "package" has arrived. He looks very well, but his right arm seems to be totally useless; he drank his coffee with his left hand, poor man—I suppose there is nothing more to be done.

In your last letter you asked about Karl and Karli and whether they contribute anything to our cuisine. Oddly enough, on the very day that the letter arrived, Karli came in the afternoon bringing a chicken, her last one. Up to now she has occasionally given Tante Tonscha something, but not us; but I knew that they had nothing themselves.

Cítov[1] has long since been under the direction of the commissariat, and they receive only a very restricted allowance of foodstuffs and 250 Crowns weekly. Their stay there will also be of short duration; the only lucky thing is that a nephew of theirs has leased a place; he is a bachelor and will take Karli and the children to stay with him; she will keep house for him and take care of the chickens, vegetables, etc. Karl is not allowed to live there and will find a place to live here or nearby and try to earn some money.

The daughter, Vera, is often sick and seems to have something wrong with her lungs. I happened to find out that our good old chief doctor, Dr. Adler, formerly chief of the Aussig sanitarium, is here, and on Karli's request I looked him up so that he could have a look at the child. She is to go to him the day after tomorrow.

He was clearly delighted to see me, and I had to tell him everything about you and all of us, including Pepi, Willi, etc. He looks marvelous and is about to start a new job as the head of a new J. lung sanitarium near here.

After seeing him one time, I had him examine me too, mainly to ascertain whether I could go to the tropics. After a thorough examination he declared that I am in perfect health and could easily

1. Karl and Karli's home

travel to Havana; but he advised me strongly against taking such a trip under our understandably unfavorable circumstances and proposes waiting until one can take the trip in peace and without destroying one's nerves. And we really are fine; one gets used to everything if one is healthy and if one can live, as we have, at least up to now, sheltered from financial privations.

We must postpone what you write about Italy and other travel plans. We have firmly decided to stay here and not to plunge ourselves into some adventure. To go there now would be an adventure; one cannot know what the immediate future will bring, and we cannot now immediately surrender everything that we still possess in order to go and live somewhere on alms. It's totally impossible to go to Eugen, as well as to sister Ella—that much we know for sure.

So, dear, good boy, don't rack your brains any longer, but stay calm and hold out, as we do, for a better future to come soon and a reunion in quiet and peace.

A thousand kisses,
Your Mamina

▸ Karl and Karli were the son and daughter-in-law of Mamina's sister Olga. With their children, Vera and Karel, they lived at Cítov, a farm near Prague. Cítov had been confiscated by the Nazis (it was "under the direction of the commissariat"); still, for a time they were able to bring foodstuffs to augment Mamina's and Toncha's diet.

Karli was a Gentile, thus the marriage was a "mixed" one, and the children were *Mischlinge,* "half-breeds." The fact that Karl was Jewish no doubt accounts for his not being allowed to live with the bachelor nephew, who apparently had leased an Aryans-only dwelling.

January 13

My dearest ones,

Since the day before yesterday we have a new "daughter" living with us—Karli's Vera, whom we asked to come for a few days.

The poor people had a terrible scare just before their departure: on Monday night their house burned down to the cellar. The cause of the fire was some carelessness in thawing the frozen water pipes in the attic; there were no firemen, and the only water was frozen, so that it was only with the greatest effort that they were able to save some furniture, clothing, and linens. On top of that the terrible cold—for nearly three weeks we regularly have had between −10° and −20°!

Karl and Karli are living in an inn in the village, and the girl, who catches cold very easily, will stay with us until her mother has moved into her new home. Dr. Adler examined her and advised great caution, since, at 16, she is at the most dangerous age. She is a dear, well-brought-up child, helps whenever she can, and Lene is happy with her windfall daughter. Today, in fact, she made dumplings all by herself.

This afternoon Otto was here and sent his greetings; he, as well as our friend Dr. Fritz K., will come more often now in the afternoons—the doctor has forbidden them to go out in the evenings. When the weather changes they will be able to do so again; you can imagine, dear son, that sitting in the house all the time is very boring for them, as it is to Ernst; the fellows always liked coming here in the evenings.

Since last night the weather has suddenly begun to get warmer. The skaters will be sorry about that, because as recently as yesterday the Moldau was frozen all the way across and covered with skaters. The children start skating here at four years old, and I kept thinking of our little ones—how they used to skitter about on the ice while we watched from above. The memories simply don't let one go, ever, anywhere. Renate would surely be a great figure skater by now, and I imagine that she as well as Hans must be equally skilled on roller skates.

I would love sometime to see some lines from them in English. I got out my English textbook again and am busy studying, since I no longer have any wool for knitting. I made eight pairs of gloves out of various remnants, but now there is nothing left. I will still probably have Lene teach me to type; in the mornings of course we are busy with the household, but in the afternoons and evenings we have plenty of time, and we miss the knitting.

Now a thousand kisses to you and the children, from Lene too.

Your Mamina

▸ The phrase "dear son" again alerts us to a code message: the fellows stayed home at night not because of doctor's orders, but because of the curfew, which was now evidently being enforced.

Rumors of deportations had started: *Aufbau,* the German-language Jewish paper published in New York, reported on January 19 that ninety thousand Jews were to be banished from Prague by February 1—healthy persons between the ages of seventeen and fifty-five to work camps, others presumably to prisons or concentration camps. The February 9 issue, however, reported a postponement of the deportations.

January 26

Dear Friedrich,

Let me introduce my best pupil and send you my heartiest greetings.

Your Lene

[typewritten]

My dearest children,

Because of lack of wool I have taken up typing; it still goes very slowly, but since nobody is after me to hurry, I can play around with this new hobby.

For the past three weeks we have had terrific cold and lots of snow—it would be skiing weather for you; we have no use for it and think with longing of the sun that shines on you. To warm myself I read your letters over and over.

Because of the cold, we also go out very little; it always takes an hour to put on all the stockings, pants, and overshoes. Only with Vera I go out every day; she is a dear child and isn't at all in the way. On the contrary, Karli brings us fresh eggs and butter, a luxury we have long done without.

After an agonizing battle with her conscience, Karli has decided to get a divorce; it is her only possibility of finding refuge for herself and the children. Karl hopes to get some sort of job in farming, and then they will wait for better times.

Lene finally had a letter from her husband again today, he writes that Peter is working hard; he seems to have been gripped by ambition to reach the goal that he missed earlier. Unfortunately Mama Sophie is not too well—she cannot walk by herself. We are terribly sorry for the poor old people.

Tante Tonscha has heaps of mail too from her son. Meanwhile Mimi has landed happily there,[2] and now they will have to find work.

Just now Otto was here and admired my typing art; just for that I promptly made an error. He sends his greetings. He is skinny as a rail, but to our pleasure has become an optimist, as we all are.

Today I went to find out what's happened to Santa Claus, about whom František took so much trouble a while ago; I've written you about that. The gentlemen assured me again that it had been transmitted by cable on December 12th to the address you gave, and now I wait impatiently for confirmation from you.

[The letter continues handwritten.] The typewriter is an old piece of junk and omits letters, especially at the ends of the lines, and it has a special hostility to the letter *d;* we must have it repaired. The typing gives me much pleasure, and I will work on it further. Hansl must surely know more than I by now; it's amazing that he works on French now too, and Renate, the good child, works with him. What won't those sweet children know by the time I see them again!

In return for Liesel's recipe for the bean dish, I will send you a good recipe for a kind of antipasto, as follows: cook all sorts of diced vegetables—celery, carrots, small Brussels sprouts, onions or leeks, cauliflower, peppers (one), French beans (two), peas—in short, whatever you have on hand. Let them cool. With the broth, make a good, thick tomato sauce, and let that cool also. On a platter, set out a can (or two, if you like) of sardines or tuna in oil, cut in pieces, put the oil into the tomato sauce; capers, some small pickles, pieces of cucumber, or whatever spicy things you wish, and the vegetables, and pour the tomato sauce over it all. You of course have much greater possibilities; here vegetables are very rare now and expensive too, like everything else, in fact.

2. Peter's "goal" was to join the army. He joined the Czech Army in exile at Agde, France, on October 17, 1939, fifteen days after its formation. Mama Sophie was Eugen's mother. Mimi had landed in the United States to join her husband, Fritz Bischitzky. She had missed the connection earlier and had to travel separately (see letter of September 2, 1939).

A thousand kisses to you; please have the little ones write me a few lines in English sometime; it would give me much pleasure.

Mamina

▶ The above letter is noteworthy for two things: it is Mamina's first typewritten letter, and it is the first letter with the censor's marks. The marks are numbers stamped or written on the corners of the letters; no words were censored in any of Mamina's letters, probably because of the care she took in writing them. The letter is introduced by Lene's brief note.

Karli's decision to get a divorce was based partly on the Nüremberg Laws, a version of which was issued in Prague by *Reichsprotektor* von Neurath on June 21, 1939. According to the laws, an "Aryan" married to a Jew would not be affected by anti-Jewish legislation, nor would the children of such a marriage—provided the couple divorced. By 1942, "mixed" couples were forced to divorce. By divorcing Karl, Karli hoped to preserve herself and the children. She had been advised to do this by Lolly, a lawyer, the husband of Onkel Fritz's adopted daughter Daisy. But another reason for the divorce may have been the fact that the marriage was not an altogether happy one. Since Jews married to Gentiles were, in fact, usually safe in the Protectorate, an unfortunate result of the divorce was that Karl lost this protection.

Otto's optimism, as well as Mamina's determination not to leave just yet, were apparently typical of the mood of the time. H. G. Adler states: "Though morale suffered, there was always humor, albeit gallows humor, and people gave in to optimistic fantasies. People learned practical skills, and almost all believed that Germany would soon be defeated. This mood was also fed by the boundless optimism of the Czech people" (1960, 15) (my translation).

The Czech Gentiles, as noted earlier, were on the whole friendly to the Jews, and together with them, hoped for an early end to the Nazi occupation and a restoration of their independence. Thus the decision to leave was all the harder for Jews to make, surrounded as they were by a sympathetic majority—a situation markedly different from that of German or Austrian Jews.

February 1

My dearest children,

A thousand thanks for your dear letter No. 24 from Friedrich and Liesel, and for the adorable English letters from the children. I showed them to Otto, and he could hardly believe that they had really written them. Lene and I were very happy about the report of your Christmas Eve; it must have been charming. I wonder if I will ever again hear Liesel and the children singing. I would give Caruso for that. I can imagine the joy; there were of course lots of presents, and my only worry is how the kitties will get along with the little bird.

What makes me happiest is that my little surprise arrived; a stone has audibly fallen from the heart of the person who sent it. A sequel is, however, quite impossible for the moment; they no longer manufacture that particular article,[3] and I beg you not to mention it again. I should also like not to mention business matters: they would only delay our letters, as would addresses.[4] Let's leave all that for later.

Today was our farewell visit to the company offices. We received a pretty memento; they have taken a lot of trouble for us.[5] Still, it was a melancholy moment to see the few last Mohicans there together for the last time. Thus blow follows blow.

Our guest Vera is still here. We have become very fond of the girl; she cheers us up, helps where she can—that is, as far as we allow her to, since she has to be very careful. Our old chief doctor insists on it, if she is to become fully healthy. Unfortunately, to Karli's great regret, he is going to leave Prague in order to go, with his wife and children, to Norway, where he has a work permit as head of a lung sanitarium.

As for us, we are quite well and in good health and have withstood the abnormally severe winter well up to now. The oldest people can hardly remember freezing weather of such long duration: for six weeks we have had temperatures below −10°! Only the young people are happy: the whole Moldau is one big skating rink; we often stand and admire the little children who are already real figure-skaters! Our little rascals would love that. But we who engage in no winter sports are already heartily tired of the winter.

3. The "little surprise" was the money transfer. A regulation of November 14, 1939, prohibited Jews from disposing of the income from houses or lands. Instead, receipts were to be placed into blocked accounts. Thus no "sequel" was possible.

4. No doubt because of censorship problems

5. The "pretty memento" was probably cash.

February 5

I let the letter wait in order to make the connection with the Clipper tomorrow. In the meantime the typewriter has been taken to be repaired, which it is really in need of; and today I received your letter, delivered by Ernst, No. 25 of January 9.

If it is possible to get the visa, then it would be quite right, as you say, to do it, and a comfort just in case. Nevertheless, for the time being we aren't thinking of leaving, because everything is much more difficult and complicated than you imagine. A lengthy stay in Italy (possible only if one possesses ship tickets) is not assured. Elsa,[6] for instance, wrote just recently that she is having great difficulties, she cannot get to where Franz is either and will probably have to come back here soon. We could not do that, since a return here would be impossible. A life abroad, without means, without friends and occupation would be very sad for us.

In short, we cannot for the moment make up our minds to leave. Please don't press us. You know how much my heart draws me to you, but it is a wild adventure from beginning to end, one that I can't draw Lene into. Just what you write about your crates shows how poorly informed you are: there is no possibility of sending even one or two; they lie well stored in the cellar awaiting their resurrection.

Don't worry too much about us; after all, we are not alone here, and we are really quite all right; even the weather seems to be changing and getting warmer. We thank you, my good boy, for your love and for everything that you wish to do for us.

A thousand kisses for you two and the children, and the same from Lene.

Your Mamina

▸ In a letter dated February 2, Mamina reports that Walter Skutsch was now giving courses in making artificial flowers, that Paul Gibian, another acquaintance, was no longer able to do office work and was studying watch repairing, that

6. The wife of Franz Bischitzky, another son of Mamina's sister Olga. Franz had gone to Sweden.

Eugen Mahler, Friedrich's former law partner, was home from the "sanitarium," and that Erwin Chobocky, a cousin, had arrived in Palestine.

February 24

My dearest children,

Yesterday morning the mailman brought a package with delicious contents from Onkel Fritz. Earlier, I had received a package of cheese that he had announced, so I can guess with certainty that this welcome gift originates with you. A thousand thanks.

And then an hour later came my dearest and secretly most longed-for gift, your adorable pictures. At first I couldn't help crying bitterly at seeing you there all together, such a perfect likeness; but now I am boundlessly happy and keep looking at the pictures over and over. You do all look so splendid, Friedrich in fact really sturdy, but Liesel too, and the children—how big they have grown and how adorable Renate is with her new hairdo. Liesel has changed her hair style too, I see, and it suits her charmingly, and everyone in the building comes to admire the pictures.

I begged Lene to celebrate my birthday as quietly as possible; this is no time and no spirit for celebrating, and it would only give me pain to pass this day without you, without Eugen and Peter, so we invited Tante Tonscha for lunch tomorrow, Sunday—a relatively elegant lunch, considering the conditions. There will be roast chicken, cabbage salad and stewed fruit, and afterwards something sweet from the confectioner; for afternoon coffee our beloved *kolaches*[7] with all sorts of fillings. That will be the end of the celebration.

We finally have warmer weather, which we welcome especially since there is only very sparse heating. The heat is turned on only mornings and evenings, and there is warm water only on Wednesday and Saturday. So we can say with conviction: "I can't wait until Saturday." It's only on those two days that we take baths, wash, and clean. In the afternoons we take as long a siesta as possible, covered with blankets. For this, Friedrich's beautiful plaid blanket serves me well, since my various travel robes remained in Aussig.

7. February 26 was to be Mamina's 70th birthday. *Kolaches* are coffee cakes filled with prune jam, apples, or other fillings.

Sunday: Well, we survived the birthday happily. Thanks to Lene's discretion, only a few people knew about it. I didn't want the poor fellows all coming by with flowers, which are sinfully expensive. The high point of the day was your dear cable, which arrived at eight in the morning and made me endlessly happy. First thing tomorrow I will let Pepi know.

She and Willi's family are touchingly kind; this morning a beautiful flower arrangement came, a big ceramic bowl filled with hyacinths, tulips, and primroses, and charming letters from Pepi, Willi, Lisa,[8] and her mother; also Onkel Ernst sent flowers and a cable. From Lene I got a splendid big bag for the journey to the USA; from Tonscha, black silk yarn for knitting a blouse and a bag of rice—the rarest article; from sister Ella, the cocoa and chocolate that I erroneously attributed to you and that Onkel Fritz had mailed; and further still, flowers from my old friends Friedländer and Libitzky.

I thank you all again for all your love, and kiss you fondly,

Your Mamina

March 6

Dearest children,

The following sad but true joke is making the rounds here: children become letters, apartments become crates, grandchildren become photographs.

Our winter doesn't want to stop; it is always cold, there is frost and snow. We have never before been so tired of this season, especially because of the sparse heating, which I mentioned earlier. Fortunately, though, the hot water is working again; they found that they used more fuel when they heated the boiler only twice a week.

On Saturday Vera is leaving us to go to her aunt's in Sedl. I hope she will recover her strength in the good air there. She was very happy here but ran around too much with her girlfriends, to the movies almost every day, and that was not what the doctor ordered. We will miss the dear girl very much.

8. Liesel's brother Willi Lederer's wife

March 7

Just this morning I had a letter from brother Fritz. It's become too comical now with his packages—he just now let me know that he had sent me a package of cocoa and chocolate in your name, and another one from sister Ella, which has not yet arrived; but at any rate it will be all right if I thank you once more. Pepi has received hers too, as she writes me. Now there is a strict prohibition against exports where Onkel Fritz lives,[9] and so this pleasure is finished also.

It will soon be Easter now, and you have been gone a year. I can't think of Easter at all, it is so cold; Vera is sitting with her feet in Lene's little footwarmer. I am dressed as if for a walk, and I'm still shivering. Just now Lene appeared with some hot soup; when I add thoughts of Havana it makes me warm, and then comes the high point of the day: the siesta on the couch covered with a warm blanket. Perhaps I'll dream of Havana!

Now that's all for today. I kiss you all a thousand times; Lene and Tante Tonscha as well as Madeleine, who wrote me for my birthday, send all their best wishes.

Your Mamina

Karli just phoned to say that Vera won't leave until next week; Sedl cannot be reached because of snowdrifts.

March 25

Dearest children,

I just received your birthday letter via Pepi, and the wonderfully illustrated one from the children—I have never had such a splendid letter; everybody was terribly happy about it, even though the wishes came just one month after the birthday. I am just glad that my mail gets to you relatively fast.

Now I will answer right away in order to settle your question about the visa. The business with Eugen[10] is completely out of the question; we are in favor of your getting us the visas, but to Geneva,

9. i.e., in Switzerland
10. Evidently a plan for the two women to travel via France

since we can reach neither Hamburg nor Bremen.[11] An official statement from the consul in Geneva confirming our passports as soon as we need them would of course be very valuable for us. It could easily be that one will need such a document.

Today a Miss Goldmann came to see me. Her brother is leaving for Havana within the next few days, and she wanted to know whether I have a message for you. She herself will go there soon and will look you up in order to bring you our greetings; I wish she could take me with her.

I wonder how you spent Easter—I hope well and in good health. Here, too, it was quite bearable. We cooked Sunday dinner the day before and left at nine in the morning. We took the streetcar to the Hradčany. It was a beautiful sunny day. We wanted to hear the Easter mass in the cathedral and got there just in time. It was wonderful, fabulously splendid. Aside from the representative of the Archbishop, who is still sick, there were 12 high clergymen; the choir and the organ were an experience in themselves, especially for us poor ones, who never get to hear a note of music.

In the afternoon Tante Tonscha was here, as were Ernst and Mimi. We enjoyed our "half and half," half coffee and half Ersatz; there was also *stollen*,[12] and we thought much of you and of other lovely Easters.

This afternoon Lene has visitors, but I vanished and went to the Botanical Garden. It was warm and sunny but everything still bare without a green leaf—instead, however, a flood of people; after all, it was the first day of spring.

A thousand kisses,
Your Mama

March 26

Dearest Liesel,

Thank you for your birthday wishes; I long for the fulfillment of our deepest wish—again to be able to live quietly and in peace

11. Visas were not sent directly to the recipients, but rather to a consulate of the issuing nation, where the recipients picked them up. Switzerland was apparently easier to travel to than Germany.

12. A sweet yeast bread, usually made at Easter and Christmas

and again to see you, my dearest ones, now so scattered in the world.

If Miss Goldmann comes to see you, she will be able to tell you many things, things one cannot write or else the postage would be too high.[13] She hopes to get away in three to six weeks, but it could also take longer, and since only Italian cargo ships are sailing, her trip will no doubt be a long one, unless she can manage to get to Panama and go on from there. I think her brother expects to take this route.

Today we have a springlike day again at last, and I am using it to air out our down comforters and feather beds on my balcony; they lay all winter stuffed into the trunks. I sold the linens, but I've kept the pillows and covers: perhaps there will be a reunion in the USA.

Within the next two weeks we have to deliver all the silver, gold, and jewelry to the banks: these things already had to be registered some time ago.[14] So, to all these dear, beautiful things, too, we will have to say farewell forever. One can keep only nickel silver and two knives, forks, and spoons, a total of 20 grams of other utensils, one silver watch, and one's wedding ring. It hurts, but this too must be borne.

My heartfelt kisses,
Your Mama

April 5

My dearest ones,

I was deeply touched by the children's offer that I could sell their stamps and use the 300 Crowns for myself; things have not yet come to that pass with me, but I kiss the sweet little rascals for that. Tell Hans that Tante Lene is busy collecting stamps for him; Ernst Skutsch helps her a lot in this, and they trade diligently; he saves

13. The reason that Mamina could not write of "many things" was not the postage, of course, but the censorship

14. Early in February, all Jews were ordered to produce a detailed list of their belongings. On March 18, the Nazi authorities issued the order requiring the "depositing" of valuables.

stamps for Mimi's Harry, who is now in the USA. I give him the Cuban stamps, which I rarely get now since the mail comes via Aussig. Pepi of course saves her stamps for Hansl, and I am happy to do Ernst a favor, since he is so touchingly kind to me and always doing things for me.

You know that your suggestion of having the Cuban visas transmitted to Geneva is the only one in question now. The other plan,[15] like so many that make the rounds here, is just a business, usually a pretty expensive one—in short, a swindle. To go to Eugen at this time is certainly impossible, not to mention any longer residence there. To join Erwin Chobocky remains as a last possibility, but we scarcely have enough money to pay the fees and then to take the most necessary things along and have enough left to live on there. Erwin was able to afford that.[16]

On the 2d we thought of Liesel; I wonder whether I will be able to celebrate her birthday with her next year? What surprises did she get? How happy I would have been to send her something. If the young lady really comes to Cuba, she will bring along a little cotton dress for Liesel that I have long had ready. I'll also ask her to bring the arch supports for Friedrich, and chive seeds. Try to sow them if possible in the shade, in good rich earth, not sand, since this plant does not like heat and dryness.

Here in the stores one still sees quite attractive clothes, considering the circumstances, but we can buy nothing at all, even if we wanted to, since we received no clothing coupons.[17] I am sorry about it for Lene's sake; she always liked to dress nicely. I myself have more than I need and am not the slightest bit interested in these things anymore.

In an old letter, dear Friedrich, you ask about the houses, if we hear anything about them: How you do go on! Lene was told by a reliable source that her people there without exception behave scan-

15. Friedrich's "other plan" might have involved emigrating to some South American country. Regulations everywhere were tight, large landing sums were required, and there were a good many swindles: fake visas, fake landing permits, and the like.

16. Erwin Chobocky and his wife had emigrated to Palestine.

17. As of February 6, clothing ration coupons were withheld from Jews. On April 1, all shops selling clothing, fabrics, etc., to Jews were closed.

dalously, and there is never a word from the whole bunch.[18] So what else could we expect?

My letter became too heavy, and I had to cut a piece off.

A thousand kisses to you all,
Mamina

Confirmation of a cablegram sent 10.VI. 40
"VIA WESTERN UNION"
LC=Fredpol
GINIAVISUM GRANTED HENLEN NOTIFIED CABLE WHEN FORESEEABLE COMPLETION OTHERS PETSCHEK
Franz Petschek
Hotel Richemond Geneve

▶ The cable from Franz Petschek, Mamina's husband's former employer and the Pollatscheks' friend, is addressed to Friedrich. Franz Petschek was notoriously fond of abbreviations: "Giniavisum" apparently means "Swiss visas"; "Henlen" means Henriette (Mamina) and Lene; "others" refers either to visas to other countries, or to other people attempting to get Swiss visas.

Applicants for Cuban tourist visas had to pay a fee ranging from $150 in 1938 to $250 or more in 1941. In addition, the following were required:

1) A letter of credit for $2,000, which could be withdrawn in six consecutive monthly payments.

2) $500 as a guarantee that the "tourist" would leave the country, to be forfeited if he or she did not do so by a specified time.

3) $150 security for the fare from Cuba to the "tourist's" destination.

In a letter marked "urgent," written to the Chase National Bank on April 9, Friedrich requests two letters of credit for $2,000 each to be made available to Mamina and Lene. After a considerable exchange of letters, this transaction was finally acknowledged on April 20.

18. Lene's "people" would be the Fürths' former employees, many of whom were Nazi sympathizers. The houses were the Pollatscheks' and the Fürths' properties in Aussig and Nestersitz.

April 12

Dearest children,

We live, as you may imagine, entirely under the weight of the happenings[19] about which you are surely better informed than we, who are entirely dependent on the newspapers here, since we have no radios. Almost all of our friends have now received eviction notices and are very unhappy about it; small wonder, since it is very difficult to find another apartment. We hope that that will be spared us; the building belongs to a foreign company, which has dealt very fairly with us.

How inexpensive your groceries are—like a fairy tale in comparison with ours! In the way of fruit there is only imported stuff, e.g., apples at 14 Crowns; Italian spinach, 20 per kilo.[20] Everything is very late here this year because of the abnormally long winter. Other than that, we get enough meat with the coupons, even though very expensive; as for butter, which is especially tightly rationed, I have a supplement coupon from the doctor, which is very welcome because of my stomach. I had a standing feud with Lene, because she insisted that I had to eat the whole week's ration of 35 grams per person. In general we eat quite well. Lene is a real artist at inventing new menus, in which casseroles play a large role.

I am always happy to hear that you have such a nice social life and don't miss the gang in Aussig at all; none of them are worth thinking about. Of Lene's dear friends, who used to stuff themselves so happily in Nestersitz, not one has asked after her.

Many thousands of kisses, stay well and happy,

Your Mamina

April 21

My dearest boy,

One can never start too early with the birthday wishes, and I fear that these will arrive too late, but you won't think ill of me; af-

19. On April 9, Germany attacked Denmark and Norway.

20. Before the war, 14 Crowns would have bought a kilo of pork, two kilos of sugar, or seven men's haircuts. George Kennan in *From Prague after Munich: Diplomatic Papers 1938–1940* (1968) reports that the cost of living was rising at a rate of over 20 percent per year.

ter all, we are helpless against the mails, as against many other things. Thus last year I determined to be reunited with you for this birthday of yours, and what else can I do but hope further for next year?

In the meantime I wish you all the good things there are to wish on earth, that you and yours may stay as well and happy as you now are. What is past we cannot have back, but the new life which lies before you can, despite everything, be better and happier. Europe is an eternal seat of unrest, and I wish that I could already shake its dust from my shoes.

It must be quite hot there by now, while we have finally stopped shivering. It became warm almost overnight, with no transition, and we bask in the sunshine. Today we had our coffee on my balcony. You mustn't imagine too much of it; it is a courtyard balcony with a view of a whole row of garages, of which, however, almost all stand empty, and so they don't bother us particularly. It is quite roomy. My four red chairs and the round wicker table stand on it, so it is decidedly the most elegantly furnished balcony in the whole building. The main thing is, one can get a breath of fresh air without having to go out.

Today Madeleine surprised us. We haven't seen her since she left Prague. She is looking for a position here, as she is terribly taken advantage of by her cousin. She looks terrible.

I kiss you from the bottom of my heart,

Mama

1940 Apr 25 PM 11:49

NLT CONSUL CUBA GENEVA

ISSUE VISAS HENRIETTE POLLATSCHEK AND DAUGHTER HELEN FUERTH AS TOURISTS NATIVES OF BOHEMIA MUST DEPOSIT [with] IMMIGRATION [upon] THEIR ARRIVAL CUBA AMOUNT RETURN TICKETS IN ORDER TO DISEMBARK

CAMPA

▶ The preceding night letter (NLT), a cable, was sent by a Mr. Campa, the Cuban consul in Geneva. The "amount return tickets" appears to be a euphemism for the $150 security deposit required to guarantee fare for the refugees' next destination.

The business of emigration certainly did keep changing, as Mamina notes in her letter of May 5. In the early summer of 1940, the United States instituted a new, little publicized immigration policy, which remained in effect until June 1941. Under this policy, immigration was actively discouraged. The reasons given to United States consular officials by Avra Warren, chief of the U.S. Visa Division, were: the threat of fifth-column activities, rising American anti-Semitism(!), and the need to use visas to move refugees out of England and Shanghai. In July 1940, the Stuttgart consulate issued only three visas, the Vienna consulate, one hundred. This rate was to decrease still further. Officially, however, visa applications were still encouraged.

May 5

My dearest children,

I am very busy now trying to find a job for Madeleine. I put an advertisement in the J. newspaper and also registered her at a bureau for these matters, but since nobody knows what a gem she is, it will not be easy. I have already received a number of inquiries, but most of them are scared off when I tell them her age.

I just spoke with Ernst on the telephone: he has found out the following at the American consulate: You, as well as I, who registered one month later, come under the 1940 quota, which covers the time from June 1940 to May 1941; but this all is not binding, since the matter keeps changing, according to emigration and other conditions. But as soon as I find out your quota number—send it to me when you have a chance—I will keep making inquiries.

A thousand kisses to you all,
Your Mama

[original in French; photocopy]

CONSULATE OF THE REPUBLIC OF CUBA
GENEVA

Geneva, May 7, 1940

Mrs. Henriette Pollatschek
Dear Madame:
I am pleased to inform you that I have received a cable from the Minister of Foreign Affairs of Cuba authorizing you to go to Cuba as a tourist.

As soon as you come to the Consulate, 8 rue Rive, I shall take the necessary steps to issue you a visa.

Very truly yours
/s/ Luis Valdes Roig
CONSUL

May 14

My dearest children,

Whitsuntide, that lovely holiday, brought me some pleasure after all—on Monday two pieces of mail from you, the photographs and the Clipper letter No. 38. Many thanks for everything. I sent the pictures and your two letters off to Pepi right away. Lene and I are especially happy that the visas have now really been granted, and we both thank you, dear Friedrich, for all the trouble and expense you have had with them. May God reward you; now we can sleep in peace.

Other than that, the holidays, like all of them now, passed quietly; the somber times in which we live cast their shadow over all our days.[21] On Sunday Tonscha was here, also Karl and Karli; the latter brought two beautiful squabs and two magnificent trout, so that we were able to prepare a feast for our stomachs at least.

Our thoughts are now with our distant loved ones from whom no news reaches us—with Eugen and Peter, with Tante Ella and her family—and we thank the Fates every day that you are well provided for, even though it must be quite hot there already. The beach must be splendid, the flying fishes and the pelicans like in a fairy tale, and the children in their element that they love so.

May 15

This morning the mail brought two registered letters, the expected confirmation from Geneva with a few friendly lines from your friend; we are much envied for this treasure. Now I want to start in earnest to learn English; even though studying by oneself

21. Germany had attacked Belgium and the Netherlands. The Dutch army capitulated on the day of this letter.

isn't the right thing, I just can't summon up the patience right now to take lessons—for that, one needs a calm mind. I have time enough; the walks have stopped by themselves, since parks and public gardens are closed,[22] so we go out only when we have errands. Otherwise, when the weather is warm, we sit on the balcony.

May 16

I just came from the crematorium where our old Aussig lawyer, Dr. Singer,[23] was cremated. He's lucky, as one says now in such cases. There were many of our countrymen there, a sad little group of stranded lives. Lene and I send many kisses and look forward to your next letter.

Your Mamina

May 25

My dear, good children,

Yesterday on your birthday, dear Friedrich, I thought of you more than ever; and indeed on just that day came your letter No. 35 with Liesel's enclosure and the report about the school performance. What I would have given to be there, and to see Renate tap-dancing![24]

Today Pepi sent your letter No. 39; it really went amazingly fast, and I am especially happy about everything you say of the children; they must really be the lights of the school. Above all, their talent at languages is amazing.

That Liesel now sews Renate's wardrobe is charming. Lene and I would also love to learn sewing; there are a great many courses of all sorts here now, but unfortunately no possibility of buying fabric and other necessities: everything is sold by ration cards, and these we don't have, as you know. Instead we want to learn to bake

22. i.e., to Jews

23. An attorney from Aussig

24. The children's school was planning a performance at the end of the school year. Renate's class, dressed as lollipops, did a tap-dance to "The Good Ship Lollipop." Renate was not a success at tap-dancing.

oblaten;[25] Mrs. F., a relative of Liesel's, teaches that course—she used to live in Liebwerd, and the Oblaten are as fantastic as the Karlsbad ones. Perhaps we could earn some money in Havana with that talent.

By now Mr. Goldmann must have been to see you; it's a funny coincidence that we have a mutual friend there now. I hope that his sister will be able to come there also—the poor thing is quite beside herself about having such difficulties now in the last moment.

We now get regular mail again from Fritz in New York. He is very well; only a job is elusive, but other people aren't any better off either. He has a friend in California who urges him to move there, but he would like to have another contact there—could you send him an address?

Yesterday we got the unpleasant news that within the next few days we would receive an eviction notice, a measure that will also affect forty other parties in our building. But this means, like all other evictions up to now, just a change of residence within the same neighborhood. At any rate, it is highly unpleasant, and we would most of all like to move into *Calle* 24;[26] unfortunately that isn't possible at the moment, so we started in right away to find something else.

This morning I went to a rental agency that recommended a new building in a residential suburb, not far from where Ernst and Mimi live now. The building is not quite finished, but we hope to be able to stay here until October 1; there is a lovely apartment available, two nice rooms, hallway, and all modern conveniences; the best thing about it is two large terraces with an unobstructed view of trees and gardens. You can imagine what that means to us, since all parks and gardens are closed to us now.

One thing is a pity: that we will lose the company here in the building. Lene in particular will miss her friends very much, and the evenings will be quite lonesome. But that, too, we will bear and be happy if we can just stay there; of course nobody can guarantee

25. Waferlike cookies, a specialty of Karlsbad

26. Regulations regarding Jewish residences kept changing. By this time, Jews were probably restricted to certain neighborhoods, though the official order for this ghettoization was not issued until somewhat later. *Calle* 24 was the Pollatscheks' street in Havana. *Calle* means "street" in Spanish.

that. Our great worry now has to do with our boy and his father; we've been without any news from them, a very irritating situation; from Ella, too, we hear nothing at all. I just pray that our dear old Clipper keeps on functioning as it has recently.

Pepi sent me the snapshot of the children in front of the bamboo forest; it is enchanting, like an illustration for a Malayan fairy tale! I beg you for a copy of it too. Who took it?

I sent the children the first of the *Bibi*[27] books and hope it will still arrive; one never knows how much longer the mail will still go.

I kiss you all a thousand times,

Your Mamina

Tell the little ones that I am very proud of them.

June 3

Dearest Liesel,

This week we were very busy looking for an apartment. First we almost rented one starting October 1 but then thought it over and asked the management of our building whether they could terminate our lease on July 15, since we had the opportunity of getting something for that date. They told us that this was 99% assured, and so we took that apartment in order to get it over with as rapidly as possible and will therefore move in six weeks.

It is in a new building five minutes from Tonscha's. Mrs. Libitzky lives on the same street and has all sorts of acquaintances in the neighborhood. Three rooms, a small hallway—very nice but oddly situated: the building is on a slope, thus the entrance is in the basement. The front facade, kitchen, maid's room, and one other room are just barely above ground; in the rear on the ground floor are two very pretty, sunny rooms, one with a balcony and a beautiful unobstructed view over many gardens and villas.

June 4

Today is our little girl's birthday, and Lene and I are always with you in our thoughts, seeing in our mind's eye Renate's beaming lit-

27. A series of children's books by Danish author Karin Michaelis

tle face when she sees the presents (I wonder whether my book arrived, and the first *Bibi* volume, mailed later?), the chocolate cake with the eight candles and everything else that belongs to such a festive day. Where are the times in which we experienced all this together, and will we ever live to see it again? My heart is often very heavy, and only Lene's courage and conviction keep me upright at those times.

I am now being treated by the dentist, Lene too, and then we still want to start with the baking of the oblaten before the move occupies us. If only one could know for how long all this work is to be done; everything is so uncertain, and it's best if one doesn't think at all but just lets things happen as they may.

In the *Weinberge,* the site of our new apartment, we will be a few minutes from the cemeteries; that will be for our walks. It's lovely there, flowers, trees, benches on which anyone can sit; and the dead are not such bad company either. A second resort for us are the Prague churches; there are so many beautiful ones, large stately ones, small quiet ones, something for every taste. I often sit there when I happen to be in the city, and I already have a couple of favorites. The quiet does one so much good, and for a while one forgets the ugly world and all one's troubles.

Tomorrow Vera is coming, after a long absence; she was in Sedl for three months with her aunt, supposedly gained weight nicely and looks marvelous. She already looks forward tremendously to seeing us and Prague again, and has, as she says, much to tell us.

What a pity that Hilde Goldmann won't be able to take along the dress for you; I doubt that she will still get away. I also had chive seeds prepared and will now sow them in the little front yard of our new apartment. That the ants ate up your violets and rose bushes is mean; but surely they won't harm the bougainvillea.

Vegetables of all kinds are already available here but very expensive. Only lettuce is within our means, and radishes, which we eat daily. Asparagus, at 17 Crowns per kilo, appears only now and then by the quarter kilo in soup or pickles, together with radishes, which taste very good for supper together with new potatoes. Altogether, despite everything, we still eat quite well, though simply. We have both got thin, but that doesn't matter. That's all now, my child, I kiss you, Friedrich and the children fondly—from Lene too.

Your Mama

June 9

My dearest children,

Yesterday evening your dear letter came. What you write of the children is a real tonic for me; their weight gain makes me especially glad and is a sign of how well the climate agrees with them. It makes my heart ache to see these poor little creatures here being taken for walks in the dusty streets and the bad air. I thank God that you are there, and I bear everything more easily. Then the thought of a reunion beckons, though in the far distance, like a fata morgana. If only we had some idea about how the rest of the family are: this uncertainty is the worst thing of all.

We are very much looking forward to the promised snapshots. I hope that there will be one soon of Hans in long pants; he must look splendid in them. On the other hand, I can vividly imagine Renate's discomfort with a dolly in her arms;[28] kittens are much more her style. Now there will be great excitement about the school program. I can already look forward to Mummy's report on this event. Do write in detail about it; it is my favorite reading matter.

We now often go to our new apartment to see how far along it is. It still looks quite disorderly. We hope that our present one will be rented by July so that we won't have to pay the quarter's lease. In the worst case, the new one won't be quite finished. It is now almost impossible to find an apartment, and we are glad that we decided so quickly.

We've also found acquaintances of Lene's here who have borrowed some of Lene's furniture from us. The apartment was so overcrowded that one always bumped into something; now we'll have fewer things to dust and fewer carpets to beat. It's awful what ballast one drags around, and I am glad that I own hardly any furniture

28. At the performance that the school put on, Renate's class performed a number in which each girl held a doll. Since Renate did not own a doll, she had to use a borrowed one.

anymore. Lene still clings to each piece and can't make up her mind to sell the things.

I was happy to hear that Mr. G. came to see you. His sister probably won't get away anymore. Now there are incredible difficulties in traveling, and for the moment we aren't thinking of it at all.

You will not be impressed with the typing of today's letter; I make error upon error. I have too little practice and am too nervous. I must write more when I have the time. But I hope, as do you, my dear boy, that there will soon be quieter times.

For today, a thousand kisses. Lene sends her heartiest greetings; from Otto I include a letter that he gave me yesterday before receiving yours.

Your Mamina

Today at 10 a card from Eugen came dated—August 28 of last year!

June 15

My dearest ones,

I know that you have thought of us more than usual in these fateful days;[29] you know too where our thoughts are, by day and by night. May God grant that mail with you continues as well as it has in recent times; it is such a joy for me when your letters come, and I tremble to think that this too might be lost.

Yesterday I had a letter from Miss G.; the poor thing has now had to give up her trip completely; it is doubly painful so close to one's goal. She spent a fortune for the preparations, and now her, as well as our, visas are invalid,[30] and we must wait and not despair, difficult as that is. Today the package that she was going to take along for you returned in the mail.

Moreover today in the J. newspaper there appeared the following article that will interest you; I'll copy it so that the letter won't get too heavy:

29. On this day the Germans occupied Paris.

30. Why the Cuban visas became invalid isn't known.

As a result of transportation difficulties connected with emigration abroad, a certain nervousness has overcome especially those travelers ready to go to the USA as well as all other registered persons, since they are afraid that the quota numbers set aside for them will expire, that is, that the distribution of visas will in fact be completely halted. This fear is totally groundless. Reliable information about the granting of U.S. visas puts us in the position to inform you of the following:

1. Nothing in the work system of the American Consulate in Prague has changed.
2. The American Consulates of central Europe have been advised to issue visas for the USA only when the traveler has actual possibility for transportation. Before such time, no visa will be granted.
3. There is no danger that the quota number of a registered prospective emigrant will expire, even if a journey were not possible for a lengthy time.

It is not opportune to overload the American Consulate now with inquiries regarding the waiting time. The situation at this moment does not allow for a precise prediction. The new quota year begins on July 1, as always; all persons whose turn comes will be summoned now as always, regardless of whether there is a possibility of transit or not.

Intensive negotiations by the aid organizations are now taking place regarding the journey to the USA as well as emigration in general; we will report the results of these as soon as the discussions are terminated.

To sum up: no one should fear that anything stands in the way of his emigration to America as soon as the possibility of transit has been granted. The immediate granting of a visa without the possibility of the visa's possessor being able actually to leave, would only have the consequence of the visa's possibly expiring, and its renewal would be involved with great difficulties.

How strange, what things one has become accustomed to, and what one has become accustomed to being without, and how much ballast we have thrown overboard. We wish only for quiet, and we will not stop hoping to find that and to find it together with all of you. Otto is just here and we are building castles in the air; how beautiful it would be if we could someday all together leave for America. What we should actually all do there, not one of us knows. But there is no use making plans anyway. Otto asks me to send you his best regards; Lene and I send you a thousand kisses; stay well and happy,

Your Mamina

June 21

My dearest children,

Yesterday I had just said to Lene, "Now another letter from Cuba could come," and there it lay in the letter box, this time your No. 41 from Pepi together with Liesel's dear, thick letter and that of the children.

This last one made me especially happy, even though Mummy pronounces that they scribbled dreadfully; it's true enough, but what does that matter to such a starved grandmotherly heart. Renate's enumeration of her presents is really overpowering, and Hans seems not to have forgotten his German. Now the performance must be over too, and the children enjoying their vacation, going to the beach and playing with their toys. I think I will forget how to play entirely. I never see children here; there are none among our acquaintances. But I will work hard at learning it again.

I am really glad that your old friends the Wertheimers are doing well in the U.S. But Miezl is in error if she thinks that we cling to old cupboards here; we would easily part with these if we were able to go over there under the same circumstances as she and her family did; she just has no notion what emigration means today. With 10 Marks in your pocket, the husband without any means or prospects, as in Lene's case—this is hard to compare with Miezl's position, even granted that she is far more hardworking than Eugen ever was. That is my greatest worry at the moment.

It is indeed gratifying that a few of our acquaintances have managed to get established over there; unfortunately it is only a few. Most have to struggle hard—among them Fritz B., who experiences one disappointment after another. Another prospect that he was told of in California has come to nothing. Mimi has already had to quit her twentieth job, because she was not able to stand the drudgery. He is selling cigarettes now, and she is looking for a new position as a maid.

June 24

Now I will give you our new address; you can already start using it next time: the post office will be notified at any rate. Prague XII, Horní stromka 618/196. There will soon be a German name, for the street signs are just being changed to German/Czech.

We have hot summer weather now, thunderstorms nearly every day, and in the evenings we always sit on the balcony until 9:30. Since we have daylight saving time, it is quite light until then. Below us the people play tennis, everybody, men and women, in shorts and as naked as possible.

Other than that, to our joy there is an enormous amount of fruit and vegetables, at manageable prices; and the mountain of strawberries that are sold everywhere make me think of Liesel and the baskets full that we got together in Ziebernik, and how we all feasted on them. The change is very welcome. There is little meat, expensive and poor; instead we devour heaps of cherry dumplings and such things.

A thousand kisses to you all, one after the other,
Your Mamina

July 3

My dearest ones,

We will now be living far from all our friends, especially from Otto, Ernst, and Dr. Fritz K.; but they plan to come regularly on a specified day, and we will also keep the telephone, for safety among other things, and Tonscha is very near us. I hope we will stay in the apartment as long as we have to be in Prague—it can't last forever, after all.

Lene has lots of work now with the move, above all because she still has far too many things. It's only when one moves that one has to clean things out—especially the many books. She had several crates of them in the cellar. Now she wants to keep only those that are most valuable to her and sell many, if anyone wants to buy them, and give the rest to J. organizations. A few especially pretty ones are reserved for the children; I hope it will someday be possible to send them.

I am very eager to hear how the hot season has started with you and how you are bearing it, if you go to the beach often and how the children are spending the vacations. Here it is very hot too, and we often yearn for our late garden, for a little fresh air and walks. Our balcony has to substitute for everything, but there are people who don't have even that. Liesel is right, one must always look at those who are worse off, and then one is content.

A thousand greetings to you all; I hope a letter from you will come soon.

Your Mama

▶ In a letter of July 14, Mamina reports that they had to move into a hotel for a few days because the new apartment was not yet ready—floors, electricity, water, and so forth, were not in yet. She adds: "In the meantime the world's face changes, and I can imagine with what tension you hang on to your radio; that we cannot do and only know what our papers say." In June, Italy entered the war and France capitulated.

The newspaper that Mamina would have had access to was the *Jüdisches Nachrichtenblatt (Jewish Newsletter),* the official organ of the Jewish Religious Congregation, published weekly in both Czech and German and censored by the Gestapo. It began publication on November 24, 1939, and was the only newspaper available to "Protectorate" Jews.

August 1

Dearest children,

Today Mr. Johann B., the uncle of your friend and well-wisher, and his wife Erna[31] visited us in order to announce that they are

31. Franz Petschek's aunt and uncle, Erna and Johann Bloch

moving into our building on September 1. Like many others, they were evicted and searched long and in vain for another apartment until one here, which had already been rented, became available—a studio above us. The poor old gentleman was overjoyed to get it. Who would ever have thought it? We are very happy about the new neighbors. Lene was friendly with Erna in the past and is trying to help them with everything she can.

Our apartment, now that it is more or less finished, is lovely. When Lene has time she will make a sketch of it for you. It's much nicer here than in Svehlová Street, nor do we miss our old friends especially. Lately Lene did not socialize very much upstairs; and we have a very nice lady here too to chat with now and then in the evenings.

While you are enjoying the most beautiful summer weather, we have had hardly any summer up to now, it pours rain almost every day, always cool; and now it is harvest time, and high time for it to become warm and dry at last, for we wait more than ever for a rich harvest. There is still enough food; one simply cooks what one has or whatever one can buy; but fruit, which was abundantly available at first, has now completely disappeared from the market, and there is only imported fruit, totally tasteless and very expensive.

As for the travel plans of our friends and acquaintances, at the moment there is no chance for traveling. Walter makes artificial flowers, cooks occasionally at his friends', Ernst studies watchmaking and at the moment has Lene's kitchen clock to repair, and all the others too are taking all sorts of courses, of which, however, many, such as the cooking courses and oblaten-baking course, have been suspended because of lack of the necessary materials. The American quota has reached October 15, 1938, but no visas are being given out as long as there are no travel possibilities. The Yokohama route is like something out of Jules Verne.

August 2

Thanks to Liesel for her dear letter. I can imagine that she has plenty to do. We only have to keep house for us two, and even so we are busy all day, although the maid comes four times a week. She is very nice and hardworking, like most of the Czech girls, a much more agreeable strain of humanity than our former friends.[32]

We finally want to start studying English in earnest. On Tuesday Ernst and Mimi are coming; I want to consult with her about her teacher—she has one who was preparing her for the examinations and is supposed to be good. It won't come easily to me, especially since I don't hear well, but I want at least to try.

Bobbo[33] was just here. He would love to leave for Chile soon but has to wait like all the rest. Meanwhile he is giving lessons in all sorts of languages and is himself studying new ones, especially Spanish. He has no news from his parents; the mail connection from there seems to be especially wretched.

Stay well,
Your Mamina

▶ The constantly changing entry requirements of countries for refugees helped to make emigration a nightmare. During 1940 and 1941, only 120,000 immigrants—less than half the number permitted under existing legislation—came to the United States, because the government refused to reallocate quotas in order to make up for countries from which no more immigrants were coming. Nevertheless, in 1940, 6,176 persons managed to leave the "Protectorate."

One travel possibility was via the Far East. The Russo-German Pact and the peaceful relations between the Soviet Union and Japan helped to make this feasible. Tickets, of course, had to be paid in Reichsmarks. Once in Japan, however, the émigrés could obtain passage on Japanese ships at reduced fares; the Japanese steamship companies even offered to obtain transit visas across Manchuria and Japan for their passengers. But the trip was a long one: six thousand rail miles, then forty-five hundred sea miles to the United States. The ships were often filthy and overcrowded. And, most important, one had to have the Reichsmarks and an American visa. It is thus with some justice that Mamina dismisses the possibility as "something out of Jules Verne."

32. i.e., the German-speaking population

33. Robert Bischitzky, son of Mamina's sister Ella and her husband Emil, who were living in London

August 11

My dearest children,

I long for mail from you; I hope that something will still come before this letter goes into the mail. Today is Sunday, and I have hurried to finish my household chores in order to start this letter, for in the afternoon there is no chance for a quiet moment.

At the moment we are disturbed about the new regulations about shopping hours for us: from 11 in the morning until 1, then from 3 to 4:30 in the afternoon. We have to change our whole daily schedule around, though the main question is whether one can get anything to buy, and what.

On Friday I started taking English lessons; I am to give the teacher a try, and then Lene will go to her too. Mimi Skutsch recommended her. She was born in England, and I find her, as well as her method, very agreeable; in return she thinks that something can still be done with me. It's a good thing that no materials are required for this sort of study, aside from a notebook and a *fountain pen;*[34] a good textbook showed up among Eugen's belongings.

By now it must be good and hot where you are, and I imagine you spend much time with the children by the sea. Here, too, it's very warm, and we use our balcony a great deal, have breakfast, afternoon coffee, and supper outside; at noon it's too hot, and more comfortable inside. We rarely take walks: In the afternoon we're too tired, and in the morning there is no time. Lene sometimes goes out on Sunday morning with Harry[35] since we've usually cooked in advance then; I sometimes go to mass or stay on the balcony and loaf, which has its charm also.

I get to the city only when absolutely necessary; nothing draws me there. Prague has lost all of its former attractions. I'm only sorry that I often have to go to the dentist. I have been there at least 15 times—the cause of that is the man's incompetence: first he treated three wrong teeth before he found the right one, and all of this despite X rays and all that modern claptrap. The main concern of these gentlemen here is earning money.

34. Practicing her English already, Mamina writes *fountain pen* in English.
35. Harry Lentner, a cousin of Eugen and widow of Friedrich's former tailor

How are things with your chances for the USA? Recently someone said that Kolbert's[36] cousin, who lives where you do, wrote that his turn would probably come in three months, and also that of his friends there—could he have meant you? When the time does come, the parting from that beautiful island will be quite difficult for you, especially for the children, who are so happy there. How does Hans feel as head of the class, and how was Renate's report card? You write nothing about it, and it was certainly very nice.

I must close now, and without getting a letter from you; the Clipper won't wait. I kiss you a thousand times from my heart,

Your Mamina

▶ Restricted shopping hours for Jews were announced early in August. In February 1941, they were further reduced: Jews were allowed to shop only from three to five p.m. Further restrictions were also in effect: Jewish doctors and dentists, for example, were no longer allowed to practice. Thus the dentist whom Mamina was seeing was undoubtedly a Gentile.

The acceleration in the Pollatscheks' and other emigrants' receiving their visas was caused by the reassignment of large numbers of visas to emigrants residing in "transit countries" such as Cuba, Portugal, Great Britain, etc. The Pollatscheks received notification of the granting of their U.S. visas on August 20 (Hans's birthday) and were given the visas on September 4.

August 30

My dearest ones,

For over a month I have been waiting in vain for a letter from you, dear Friedrich; only Liesel's old letters have come, and I fear that you have changed over to surface mail, which functions very irregularly. If an item ever arrives quickly, it's just an exception, and that is why I do not use it. On the other hand, though, Lene received a letter from Eugen the day before yesterday; he is with his parents in the well-known beach resort[37] where I was once with Mrs. Friedländer.

The time for your quota has, one hears, become significantly

36. Ernst Kolbert, a friend from Aussig
37. i.e., Nice, France

closer; I hope nothing disturbing will come up and that you will reach your goal soon. Your friend and well-wisher is ready now, one hears, and probably reunited with his mother. We have become good friends with Conrad's aunt, Johann Block's wife. They will move into the building in two weeks, though only for a limited time, since another family is thinking of buying that apartment and enjoys certain advantages.[38] At any rate, we will make ourselves at home as long as possible; what will come after, one cannot think about.

Just now, to my great joy, a big pile of mail from you arrived. The Clipper went terrifically fast this time, barely two weeks, and brings much interesting news from you, above all the arrival of your friends,[39] which surprised us very much. Of course we will be discreet; only Uncle Johann will know of it, that goes without saying. I can imagine that you are devoting much time to your friends and giving them the benefit of your previous experiences.

That you will be going to the States in the foreseeable future makes me very happy; it is, after all, the destination of your new future; may it bring you happiness and bring us all together again one day.

Many thousands of greetings to you all, and give my regards to your new old friends,

Your Mamina

[original in English—carbon copy]

September 11, 1940

The Chase National Bank
11 Broad Street
New York

Foreign Department
Subject: Credit Nrs. SC2100, SC2101

Gentlemen:

On April 16, 1940 you debited my account with twice $2,000.00 for the opening with your Havana branch of two Special Credits in

38. Because they were Gentiles

39. The Petscheks. Franz Petschek is Friedrich's "friend and well-wisher."

favor of Mrs. Henriette Pollatschek and Mrs. Helene Elizabeth Fuerth [*sic*] respectively.

These credits should be available to the beneficiary "provided she presents herself for initial payment on or before May 1, 1940."

Until today neither Mrs. Henriette Pollatschek nor Mrs. Helene Elizabeth Fuerth presented themselves at your Havana branch.

I spoke about these credits with your Havana branch. I was told that the credits are now invalid, because the beneficiaries did not present themselves in due time and until today respectively, and therefore the credits should to be canceled. I have been adviced by your branch to give you notice about these facts.

I request you therefore to cancel the mentioned Special Credits and to credit my account with $4,000.00.

Since I will leave Havana in a few days to establish a permanent residence in the United States I kindly request you to arrange this matter as soon as possible.

Yours very truly,
Dr. Frederick Pollatschek[40]

Air Mail

▶ In fall 1940, anti-Jewish decrees continued to multiply. On September 12th, Jews were forbidden to approach markets on market days. As of September, Jews were no longer permitted to rent vacant apartments but could move in only with other Jews. On October 7, Jews could not renew apartment leases once they had expired without consent of the Emigration Office. On the 25th of the same month, Jews were forbidden to move to other residences (except, presumably, when evicted) or to leave the city.

On September 23, the Pollatscheks flew in a small seaplane from Havana to Miami, where they spent a few days. Then they took the train to New York, stopping briefly in Washington. They arrived in New York on October 2 and rented a one-bedroom apartment in Forest Hills (Queens). Hans and Renate slept in the bedroom, Friedrich and Liesel on cots in the living room.

40. Friedrich had by now anglicized his name. His doctorate was in law. The oddities in name and word spellings and punctuation were in the original letter.

September 14

Dearest children,

I will start writing again today, and perhaps this letter will already reach you in New York. I have never been with you in my thoughts more than now: I keep thinking about how the parting was for you and for the children, how the trip went, and how you will accustom yourselves to the climate there after the tropical summer, and a hundred other "how's." You will surely feel cold, since winter is upon us, and I hope that you and the children won't catch colds.

We are quite used to the cold here: I have worn my winter dresses all summer long, and now we are all afraid of the winter; they will surely economize very much on heating materials. Other than that our health is good, even though there are various inconveniences: shopping is not easy, and meat especially is very scarce; we mostly live on vegetables, which are still available in sufficient quantities, and desserts made with as little butter and shortening as possible.

What will the children do without their cats? I hope you were able to find good people with whom Hans could be happy to leave them, otherwise his little heart would have pained him too much. I had always hoped that you would go to California, to the eternal springtime; but now one must take everything as it comes and trust fate to make it well.

We now have pleasant company in the building; as of yesterday Johann B. and his wife live above us, and Madeleine is with them as their familiar spirit. Since there is no room for her to sleep up there, she is living with us, to our great delight. The poor thing was very badly treated in her last job: lots of work, not enough to eat, and 50 Crowns per month wages. Now she is happy; there is enough work too, but she will surely be treated well, and she won't starve either.

It's also a good thing for us that she lives with us, or else we would surely get a stranger here; thus we hope to be spared. Otto, the poor thing—they had hardly moved but that they got their notice again for October. Perhaps he will still find something; but from now on there is no other possibility for us than to move in with another family.

Yesterday I had a card from Onkel Fritz, who complains that

he has not heard from you in a long time; other than that, they are well, and aside from coal they lack for nothing. Lucky people! I will write him that you are very busy at the moment and will soon be leaving.

A thousand kisses from Lene and
Your Mamina

September 24

My dearest children,

I am terribly eager to learn what sort of impression your new home will make on all of you, for, with God's help, that will after all become your permanent home. What a wonderful feeling it must be to have a home again! I wonder if the two little travelers will still be able to wear any of their warm clothes; Mamma will be busy opening all the seams.

Our greatest worry, aside from the larger and more important ones that you know of, is whether and for how long we will be able to keep our apartment; it is our shelter from all the miseries of these times. And the question: what to cook? Up to now we have still managed, thanks to Lene's ingenuity. Karli brought us good potatoes for the winter, as these are now rationed too, and thus an important part of the menu is assured. For the rest, I hope the dear Lord will continue to provide.

As for your worries about our livelihood, let me just say that we have enough to live on. Of all that you would like to put at our disposal, nothing can be got hold of, and any attempt to reach it could simply lead to unpleasantness for all concerned. So please let us discuss it no further.

Tante Tonscha has new worries now about her son. He, as well as Mimi, are again out of work. His cigarette factory—it was a Czech one—went out of business, and she lost her job. But as Fritz writes, one must always be prepared for such occurrences there and must simply look about for another job; I hope they will manage that soon.

Stay healthy, and be most fondly embraced by us,
Your Mamina

September 24

Dear Fritz,[41]

Here are the results of my inquiries about American visas: at the moment no visas at all are being issued, but the American Consulate awaits new orders within the next few days, and then the distribution will be taken up again. The appropriate people will then receive so-called pre-visas, that is, notification that they are in line and an inquiry whether they have all their documents and travel plans ready. These fortunate ones then have six weeks' time to complete this, and then comes another notification and possible extension of the deadline; if the conditions are not fulfilled, then the visa expires, and one has to register all over again.

Some acquaintances of mine have for weeks had airplane tickets Prague-Rome, Rome-Lisbon, and Lisbon-New York, but can't get away either because no visas at all are being issued.

Your Skutsch

My dear children,

Just as I am taking the letter to the post office, comes your dear letter from September 8 with the enclosure that I will pass on, and in the same mail Pepi announces the receipt of your cable from Miami. That really went fast, and I am very happy about it. I hope the sea voyage was pleasant for all of you and that everything else goes as you wish; all our thoughts and good wishes go with you. It is wonderful how the children adapt to everything; I am convinced that they will soon be at home in New York too.

Your Mamina

October 26

My dearest children,

How great Lene's and my joy was yesterday when your dear letters came, Friedrich's No. 2 and Liesel's to Pepi, and the charming

41. The letter is addressed to Frederick (Fritz) Pollatschek by Ernst Skutsch, with a postscript by Mamina.

ones from the children. Hans writes like a reporter, and I am delighted with his style and his sureness in writing; but Renate's English amused us very much too. Why, though, has she changed her first name—is her old one not American enough, and where did she borrow *Harriet* from? How many things these two little scamps have seen and experienced by now! I sent the letters to Pepi right away, so I do not have them in front of me but will answer those of your questions that I remember.

The consulate is not here anymore but has been moved to Vienna. I only know that we, as well as everyone who registered in December, are already on the waiting list, which is because there are no travel opportunities at all. I will still find out whether there is any point in working on obtaining an affidavit at this time. As I have written you, these are not recognized by the consulate in most cases; all our acquaintances are in the same position, but as I said, nobody can get away, as much as we all would like to. There is only a so-called possibility via Japan, and that is something out of Jules Verne.

On the other hand, I am very happy to know that you have found an apartment and by now have probably already got the most necessary furnishings. It must be a good deal of work, and I would give much to have been able to help you with it. Now the children will be going to school too; I hope you decided on the original apartment you mentioned and that it is close enough so that they can walk there alone.

I am happy that you have so many old friends there, more will probably show up too; at any rate, acclimatization won't be so very hard for you. After all, everything is more familiar than in Havana; and you'll soon be seeing snow too. Here we have it earlier than we had hoped for. Today it snowed all day without ever stopping, with 1°! It looks like Christmas, and it's lucky that the building is well heated.

That is not the case everywhere; today Lene was at Ilse's in Svehlová Street and shivered terribly. I pay no calls at all; in the mornings I have no time, and in the evenings I don't dare go out; one can go only with a flashlight, and I am not steady enough for that.

Greet all our acquaintances, my fondest embraces to you,

Your Mama

▶ Mamina seems to have forgotten that Renate's middle name was Harriet. Actually, she had two middle names: *Harriet,* more or less in honor of Mamina (Henriette) herself, and *Josefa,* more or less in honor of her other grandmother, Pepi (Josefine). It was Renate's decision to reverse the order of her names (Josefa got dropped) because she did not want to sound "German" at that time, and she was also worried that people might not know how to pronounce Renate. She later re-changed her name, revising the spelling to *Renata.*

Hans anglicized his name to *John,* and Liesel (Elisabeth) became *Elizabeth.* Friedrich had already adopted the English *Frederick* in Havana.

[original in English]

October 26

Dear little Harriette Renate!

Y did not know that little girls get a new name if they are coming to Amerika, but Y like Harriet very much and Y thank you heartily for your nice letter. But Y would miss my beloved Renate and therefore Y write to both. Y am so glad you have had a beautiful journey, in the Clipper first and in the fine Pullman-car, which a lot of famous things have you kiddies seen! Y am sure Franz[42] will envy you very much, Y think he will never have to see the Capitol and the World-fair. Y hope you will be very happy in your new Home and have a nice little flat and a nice little school too, with many friends to chatter with.

Do write again very soon, Y am so fond of getting your letters.

Lots of kisses my sweet little girl,

Yours Mamina

Dearest Renate,

What do you say to Mamina's good english? Many regards from your

Aunt Lene

42. The children's cousin, Willi and Lisa Lederer's son

November 10

My dearest ones,

I wait with longing for mail from you, but I will start my letter now and hope that one from you will come before I send it off.

We have been thinking often of you during your election days.[43] It must have been an exciting time, and I imagine that Hansl already took an active part. We were very happy with the outcome.

Recently we had the happy visit of Fritz O., who was finally able to get permission, after many attempts, and came here to visit all his old friends. He was obviously happy, very nice and friendly. Otto came with Kettner, Peters, and finally Maňka R. came too; it was almost like back in Nestersitz. Our coffee tasted so good to him that he mistook it for real coffee, and when I assured him that it was *half and half,* he said that it fitted perfectly, as he after all was *half and half* too.[44]

Poor Otto had a terribly scare: his sister Paula fell under a streetcar but was lucky enough to break only her collarbone. But it was a great scare. Lene and I visited them this week and found her quite cheerful despite her pain. Otto takes care of the household, with or without the cleaning girl, and cooks under Paula's supervision. When Fritz O. was invited to their place, he prepared a delicious *cholent. Es wächst der Mensch mit seinem grösseren Zwecken.*[45] On the happier side is the news that Otto doesn't have to move again for the time being.

Madeleine had bad luck too a week ago—she poured boiling water over both her feet and burned herself badly. I made a bandage, but the next day I called the doctor, who was very much satisfied with the bandage but less so with Madeleine's feet. He took over the treatment. She had to stay down with us for a week, and despite the pains, she was happy for once to be taken care of and spoiled by us; the result was that in that short time she gained one-and-a-half kilos.

43. The presidential election in which Franklin D. Roosevelt was elected to his third term

44. Fritz Osthoff, a cousin of Liesel's, was half Jewish and half Gentile—thus "half and half," which Mamina writes in English.

45. A well-known quotation from Schiller: "Thus man grows with his higher purposes." *Cholent* is a Jewish stew.

Life goes on uniformly for us, and we are happy when nothing new happens. I am still going to the dentist, but this new one is very skillful, and I hope to be finished soon. Lene goes to him now too. Other than that we have our housekeeping, the hunt for our daily bread and the other things that belong on the table; but I go for an hour's walk nearly every day since Lene usually does the shopping herself, and I wouldn't get out at all. Once a week I go to the English teacher for a one-and-a-half-hour lesson. In the evenings I usually study, read English, write letters, and play solitaire while Lene knits and Madeleine rests from her day's work.

Recently her cousin, your children's dentist, was here to see her; he saw your pictures and could hardly believe how the children have developed. He is very depressed because he has no work; he had after all risen very high in his profession but now has lost even the job in the J. Hospital, which he was allowed to keep for a while.

I braved it out after all! Yesterday I said to Lene, I won't mail the letter yet, maybe tomorrow there will still be mail—and there it is, I just got Pepi's letter with your dear No. 3.

We are especially happy this time about all the things you write about Peter and naturally that you are all so well and have your apartment now; even though it will of course give you, especially Liesel, a lot of work. I am very happy to hear that you have work, dear boy, and the new name pleases me too.[46] If your dear father could have imagined that his son would ever set foot on the land of his dreams and make it his second home!

Now it has become my dream too, to come to this blessed land in the not too distant future and to be able to live a few more years with you and all our dear ones. It would then be the same for me as for all of those who have had the good fortune to get away from here: in that instant, everything that one has left behind is forgotten.

A thousand greetings to you and to my sweet little rascals, and greetings from all our friends; Madeleine just stuck her head in and begged not to be forgotten in the greetings.

Your Mamina

46. Frederick/Friedrich was working as a financial advisor in Manhattan.

November 24

Dearest Liesel,

It is now twelve days since your dear letters came, and I already look for the mailman, even though I know that you have other things to do besides write letters; but it is our only pleasure. I can imagine that you have a mountain of work now, and Friedrich too, I hope, setting up a household from scratch and getting everything new, from the kitchen spoons on up; but it must be wonderful to be able to go into the stores at any time of day to buy what one wishes—naturally so long as the money holds out. And the magnificent groceries—our mouths watered as we read in your letter of all the things that there are. We are not used to that.

I asked you one time whether you could send a little package; anything would be welcome—tea, coffee, rice, almonds, chocolate—a lot of things that are no longer available here, or at insane prices. We would gladly pay the duty. It would however be possible that the mails might not function perfectly. At any rate you could sometime include a greeting for us in a letter to Onkel Fritz.

A thousand kisses, especially to John and Harriet.

Mamina

December 6

My dearest children,

Your dear, long letter No. 14, my good boy, was a real joy, not only for us, Lene and me, but also for our friends, to whom I had to read aloud, at least piecemeal. Of course Tonscha was here too and was especially happy since there was mention of her Fritz in it. She has not heard from him in ages.

Everything that you write about your new home is so interesting and gratifying, and so well observed. Coincidentally, I am just now reading an English book by Edward Bok, a Dutchman who came to America as a little boy with his parents, became a well-known publisher there, and after he was 50, wrote his memoirs, that is, the story of his Americanization. This man agrees with you in many particulars, and despite some things that he finds fault with, he is so delighted to be an American that he closes the book with "God bless America."

If my heart is often heavy, full of longing for you, still I am unceasingly happy to know that you are satisfied and happy and that you have work that suits you, even though I fear that you are exerting yourself too much. Liesel too must have plenty to do, but I hope you are all in good health and the children have accustomed themselves to the winter and can tolerate the cold. It is wonderful how they get on so well in school and that they can keep up. I hope Santa Claus will be good and bring them the reward they deserve; how sad that I can't even send them a book.

Today is St. Nicholas's Day; I keep thinking of what a joy it used to be with the children's filled stockings, and how they would come downstairs to see if St. Nicholas had left a little something for Mamina too. Do they still believe in these sweet fairy tales?

This time I hung a stocking in the window for Lene, and it was great fun: There was nothing of course by way of treats except for a couple of little pieces of chocolate that I still had, tucked away from your last package from Lucerne. There is nothing of this sort to be bought anymore, neither fruit nor nuts nor citrus fruit nor the other things that belong in a St. Nicholas stocking. Among the things that I had once bought for Liesel's kitchen I found a few practical odds and ends, which are now no longer available in the same quality, and Lene was very pleased. We have become more modest, and a fatted goose would nowadays make a woman as happy as, or more happy than, a string of pearls would have in the past.

We are altogether so preoccupied with food now that you can't begin to imagine it. The main topic of all conversations now is recipes for dishes with no eggs and as little butter as possible; but at the same time they should taste good, and what oatmeal and poppyseed cakes, *schnitzel* made of savoy cabbage or barley, and mayonnaise made of milk and flour and colored with food coloring make the rounds in each group of friends! It's especially interesting when the gentlemen eagerly copy these recipes down; the poor things after all have no other occupation than to make their wives' work as much easier as they can.

What you write about affidavits, dear Friedrich, I must answer in this fashion: nobody here has had one acknowledged, and all inquiries to Vienna have been met either with no answer or with a refusal. If the Americans are kind and amiable in their own country, then they are just the opposite in the consulate, and unfortunately it is impossible now to think about a journey until this tactic is changed. Harry, the wife of your Viennese tailor, for instance, is in possession of a first-class affidavit, also a first-class bank guarantee; she is nonetheless unable to bring about her emigration, and she told me of other such cases when I asked her opinion in order to answer your questions. I've heard the same from others; and so there will unfortunately be nothing to do but wait until a compassionate Fate takes pity on us.

I hope it will be the last Christmas of our separation. We will try to get through it as well as possible. Tonscha will be with us, and Madeleine. If we can get one, we'll have a fish and some yeast dumplings, and there will be a stollen too, and with that we will think of all you scattered dear ones, large and small, and be with you in spirit.

Stay well, have a happy holiday, and may the New Year bring you only good things.

A thousand kisses. Give my greetings to your friends, who are so nice to you.

Your Mamina

▶ The book Mamina was reading was *The Americanization of Edward Bok: The Autobiography of a Dutch Boy 50 Years After* (New York: Charles Scribner's Sons, 1922). Bok, a publisher and editor (of *The Ladies' Home Journal,* among other publications) doesn't literally close his book with "God bless America," but that is his essential sentiment.

Affidavits, or affidavits of support, certified that the giver would support the immigrant should the need arise. They had no prescribed form, but they had to be notarized and had to contain certain information relating to the giver's financial situation. American consuls had autonomy in determining the validity and sufficiency of the affidavits. Some consuls accepted affidavits from friends of would-be immigrants, others only from relatives. In some cases an affidavit from a person with a fixed income was sufficient; in others not. Some consuls demanded a $2,000 deposit in a blocked account, regardless of the giver's means. Some also required sworn answers to certain questions. There was no appeal from the consuls' rulings.

[original in English]

[no date]

My two darlings!

Y thank you so much for your nice letters and your good wishes for New Year. I am praying every day before going to bed, our Father, let me come to New York and see again my kiddies Hans and Renate.

I am so happy you are going well at school and have friends to play with, and to snowball together. If I shall come, you ought to take me up to the Empire State Building, I wonder if I will feel giddy, but I am sure Hans will hold me fast, and I will not fall down on Manhattan, will he?

You must write to me and Tante Lene all about Santa Claus and Father Christmas, I hope they have filled your stockings with good things and brought a big bag with presents for you. I am sending you a lot of kisses, and so does Tante Lene.

Your Mamina

December 18

My dearest children,

Yesterday, to my great joy, I received your letter from Pepi, dear Liesel, with the two children's letters to Franz. We were very much interested in everything that you report about your apartment and its furnishings, and I can imagine your little home quite well. How I long to see it and to breathe the "fresh air," which we haven't enjoyed for a long, long time.

If I think that I could go for walks with the children, pick up Renate from school, go shopping and help Liesel in the household, that would be the fulfillment of my most daring dreams. I'm not good for very much anymore—one can't pretend not to be one's age, and the last two years count more than double for us all—but I am not entirely beyond hope; just let it not be too long.

Christmas will be a strange holiday this year. There are no presents to give, except for brandy, which one can still buy in great quantities and at outrageous prices; other than that, an occasional jar of jam. We are going to be very generous and give Otto, who has taken care of various errands for us all year, a little coffee; in other times he would have received a fatted goose for these services. Other than that there won't be any presents; instead, I have given money to those poor creatures who have still less than we do, and to Herbert in addition a box of cheap cookies. Among these poor creature is also, alas, my sister Emma; who would ever have thought that I would have to support her!

Lene and I have reached a splendid agreement: we will give each other a fatted goose. I hope that this affair will have a happy end; I will believe in it only when I see it lying in our kitchen. The expense, which is about equal to what we would formerly have spent on a suckling pig, is no luxury, since the fat shortage also influences us quite significantly, and we must make every sacrifice in order to fatten ourselves up a little.

A week ago yesterday we had an exciting evening. Old Herr Johann Bloch died quite suddenly of an attack of angina pectoris, before the quickly called doctor arrived. He was cremated the day before yesterday.

Just now Harry Lentner, widow of your former tailor, is here and told me that she finally received word from the consulate in Vienna that her affidavit will not be recognized because her documents are not adequate; they don't say what this lack consists of. That is the usual course of things now.

Recently Erich Schneider[47] came and asked to read your latest letter; since I was just busy de-sprouting our potato supply in the pantry, I handed him the letter and he buried himself in it with his well-known thoroughness and was quite taken with its interesting contents. He is making the most fantastic emigration plans, via Santo Domingo, and other Robinson Crusoe tales, but I am convinced that he will finally do what all sensible people must, whether they want to or not—wait and see. Other than that he looks better than ever and is learning how to make orthopedic arch supports.

Lene recently received a visit from her two old Czech friends from Nestersitz, Gretl H. and Li P.; they are both very frightened.

47. A physician, son of the Pollatscheks' family doctor

The two ladies are very friendly, which one cannot say of the others from the former round-table, Maňka R. naturally excepted.

But all of that seems so far away; it sometimes seems to me that I can't even remember the names of the streets. Lene on the other hand still dreams of an eventual homecoming, something that I cannot imagine at all. I would not be able to look these people in the eye—I think I would have to spit at them.

Whatever the future has in store for me, this one thing is sure. There are only two things that I would like to see again: Pepi and her family, and a beloved grave; but never the house in which we were so happy.

I send you all a thousand kisses, stay healthy and happy,

Your Mamina

Lene and Madeleine send their regards, also Tonscha and all of our friends, especially Otto.

▶ The idea of emigrating to Santo Domingo was not so fantastic. The *Jüdisches Nachrichtenblatt* reported on February 22, 1940, that an agreement had been signed between the Santo Domingo government and DORSA (Dominican Republic Settlement Association—an American corporation) to undertake an experiment in Jewish colonization in that republic. For a start, five hundred families were to be admitted, with a gradual increase to one hundred thousand persons, with full rights and freedoms, and the possibility of importing their belongings without duty or entry taxes; however, by June 30, 1942, only four hundred seventy-two settlers had come; and the Brookings Institution in a study reevaluated the country's absorptive capacity downward to three to five thousand immigrants.

December 30

My dearest ones,

Well, Christmas is happily over. We celebrated it quietly but quite cozily and thought of you and all our far-off loved ones a very great deal.

Tante Tonscha presented herself in the afternoon; there was coffee and stollen. She brought a miniature Christmas tree made of blue fir twigs tied together and trimmed with tiny white candles; we surprised Lene with it, lighted the candles and laid the meager presents by it.

Madeleine received a few little things, a package of cocoa from our supply, a jar of jam and things like that; she hardly gets enough to eat at her lady's, poor thing, and for that she has to work from morning far into the night, while the lady doesn't lift a finger and eats all day long—an evil person. The death of the old gentleman made no big impression on her.

Lene got a lot of flowers, which made her especially happy; for me there was a pretty little make-up cape that Lene had fabricated, a pot of flowers from Madeleine, bonbons and a bottle of vermouth from Tonscha. The high point of the evening, the fat goose that we wanted to give each other, was taken away in the train before it reached us.[48] However Walter, always helpful, got us a very beautiful one yesterday at a good price, and we are now reveling in long-denied pleasures.

I am so eager to hear how you spent Christmas, whether you played "Silent Night"; but I think that you don't have a gramophone. I gave your beautiful record—two, actually—to my English lady for Christmas; after all, I wouldn't have been able to listen to them anymore, and she was very pleased with them. We often speak of you, it's my favorite topic, and today she wished me next New Year in New York. Will this wish come true?

Tomorrow is New Year's Eve, the third since our exile. We are invited to our neighbors' in the building; it will be a quiet celebration, but we are happy to go there, they are charming people. Their name is Cohorn; the woman is a widow and now has a big apartment together with her brother-in-law, the brother of her late husband. They used to have a large factory in Braunau. The lady is wonderfully nice to us, and the affection is mutual. She also has a foster daughter, a singer in Havana.

Thank God the abnormal cold has left us now; in fact it is thawing, and we are happy: winter has no interest for us any more, and it has sometimes been quite cold in the apartment.

48. Who took away the goose can, of course, never be known. It might have been German soldiers, SS men, Gestapo, or pro-Nazi Czechs.

From my sister Emma I just heard that Gerda[49] still sits in Lisbon with the children and her sister, waiting for ship tickets, which are very difficult to get. The difficulties of emigration keep getting larger; one rarely hears that someone has got away. May God grant that this and a few other things may soon change.

Your Mamina

49. Emma's daughter-in-law

The Heller Family. Henriette is second from the left.

Painting of Lene, 1920

Wedding Photograph of Liesel and Friedrich Pollatschek, 1927

Henriette, probably in the 1930s

Painting of Henriette, 1931

Lene (Helene Fürth) in Her "Winter Garden," probably in the 1930s

Hans, Liesel, Renate, and Friedrich in Switzerland, 1939

Lene, Mamina (Henriette), and Tonscha, Prague, 1940

Friedrich, Hans, Renate, and Liesel in Havana, 1940

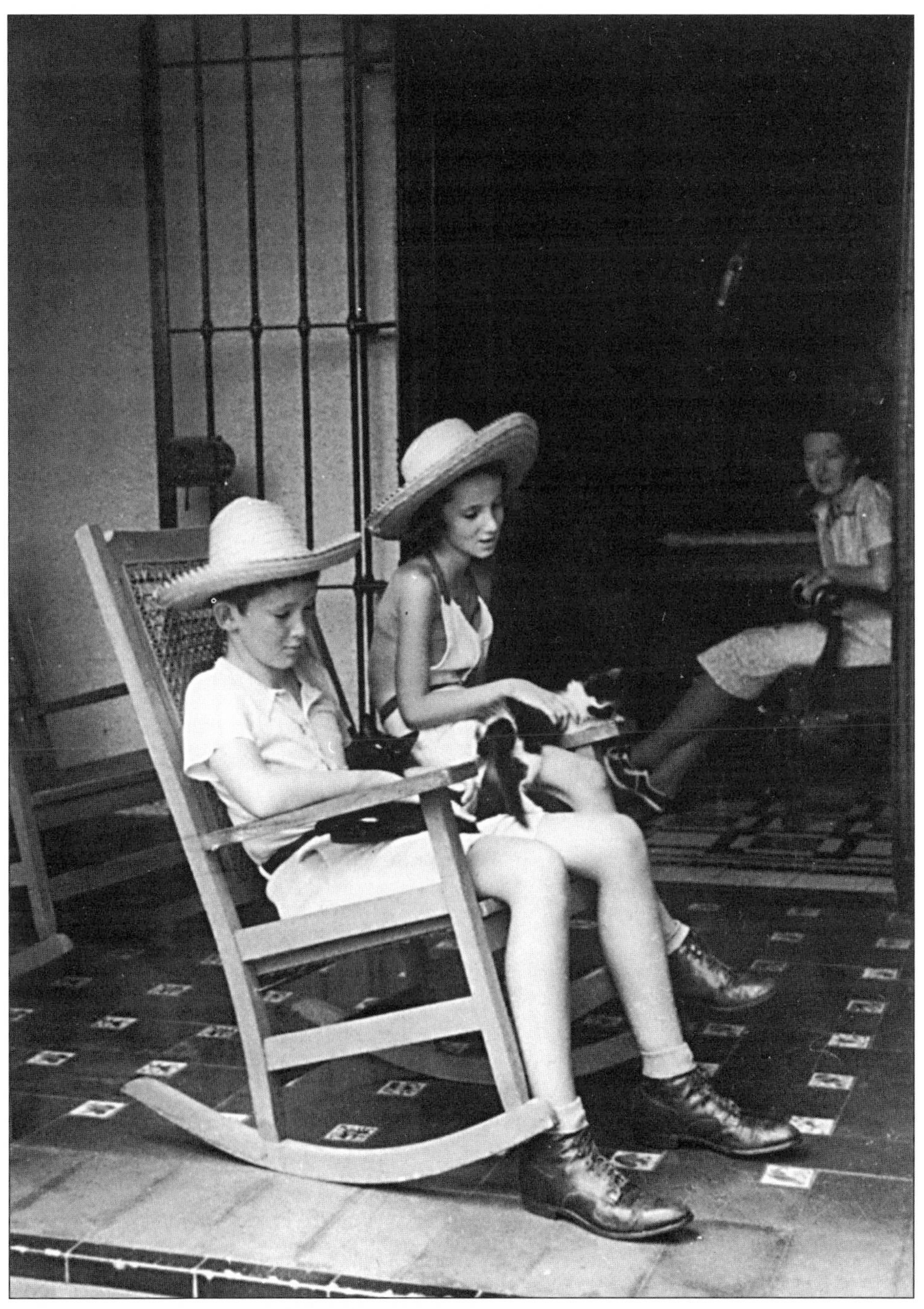

Hans, Renate, and Liesel, on the Back Porch in Havana, 1940

Renate and Hans with Kittens, Havana, 1940

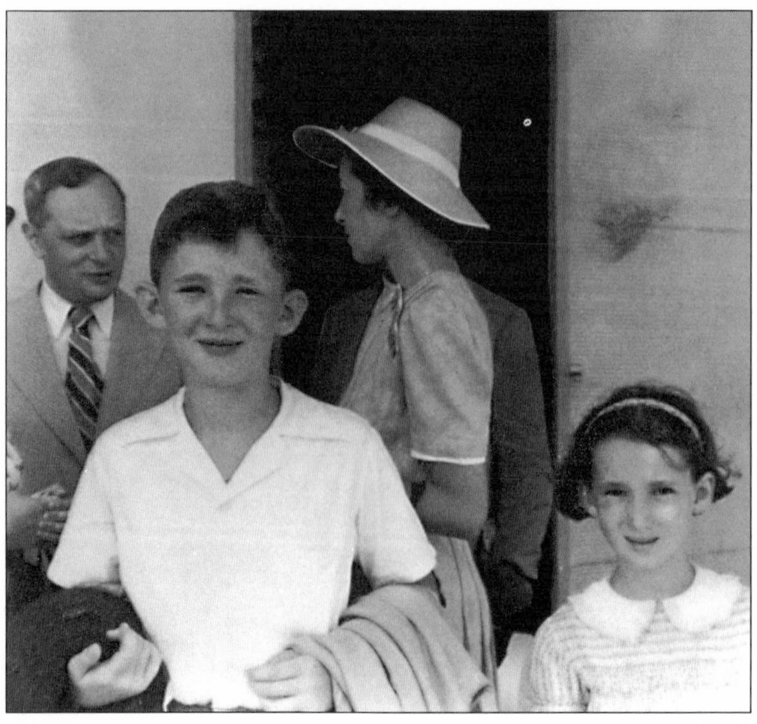

Hans, Renate, Liesel in Background, Havana Airport, 1940

1941

January 2, 1941

New Year's Eve is now over also. It was very pleasant, and quite against our intentions we stayed until midnight, sitting over a bottle of red wine, and welcomed the New Year in. May our wish for a reunion be fulfilled! Overnight it has once again become deepest winter, masses of snow and −10°! My heart pains me when I see the children outside throwing snowballs; I wonder whether our little rascals can also pursue this sport, or is the snow swept away where you are? Here one could ski down to Wenceslas Square,[1] as once in the Kroitzschgasse.[2]

A thousand kisses to you and the children,

Your Mamina

January 15

My dear ones,

Here winter rages as it hasn't for a long time, as if it were doing it on purpose. Coal is scarce, and there are masses of people who have nothing warm to wear and not much warm food to eat. We

1. Prague's main street
2. The Pollatscheks' street in Aussig

have on the average −10°!, and more incredible amounts of snow than in years. On the streets one walks between meter-high walls of snow thrown up by the snowplows.

Thank God we still have our apartment, which is usually well heated—we must be very content with that; we also have enough to eat, though in the true sense of the word we are eating ourselves up; one can no longer ask, "What does this cost?" rather, "What is there?" And that is what we do.

Lene knows nothing of her men but is such a fabulous person, always calm and full of trust that she will see Nestersitz once more, even if just to settle her accounts there. I do not share this hope of hers but am glad that she holds fast to it. It makes everything easier.

Ernst was here today. He has my tax statement to do, as he is always busy with my things; moreover he is repairing all our clocks. He is already quite an accomplished watchmaker and claims that this occupation is a fabulous distraction, since one must concentrate completely on the work. The other friends also come regularly; after all, they all have time enough. Otto and Kettner are usually here together on Tuesdays. There is still coffee, even if it is very much diluted with corn; but they like it.

Greetings from Lene, also from Madeleine; she is going to have to look for another position now, since Frau B. will hardly be able to keep her apartment any longer, as she rented it only until March 1.

A thousand kisses for you all; I pray that I will hear from you soon.

Your Mamina

February 12

My dear boy,

Your letter No. 6 plunged us into quite a dilemma, there's no denying that, but there is no other way to solve such weighty problems, if they can be solved at all. One thing is sure: you judge the situation almost entirely accurately, and furthermore you are the best and dearest son and brother one could ever imagine. But it hurts me that you pile such worries about us on yourself, on top of all your work.

As you rightly assume, we have discussed the question itself repeatedly with our friends, and for today I can answer a few questions for you. As to the first possibility: staying here would mean, if it were at all bearable, waiting until the moment when we could leave under favorable circumstances. That depends above all on Lene, who would be very hard to persuade to leave, and this task of persuasion would rest entirely on me. What troubles her the most is the fact of having to leave behind everything that she still owns and has saved up for her family: not only her furniture, which, strangely enough, she still clings to, just as she has still not quite given up the thought of returning to our former home.

Naturally I too would have a hard time deciding to give up all that I still possess, not furniture and such things, as I hardly own anything of that sort any more; but rather other things, and having to come to you poor as a church-mouse.

The second possibility, if it were feasible, would of course simplify the whole situation, even if that means only the substantial diminution of your expenses. It has other advantages too; but this possibility is not, for the reasons you give, feasible.

Now with the third, the problem of an exit permit disappears, since these are easily available. The only possibility would be the Berlin-Lisbon route. The sealed direct train runs, even if not regularly, and the necessary transit visas are available, we are told.

Regarding our visas, I wrote today to your friend in Geneva as you suggested. This afternoon Otto and Fritz Kettner were here; the latter has had quite a bit of experience and described the course of the visa application from Berlin, since a trip to Switzerland is out of the question; consequently the visa must be sent to Berlin. From there one then receives a pre-visa, after the conclusion of countless preparations—that is, when one has the ship tickets. Then one receives the emigration permit to Berlin in order to pick up the visa, and one isn't allowed to return after that. That is the situation in its larger details; I will still find out closer details at Mr. Platschek's at the Emigration Office of the Community Center.

This all still is not to say that we will take the trip, as the most serious problem still remains unsolved: that is the risk of getting stuck, and this risk increases day by day; here all friendly advice fails us, and nobody can help us. Nonetheless, we want to inform ourselves about everything in detail and report to you; that's all that one can do for the moment.

This morning your unexpected package arrived, and we greeted it with jubilation, and in the afternoon our guests were served genuine coffee, which they hadn't had at our house for a long time. Fritz K. said, "I can see Friedrich clearly before my eyes, when I drink this coffee."

That your Christmas was pleasant and a big success is wonderful.

A thousand greetings and kisses,

Your Mamina

P.S. Renate's poems are adorable; nobody can believe that she really wrote them herself; I am very proud of the little genius.

▶ The "other things" that Mamina hesitated to leave behind must have been her shrinking bank account. What the "second possibility" was isn't clear. The "third possibility" that threw the ladies into a dilemma was immediate departure for Cuba, as Frederick had apparently been able to obtain another Cuban visa for them. More will be said later about routes to Lisbon, from which ships for Cuba departed; it suffices to point out here that the "sealed direct train," which had begun just that year, running once a month, was just that—a train supervised by armed German guards, which the passengers were not allowed to leave. The Community Center, frequently referred to, was the *Jüdisches Kultusgemeinde* (Jewish Community Center).

On January 24, *Aufbau* reported that American consuls in Germany and the lands controlled by Germany were issuing very few visas. Portugal and Cuba were issuing visas, but Spain was giving no transit visas at the time. The situation was to change almost weekly. The February 21 issue of *Aufbau* reports that visas were once again being distributed.

February 20

My dearest boy,

Since my last letter, in which I answered your idea of going to Cuba, the situation seems to have changed, and for the better, since, as I just heard from one of our friends, the American Consulate in Vienna is no longer so rigorous about accepting or rejecting affidavits.

Our authority tells us that several of his acquaintances have recently been summoned to Vienna by the American Consulate in order to take possession of their visas, and the permission to travel to Vienna and back was granted them too. My friend advises me to write to you and ask you to set in motion everything for obtaining an affidavit, because if conditions are really like that, then the detour via Cuba would of course be unnecessary, and I would be prepared—oh, how gladly!—to travel to you even alone.

Lene for the moment wants to stay here, and I cannot try to change her mind, though I hope that sooner or later she will come to an agreement with Eugen and do of her own accord what you advise her to do, that is, to cancel out the past and begin a new life in a better land. This hope alone would console me for leaving her behind, if it were really true and I could leave here and travel to you.

Sometime in the next few days I will look up our lawyer and discuss with him the various matters that relate to the financial side of emigration: what is to happen to the different things that were meant for you now depends on you. I could of course leave several things in Lene's care, but still I don't want to overburden her. I do not think that she will be able to keep this expensive apartment, but, on the other hand, she would not be allowed to rent another one and would be entitled only to a room assigned to her, together with another woman.

These of course are matters that would make leaving here very hard for me; so too having to leave Tonscha here, and the few remaining ones of our people—those in Trebitsch, for example—to whom I wouldn't even be able to bid farewell, and also Pepi, since journeys aren't possible. But there would be nothing to do but to bear that too.

A thousand greetings from Lene and me to all of you, and heartiest thanks for your wishes.

Your Mamina

March 3

My dearest children,

Today above all I want to thank you for your dear telegram; it was the high point of the birthday, which otherwise passed very quietly. There were no little greeting-bearers coming first thing in the morning with their handmade presents, nor any roast lamb that gathered the whole family around the old dining table in the evenings.

I had prohibited all presents, but nonetheless there were some small ones: candies, brandy, vermouth, and other things to eat and drink, and a few bouquets. At noon we had beef roulades and *Linzertorte,* which, considering the times, was quite good. Tonscha and Madeleine came in the afternoon for coffee, and there was a genuine marble cake; so we didn't starve. It was, as I said, wonderful how exactly that morning your telegram lay in the letter-box, and at that instant I sensed your nearness.

Now I have firmly decided to come to you, if it is at all possible, and any way possible, via Cuba or directly; I know only that nothing but a higher power can hold me back. Unfortunately I have not yet had an answer from Geneva to my inquiry about the visa and also don't know when my turn for the States will come; they don't give any information about that, and one has to wait until one is called.

Ernst has put himself at my disposal to make the way as smooth as possible, and that is a great help, since it is a long and tedious road to the ship, but I hope I will manage it; at any rate I will leave nothing untried.

In the meantime I am taking medication against anemia in order to be able to bear these exertions with a little more strength. I get injections and take pills and have already gained half a kilo: I've made a start.

Here the desire to emigrate has recently increased enormously, and I'm afraid that the ships will be sold out for months in advance; but I can't do anything until I have either the Cuban visa or the notification from the American Consulate that I am in line and that an affidavit has arrived. I am at least starting by getting rid of everything that I don't need, even if I don't get away from here. If possible I will sell it. Thus I can make room and time for other work later. The money will do me no harm; I will really need it.

I will leave some of my things here, clothing and linens, those that I don't give away; since I can take along only 50 kilos, which is only the barest necessities. So I have to be careful to take along only a few very good things that will last for years; things to wear around the house will be more easily available there; everything else has to be added to the left-behind mementos: I wish I could do that already.

Harry L. is still sitting around here too and doesn't know whether she will go to Cuba or to the States. But at least she has someone supposedly totally reliable in Lisbon, whom her brother found for her, and she will pass him on to me. It would be very nice if I could travel with her, but her turn will surely come sooner than mine.

I just read in the papers that there were heavy snowstorms in the States. I hope they are over now and that by the time you get this letter it will be spring and the children will be able to play outdoors. It's already quite warm here too; yesterday I washed our balcony and aired your down comforters; Lene made use of the tempting opportunity and took her afternoon nap on it and under them in the warm sun. In the mornings we are on our feet until noon, but in the afternoons, after we've washed the dishes and cleaned up in the kitchen, we sleep like tops.

We have entered into a business arrangement with Karli, who is often here: she will take over our beloved curtains and show her gratitude in other ways. Karl is thick as a barrel; he works for some farmer and doesn't worry his head about anything, as was always his habit. The boy works for a German company. He is a handsome and nice boy; the girl is a dear thing too and extraordinarily talented in all kinds of painting and drawing. She goes to an art school here and is very proud that she has already got a job drawing fashion illustrations for a seamstress and will earn some money.

I kiss you all a thousand times, stay well,

Your Mamina

▶ Complications facing would-be émigrés kept on multiplying. American visas were being issued only to persons holding ship tickets, regardless of how early they had registered. Ship tickets, however, were almost impossible to obtain because of the flood of refugees, together with Americans fleeing Europe. Americans were given preference on the American lines and on the transatlantic Clipper airplane; by April, American Export Lines was booking passage only for Americans. By May, the shipping companies were so fully booked that they were making no new reservations for months ahead. Meanwhile, in the year from June

1940 to May 1941, an estimated thirty to forty thousand refugees poured through Lisbon.

If one did succeed in obtaining both a visa and a ship ticket, one then had to get Spanish and Portuguese transit visas. These were issued by the International Police in Lisbon upon receipt (by mail) of the ship ticket; the whole procedure took about one month. On presenting the Portuguese visa to the Spanish Ministry of Security in Madrid, one obtained the Spanish visa. (See Mamina's letter of March 14.)

One can only speculate about what specific event or piece of news, if any, prompted Mamina's sudden decisiveness about emigrating. Perhaps she had heard that German Jews were now being conscripted for forced labor or that Polish Jews had begun to be deported to the Warsaw Ghetto.

March 14

Dearest Friedrich,

The difficulties from here lie in obtaining the transit visas for Spain and Portugal, because here these are not issued, as in Berlin, by the consulates there but rather have to be mailed from here to the respective countries, which of course causes incredible delays and often puts the whole journey in question. If only you knew someone who could help with this: from here we can do nothing but wait.

What oppresses me the most is always the fact that you, my dear boy, must make such large financial sacrifices for me: I can't pay for the ship ticket, even if I had some of the money, only the ticket as far as Lisbon. This financial question is also above all the cause of Lene's hesitation about accompanying me, and I can understand her: that I would someday be dependent on you has always been more or less certain, and I just hope that I won't cause you any difficulties or expenses. I imagine that you will have to buy a folding bed; I could bring along pillows and blankets, and I could sleep in the dinette. Since I am a passionately early riser, by morning all traces of my nocturnal activity would be gone, and the dinette nicely in order. I wish all the other things could be so easily arranged.

Four weeks ago Madeleine found a very good job with a fine old lady, where she is treated very well.

A thousand kisses,
Your Mamina

March 26

My dearest Friedrich,

I just received your cable of the 26th relating to the visa, and I am very happy that the first step toward emigration has now been taken, even though it will still take much work and trouble before I will be able to take you in my arms. I only pray that I may stay well—then I will wait confidently for a happy end.

Of course it would be very pleasant if I could travel with Harry L.; sometimes I am in fact a little frightened of the long and complicated journey. She begs you to get her brother to work together with you so that we could get tickets for the same ship. Of course I do not have to travel in the same class; her people are enormously rich, and she can travel first class or even better. Needless to say you mustn't worry about this at all; everything would be all right with me, so long as I can get away from here and come to you without your having any more than the most necessary expenses.

Harry's brother seems to be quite inept—to this day she still doesn't know his address there and has to keep writing to Cuba, which means unnecessary delays. She also receives no replies from the ship company to any of her inquiries about what has happened to her ticket. She was supposed to go on March 3 but was notified much too late, had to change her booking, and since then everything has been at a standstill.

Regarding the train to Lisbon, there is nothing further to be done; that is taken care of from Berlin and usually works out quite well. What is harder is, as I wrote you, obtaining the Spanish and Portuguese visas. However, one hears that the ships are fully booked for a long time ahead; but we have poor information, and you will know more about it.

Now for something that interests Lene especially—what has happened to her visa for Cuba? Is it possible to transfer this too to Berlin? I asked Dr. Heymann distinctly to deal with both of our visas at the same time; but since in your cable you speak only of mine, I just wanted to know whether Lene's would expire, which is something that must not happen.

For the moment she does not want to leave, but she should after all have something in hand in any case; I think that Eugen will sooner or later pick himself up and take the matter in hand himself. As he wrote a few days ago, his brother Hans is back now and will stay with their parents, so Eugen could now think of building up a new life for himself and Lene—enough valuable time has been lost as it is. Even the most eager optimists have given up waiting or hoping for anything here, and if Eugen has even the slimmest chance over there, he must take the initiative.

I have now long been without mail from you; meanwhile in the last two days it has finally become warm; I look with longing at the villa gardens, where the crocus and the snowdrop creep out of the ground and old wounds are reopened. We just have no happiness here to help us through this sad spring; only your letters are rays of light and all the greater our longing for them.

Here a regular emigration epidemic is raging, and thus it will be all the harder to get out. But Ernst is very happy about the cable and will take up the matter with all his might.

Many greetings and kisses to you and the children. On April 2 we will drink a bottle of beer to Liesel's health.

Your Mamina

April 4

Dear Fritz,

Your mother today received the following letter from the Cuban Embassy in Berlin:

> The Cuban Embassy informs Mrs. H. P. that the entry permit has arrived, and in order to receive her visa, one needs: health certificate, certificate of good conduct, and photographs. The $2,000, the bond security, and the return tickets must be deposited at the time of landing.

As I have repeatedly written to you, we will obtain from here: tickets from Prague to Berlin, from Berlin to Lisbon, and pay for the travel- and hand-luggage from here to Cuba! But you have to take care of everything else:

1. $2,000
2. Bond security
3. Ship ticket and return ticket!!!!!

4. Hotel reservation in Lisbon—through the ship company, which will find out from us the date of arrival in Lisbon.

5. Money for possible longer stay by your mother in Lisbon—in case any delay should occur in the departure from Lisbon!!!!!

Your Skutsch

▶ The requirements for entrance to Cuba had not changed much since the previous year (see the note preceding Mamina's letter of April 12, 1940). In other respects, however, the Cuban authorities were more quixotic: In May 1940, the government had announced that it would admit no further "political or religious" refugees, but later in that year and during the first half of 1941, the policy became more liberal again. In August and September, tourist and transit visas for emigrants were once more suspended, but after September, Cuba once more issued nearly thirty-five thousand visas. Unfortunately, the Germans suspended rail traffic to Lisbon on November 3, 1941; hence most of the visa holders were unable to reach their destination.

On April 3, Frederick's Cuban attorney notified him that "the case of your Mama has been canceled." Presumably this meant that her visa application had become invalid—a fact that the Cuban Embassy in Berlin was apparently not aware of. The attorney waived his normal fees for his "activities in this matter." After April 18, 1942, Cuba admitted no further immigrants born in the Axis-controlled countries. Those already en route were taken to Tiscornia, the Cuban version of Ellis Island; but thanks to the intervention of the American Joint Distribution Committee, they were not deported.

April 28

My dearest children,

Yesterday to my great joy I received a letter from Madrid confirming the order booking a ship passage for July or August. I will be notified as soon as a space is available. That isn't to say when this will be the case, but it is a big step forward, and I pray day and night that nothing will get in its way.

In the meantime, the day before yesterday I received a very nice letter from Pilsen from the mother of your friend and co-worker, Dr. E.;[3] she asks how far along I am and says that she would

3. Henry Ekstein, Frederick's former secretary

be very happy to have a traveling companion. Naturally I would be happy too and will write her that. Her brother, who lives in Prague, visited me yesterday also, a very nice person, and we conversed exhaustively about our situations.

On Tuesday your second package of coffee and two packages of tea arrived. Lene was just at her English lesson, so I made use of the unguarded moment and made the package disappear, in order to give it to Lene on Thursday as your birthday present. Her surprise and joy were great; I still hunted up quite a nice umbrella and a few things to nibble on, and then there were also a whole lot of her beloved flowers from her friends; a letter from Eugen and his parents and the others over there came on time too, and in the afternoon we had the obligatory coffee with marble cake. But we all had just the one wish: to celebrate the next birthday reunited with all who are dear to us; may God grant its fulfillment.

Tante Tonscha recently had a priceless letter from her son, who scolds her thoroughly for her lack of courage; it certainly isn't easy always to keep up one's confidence here, and we all have our weak moments; but just let us once be over there, and we too will find our sense of humor once again.

I began this letter yesterday evening, and this morning to my great joy came your letter No. 14, my dear boy, full of love and goodness and good advice. I wrote to the American Consulate in Vienna for a form and have already received it. It will be suitably filled out and sent back (all further written information or requests are rejected); now we hope that it will find grace in their eyes.

Naturally we will work on Cuba as the more likely possibility with the means that we have; thanks to your special efforts, I hope to reach this goal and one day to arrive in your arms.

Today another shipment of coffee came from Lisbon—many thanks; we are now rolling in this luxury. From your letter I see to my sorrow that Liesel has caught a bad cold; how terrible that I can't already be with you to take care of her and manage the household. We think of her all the time and of how she will manage everything all by herself.

Just today I wanted to write to Renate for her birthday, but the letter would become too heavy, so I will wait another few days. Unfortunately all shipments of books to America have now been stopped. I had picked out adorable Czech books when the book dealer explained to me that they could no longer be sent; so I will bring them with me. If the children would rather have German books, I still have a whole lot from Peter and will make a selection.

Many, many greetings and kisses, and thanks for all your efforts and love. I hope Liesel will have recovered quickly.

Your Mamina

May 10

My dearest ones,

This morning I received your dear, good letter No. 17, and I won't let evening come before answering it.

Everything that you write about my trip is so clear and reliable; I am completely confident, even if, as I believe, it will still take a good while before my heart's wish is fulfilled. I know everything is in the best hands. May God grant that I remain healthy and active for a few more years and can do something for you. My dearest Liesel, when I imagine us sitting together again for afternoon coffee, then my heart pounds so—what won't we have to tell one another! And how delicious the coffee will taste! And the children—I dream of them every night, because I think of nothing else but being with you.

Lene is not exactly hurrying to get a visa but will be very happy to get one anyhow. I think she would be ready to leave here immediately if Eugen would do the same; but she doubts that he wants to leave the old people. His Mama seems to be doing quite poorly. But it is a pity to drag out the time so uselessly.

I am happy to hear that you are all well again, and I have high hopes for Liesel when the children are settled in summer camp and she has less work and more rest. I hope you will be able to get out of the city too for a bit and that you will do something for yourself, my good boy.

That you don't want to force yourself on Mr. G.[4] I can well understand; he seems to be a difficult gentleman, and his sister Harry is furious with him. I wish for her that she could finally reach her

4. Harry Lentner's brother

goal, but if we cannot travel together, that doesn't matter much; as you know, there is no lack of company on this voyage.

I recently heard that the Berlin people[5] are very well organized—so long as no unforeseen events occur. One must simply hope for the best. Of course it would be very valuable if I had someone to help me at the port in Lisbon, since I don't know a word of the language and have little experience at all in traveling. You will, I know, do everything right.

Just now a German gentleman was here to look at the apartment, and it is surely just a matter of days until we will have to vacate it. I had so hoped that would be spared us. We are all in this situation; one must always be braced for it and only hope to find a halfway decent room with a decent family. At any rate, it will help make my parting easier.

I already wrote you that we have such charming neighbors here in the building—Cläre Cohorn, the widow of a former manufacturer from Braunau; she lives with her brother-in-law and is working on her emigration (my typewriter, the old pile of junk, suddenly stopped working), so I sometimes let her read your letters, which she is feverishly interested in. Frau Cläre is madly in love with you without knowing you and considers you the most ideal son who ever lived. I think she is right.

A thousand greetings for today to you and the children. Lene sends her greetings, as does Tonscha.

Your Mamina

[written in Spanish]

COPY

Havana, May 16, 1941

EMBACUBA

MADRID

REFERENCE OUR 2370 FIRST CLASS PASSAGE FOR END JULY OR AUGUST FOR TIME BEING OBTAIN ONLY FOR HENRIETTE POLLATSCHEK IN COOPERATION WITH FIRM GESTORM[6] WHICH HAS MONEY

5. The *Hilfsverein der deutschen Juden* (Welfare Organization for German Jews), whose aim at the time was to help with formalities and transportation arrangements involving emigration.

6. "Gestorm" was a misprint for Gestorum, a travel agency.

CORTINA

MINISTER OF STATE

THIS CABLE WILL BE PAID FOR BY THE INDIVIDUAL CONCERNED

SEND:

/s/ M

L R MIRANDA

UNDERSECRETARY OF STATE

May 19

Dearest children,

This morning I received your mail from Pepi, your letter No. 18, dear Friedrich, Liesel's and the two from the children; Pepi will surely still send the photos. Everything made me enormously glad; a thousand thanks.

Ernst just sent me the enclosed lines, which will inform you. We consulted long and thoroughly before deciding about an answer to the travel bureau. July, as you see, is not possible; August at the earliest; but even though, as you can imagine, I ache to get away from here just as quickly as possible, it is necessary, according to everything we know here, to have at least three months to get ready. As you quite rightly say, one shouldn't risk an imperfect booking unless absolutely necessary, and therefore we have decided to choose September. What Ernst writes about the time of year is his idea, not mine, since for me any time of year and any weather would be all right, if only I could come to you.

It is wonderful that Hans is starting to play tennis, and I hope Renate will be consoled for it. Instead we two will go for walks or carry on some other mischief to make it up to her. Above all, we will knit lovely things for her dolly or for the little toy animals; I am learning a whole lot of such things at our neighbor's, and I make little samples in order to keep them in my memory. We have also learned from her to sew gloves, Lene and I. She is incredibly talented and has the burning desire that we should travel together to Cuba and then further.

Sending cables via the Community Center is, as I just heard, impossible again; our neighbor Mr. Cohorn, who is very busy with emigration, just told us. At any rate I will choose the route via Onkel

Fritz in order to get news to you as quickly as possible if need be. Via Pepi I have already availed myself of Fritz O.'s services to help us wind up our share of the house, since this is the thing that requires the most time and costs the most money. I will have to pay a tax of one fourth of the assessment that they set there.

Now I have finished making my list of things to take along and will see what can go and what has to stay behind. The health certificate made by the office doctor in Spanish, with the added remark that I was recently vaccinated, is already at the Cuban Embassy in Berlin; but just in case, I will have a copy made for myself. I also have notarized copies of all the other documents. That the Cubans demand notification of the ship passage before issuing a visa is something we knew.

Now our dear Lord should just help us so that everything works out. I go into every church that I pass and ask Him for that; I think He must wonder why I have suddenly begun bothering Him so much, but I hope He will do it for love of you, my dear son.

Nothing has happened yet with our apartment, but we live in constant fear that it will still happen; that would be most unpleasant.

Stay well,

Your Mamina

May 22

Dear Fritz,

That we should figure with a SEPTEMBER date as the earliest—so that we can wind up everything here—is something I wrote you in letter 11, c.f., our correspondence with the *Gestorum Nacional* in Madrid. This travel bureau seems to be a agency of the *Compania Transatlantica* in Madrid, which you mention in your letter No. 18. But because it is impossible to determine this from here, I am writing to the latter today in order to postpone the travel date to SEPTEMBER and to find out what prospects your mother has—and in order to push the matter on, so that we can begin with other important tasks as soon as we hear something positive and favorable from Madrid.

We will naturally keep in touch with Madrid, with both agencies, in order to arrange everything the way we need it. We would hate to postpone confirmed reservations, because then, as I hear from one case, one has to be satisfied with very late dates, with no guarantee of their being honored.

Best wishes,
Your Skutsch

P.S. of May 28

From the English lesson, where your mother, too, labors, admired by the teacher and all of us, Mimi brought your letter No. 20 of May 9. We are in agreement in everything and await with great interest further *news from Madrid.*

And so that your mother will be able to communicate properly with you—I hope, around the end of *September of this year*—I acquired for her a "dictionary of American slang compiled by Maurice H. Wessen, professor of English University of Nebraska"—a book of 500 pages!

Again, best wishes,
Your Skutsch

May 29

My dearest ones,

I received your two dear letters from Pepi, Liesel's wonderfully typed one and your No. 20. Both of them made me happy, especially that you liked the children's vacation spot so much;[7] I can imagine how happy they must be out in the open and hope they get a rest as well as Mamma. When they come back, I will, God willing, be there to welcome them. The happiest moment of my life will be rushing into your outstretched arms at the port. Before that, there is still much to do. Since, as one hears here, some of the younger men are not leaving—a certain age has been set[8]—demand for ship tickets has become somewhat lighter, and that would be an advantage for us.

7. A summer camp in the Catskill Mountains that the children went to in June. Renate was miserably homesick and unhappy there.

8. Probably because they were to be conscripted to forced labor.

As for the house, we have a plan: assuming that you agree, we would like to try to sell it. The amount of the sale would go into a blocked account here—that is Lene's and mine, the third is blocked anyhow[9]—and Lene as well as I, when she reaches that point, could withdraw from it for the purpose of emigration, including the fees on the house, which are quite substantial. Of course we do not know whether the matter can be brought about or how much time it takes.

A thousand greetings and kisses for you all,

Your Mamina

June 2

Dearest Friedrich,

You can imagine my joy when, on the Saturday before Whitsunday, the cable lay in our mailbox with the news that a passage had been booked for me for the middle of September. I ran to Čedok[10] right away to cable you; it is more expensive than via Onkel Fritz, but much quicker, and you must have received the cable on Sunday and been happy with me. Now the work for the trip begins full strength. I am just awaiting Ernst; we will do everything in order to make quick progress; if everything works we should be ready in good time.

Yesterday Mrs. Ekstein was here with her brother. She brought beautiful flowers. She is a pretty woman, still looks very young, but is quite nervous and distraught about the sad death of her husband and all the accompanying circumstances. She is here for a few days in order to arrange her portfolio; she has a ticket for July and will travel directly to the USA, so nothing will work out with the travel companionship.[11] However, it is possible that I might travel with our neighbors, the Cohorns; they are working full speed on their things, but still have no confirmation of tickets. At any rate they are going to Cuba. Harry Lentner also has hers for July but is terribly afraid

9. i.e., Frederick's portion

10. A Czechoslovakian travel agency, under the control of the German National Railway since January 1941

11. Mrs. Ekstein did not, in fact, travel directly to the USA (see her letter dated September 29). Her husband had recently died in Theresienstadt.

of not being ready; the poor thing has been very poorly advised and has to take care of everything herself.

A thousand greetings to all of you, also from Lene,
Your Mama

June 13

My dearest children,

Thank you for your dear letter No. 21 from Friedrich and Liesel to Pepi. I was very happy over the marvelous report cards and everything that you write about my two sweet little scamps. It would be wonderful if you could find a nice apartment outside the city, perhaps one with a garden or at least a balcony. When I get over to you, we will fix it up, and there is surely something to be had in any part of the city, just as in Prague, if it is available.[12]

Today the appraiser was here all morning; it is a tedious business to compile the lists, and then the appraising, since every toothbrush and every stocking is dealt with; but one does it gladly—it is after all the beginning of emigration. Now we are waiting eagerly for news from Fritz O. about the house in Aussig; he was here on Saturday and promised to obtain the necessary information. He said furthermore that you were the smartest, because you left so early; he would be happy to be ready for that.

A thousand kisses from
Your Mamina

June 27

My dearest children,

Yesterday I wanted to mail an air mail letter to Gestorum, but found out to my regret that air mail service in Europe has been stopped. Now our letters will be sent by surface mail to Lisbon, which will make things take quite a bit longer.

12. This is clearly meant ironically, since Jews were now restricted to certain districts in the city, in addition to being forbidden to rent vacant apartments or to leave the city without permission.

Now above all, our apartment problem has not yet become acute, and we are happy every day that, during this burning heat, we have our balcony; we sit outside evenings until 11. We have a view over villas and gardens; we can smell the acacias; it is almost like on Kroitzschgasse.

Ernst, Lene, and I have just had an earnest discussion about the current situation, and have decided to wait for now with the portfolio until travel opportunities can be seen more clearly. This is of course a difficult dilemma, but the risk of giving up all my money and some of Lene's without the least halfway secure chance of getting away is too great. After all, I do have everything ready and can start the matter at any time, with the danger of having to postpone the deadline still somewhat further, difficult as that would be for me. So I hope what I am doing now is the right thing.

Your *fishing trip* must have been very nice; I wish we had got a little of the bounty.[13] We also miss fruit very much; there is rarely any to be had, and we compensate partially for it with jam and lemonade; we also do everything else possible to get proper nourishment, but we are not getting any fatter.

On the other hand we had a very pleasant afternoon last week; we invited a few friends, one with children, to a film afternoon. One of the friends, who knows about these things, showed your films (with Lene standing by)—the Arosa films, Davos, Rome, the Salzkammergut, and the film of our home, the children with their birthday presents, skating, and in the garden. It was delightful, sad though it made us feel. What a pity that I cannot take the films with me! I do not want to sell the projector so long as Lene has the opportunity of looking at the films now and then; it gives her such pleasure, and one gets so little money for anything.

A thousand greetings and kisses to you all,
Your Mamina

13. Mamina writes *fishing trip* in English. In February, Jews were prohibited from buying fish or going fishing. That summer, Jews were prohibited from entering the city forests or walking on the Moldau River shore.

[original in English]

AMERICAN LLOYD, INC.
World Wide Travel Organization
55 West 42nd Street, New York

Pennsylvania 6-0670-0671 #1007
CABLE ADDRESS: AMERLOYD NEW YORK

July 18th, 1941

Received from Mr. Frederick H. Pollatscheck of 160 Broadway, New York City the amount of

$100.00 ($ HUNDRED 0/00)

representing additional payment on passage Henriette Pollatscheck, booked with us on April 18th, 1941.

AMERICAN LLOYD, INC.
/s/ Kurt Grossman
KG:LP

▶ One of the persons most instrumental in helping Jews to emigrate was Hanna Steiner, a leader of the Women's International Zionist Organization (WIZO). From 1938 or 1939, she helped Jews to emigrate from Czechoslovakia, her homeland. She was arrested for three weeks in 1939. Later she was the head of the *Frauen- und Jugendhilfsdienst* (Women and Children's Aid Society), helping the young, old, and ill to prepare themselves for the journey to Theresienstadt. She was deported to Theresienstadt herself in June 1943 and died in Auschwitz in 1944.

July 18

My dear ones,

We have great worries about my departure, not only because we have received no answer from Aussig regarding the house nor a confirmation regarding tickets, but because the whole situation has deteriorated markedly, and I begin to fear that I won't get away.

Today we had another war council with Ernst, and I asked him to speak with a German lawyer from Aussig, who now lives here, and ask his advice; he himself will hardly be able to do anything for me, but he may be able to show us a way that will lead to the desired goal. As I already wrote you, we contacted Gestorum on July 11th via Onkel Fritz, the quickest way; the problem is not only the cabin number, but an actual and reliable confirmation, since the telegram from the travel bureau some time ago is not anything that one can base a portfolio on.

Just in the last few days we have gone through a genuinely tragic story with Harry Lentner: she had confirmation that a first-class paid passage had been booked for her on the ship *Marques de Cammilac,* without indication of the cabin number. On the day she was supposed to travel to Berlin with the transport, she found out that her ship had left for Cuba on July 4. In addition to her, another 20 travelers were left behind in Berlin. The Spanish Consulate here thereupon declared her visa expired until she has a new booking. You can imagine the feelings of the poor thing when she left a day later for Berlin; Mrs. Steiner insists that she will be able to go and promises that the Assistance League there will take care of those twenty people who were left behind, at least so far as bringing them to Bilbao. What will happen to them after that, heaven knows.

This is just one illustration of the difficulties of emigration and the reason that I asked Onkel Fritz today to beg you via the shortest route that you should once again demand a reliable confirmation of the booking.

Thank God, some lucky people get their wishes fulfilled, as I found out today to our joy from the mother of your friend Ekstein. She came this morning to say goodbye to us, since she is, as they say, ready to march, and will leave within the next few days, for everything has worked out with her. I am terribly envious of her, and we sent a thousand good wishes and greetings with her. I hope she arrives successfully at her goal.

As soon as we hear from Aussig, I will begin with the portfolio, if no other events intervene that would put my travel plans in question.

A thousand greetings to you and the children,

Mamina

▶ On July 1, the U.S. instituted new and more stringent visa regulations: No visas were issued to applicants having parents, children, spouses, or siblings living in territories controlled by the Germans, Italians, or Russians. The reason for this change was that officials in the State Department feared the countries would use refugees as a threatening leverage against their relatives.

On July 15, the Nazis demanded the withdrawal of all American consulates from German-held territories. Thus refugees could get visas only if they first left Nazi territory. All visa applications were voided, and new documentation had to be supplied on new forms. These were limited in supply and slow to come; by fall, immigration had practically ceased.

July 25

Dearest Friedrich,

I was happy from the bottom of my heart about the news of Peter's marriage[14]—he is happy, and they are going to have a baby, and I a great-grandchild, even though the prospect of my seeing my new granddaughter-in-law and the little one is slim; even so I am still happy about it—there are so few opportunities now to be happy that one must be all the more thankful.

Our fate has indeed come to pass, we are losing our pretty apartment and with it all the comfort and ease that we still have; it is no consolation that everyone is in the same situation. Now we and all our friends, even rental agents, are looking for a small room—a larger one would have to be shared with yet another person—with kitchen privileges, in the home of clean, decent people; since we have until August 25, we hope still to find something, even though it is difficult—the two allotted parts of the city are overfilled.[15]

You can imagine that I would very much like to leave, but I consider it impossible for the moment. By now you have probably received the notice from Gestorum saying that they don't even consider making a booking, and similarly the people in Aussig don't consider sending the necessary materials. Even if I had had the ticket for September, I would not have been ready; the whole thing is very precarious, and you simply hear of those few lucky ones who have succeeded.

A thousand greetings to you all,
Mama

14. Peter, in England with the exiled Czech Army, had married an English woman.

15. In September, Jews were required to obtain written police permission before crossing the boundaries of the two ghetto sections of the city.

July 29

Dearest Friedrich,

Unfortunately we are completely occupied with searching for a room, which is a joyless business. Then there is still the packing and after that arranging the furniture, because we first have to see what we can find space for. I will now sell all the rest of my furniture, because sooner or later I do hope to come to you and thus to reach my final goal.

For the moment the outlook is very gloomy; one hears only of adventurous journeys, and I am very eager to hear how our acquaintances, Harry,[16] Kolbert's mother, and Mrs. Ekstein, arrived. However things turn out, I have decided to travel only with hand luggage: in the first place I would not be able to pay the fees, and then too the chance of getting the things is very slim. I have packed the large trunk, paid the appraised fees, and will leave it here until the time seems more opportune for sending it.

Erich was here with Ernst yesterday; he has the most fantastic plans, something new every day, but with all that, he makes no step forward, and I think he will never get away. He goes about everything in a scholarly way but is as impractical as can be.

Ernst wanted to send you a cable, but we decided against it; after all, you have been notified by Gestorum that they are making no bookings, and furthermore, you are better informed about everything than we are here; thus we found out the new regulations about USA visas in Washington one month later than you. The whole cable business would just have confused you; we must simply have patience until the trip can be carried out under halfway normal conditions. Our nerves are so used up that they cannot stand any big trials.

Continue writing to our address; the letters will always reach us, and as soon as we have found something, I will write you immediately; fortunately we still have four weeks' time.

Stay well, a thousand greetings, from Lene too.

Your Mama

16. Seemingly Harry Lentner did finally get away.

▶ In July, all the American consulates in Germany, Italy, and the German-occupied territories were closed down, and visas henceforth had to be passed on by the State Department in Washington. This move invalidated all pending visa applications and affidavits, and the would-be refugees had to start all over. An applicant was now required to have two sponsors: one financial, the other vouching for the applicant's morals, the purpose of his or her entry into the United States, and his or her attitude toward the American form of government.

Three new committees were formed, and elaborate new forms issued. If the visas were approved but the refugee was not able to get transportation during his or her quota year, the visa expired, and the applicant had to start all over again.

August 8

My dearest children,

Today I received Liesel's letter No. 5 of July 20, sent by Pepi, quite quickly this time, but unfortunately with the news that you have a patient again—while I believed you were both recovering; so for the visit to the children in camp, poor Daddy has to lie in bed and suffer. By a strange coincidence I just now have sciatica too, for a month, in fact; it isn't so bad that I have to stay in bed, but just for that it's all the more persistent. It bothers me especially when I have to walk on the pavement or climb stairs. Like you, I get shots and hope to be rid of it soon; I can use it less than ever just now, when Lene and I are busy packing and looking for a room.

Despite all our efforts, we still haven't found anything. A gentleman at the Community Center assures us over and over that we will get something, but it's a horrid feeling to know that you have to turn over the apartment, fully cleaned, on the 25th and don't know where to go, nor what you can take along or find room for—everything else has to go into storage.

Today I said goodbye to my bedroom furniture and my dear old bed; your pretty desk went along too. And even if I, like you, dear Liesel, no longer especially cling to these things—unlike Lene, who cannot part with one item—still I felt sorry about it. If only I had the hope of being with you in a foreseeable time, everything would be lighter to bear; but the journeys become more and more difficult, and their organization worse and worse. Harry, who is now at the end of her odyssey and will, I hope, soon arrive there, can tell you all about it.

I am very happy to hear that the children are well and happy; I hope that Liesel will gain another couple of kilos after the first one and that you will have a better winter this year. Too bad nothing came of California, but perhaps that will happen later. We are all in a time of transition and must only hope and pray that everything will be all right.

Lene and I received notice last week to turn over our portfolios; Grüner (for her) and Ernst (for me) are fully occupied in preparing them. My documents were all collected at any rate, and I am happy that I had to start the business, so it will be finished all the sooner, if ever it should come to a journey. Lene is not thinking of it, but I cannot imagine, however hard the parting from her would be, that I could continue living here. I just keep hoping that I would find a more favorable travel time and would thus be able to stand the strains of the journey more easily. We are simply no longer so resilient as we used to be. Now I would just be happy if this move were over; then we would have little work in our one room, and that would do us both some good.

Here it is cold and unfriendly as in fall, and we are afraid of the winter with no central heating.

Many thousands of greetings and kisses,
Your Mamina

▶ Since steamship tickets could be bought only via Spain or Portugal, applications for a "license to engage in a foreign exchange transaction, transfer of credit, payment, export or withdrawal" had to be made to the Federal Reserve Bank for the release of dollars. On August 2, 1941, Friedrich (now Frederick) made an application, stating the purpose of the transaction: "Applicant is a blocked national of Czechoslovakia. To applicant's mother, Mrs. Henriette Pollatschek, residing at present at Prague XII Horní Stromky 2403, a Cuban visa was granted by the Cuban Authorities. Said Mrs. Pollatschek is Jewish and is, therefore, exposed to different persecutions in Prague. Applicant wants to have his mother in Cuba as soon as possible and intends to buy passage for said Mrs. Pollatschek from Spain to Habana, Cuba, through the firm Simmons Tours, 1350 Broadway, New York City. A license is, therefore, required to permit applicant to pay to said firm $730.00 for this passage."

The license was granted on August 8.

John and Harriet were now in summer camp in the Catskills, near Rhinebeck. Meanwhile, Liesel had contracted tonsillitis and another, undiagnosed illness—either sleeping sickness, as one doctor believed, or a sort of "nervous breakdown"—characterized by dizziness, nausea, and severe headaches. After her recovery, Frederick had an attack of sciatica.

Regarding the journeys to Lisbon, Herbert Agar writes in *The Saving Remnant* (1960): "At least as far as the Spanish border, the trains are supervised by armed German guards. The story of some of these trains reads like a version of *Alice's Adventures in Wonderland* which happened to be written in hell. One train, organized by the North German Lloyd in Berlin, found on reaching the border that the visas for Portugal were not in order. But if a long delay ensued, the American visas for the whole trainload would expire. The agent for the North German Lloyd stormed into the office of the American Jewish Joint Distribution Committee, insisting that something be done at once to clear his passengers for Lisbon. 'Don't you people realize,' he said . . . 'that the lives of these refugees are in danger!'" (136).

Furthermore, Agar adds that some refugees found, on finally arriving in Cuba, that their visas had not been cleared with the Cuban government and were therefore invalid.

Only five hundred thirty-five Jews from Bohemia-Moravia succeeded in emigrating during the year 1941.

August 24

My dear children,

Finally, after three weeks of searching, daily new addresses and new disappointments, we have found a tiny room and moved in today. The tininess has the great advantage that we won't get yet another inhabitant in it, since it is only 17 square meters, that is, less than the permitted size, and another advantage is that we are the only tenants of a very nice brother and sister, who have made the affair as easy as possible for us. We have a whole wall in the kitchen, will have a gas cooker installed, and Lene can cook in her usual way, which is especially important. Grüner and Tonscha helped us unpack, and already it looks quite livable.

Now I would be happy if we could only stay here in peace, but unfortunately there are always new troubles, and I often yearn boundlessly to be living with you in total stillness. I wonder whether that will ever come to pass. And I would awfully much love to have news of you and to know that you, dear Friedrich, are well again and the sciatica over with. My foot, too, will surely improve now that it can get some rest; the packing and all of that wore me out very much, and so the shots couldn't take their effect.

Ernst is already trying to get some coke for our little stove. Do stay well, all of you, and write often. A thousand greetings to you all,

Your Mamina

Our address is Prague II, c/o Löffler, Malá Štěpánská 10.

September 2

Dear Fritz,

Your mother received your letter No. 27 of August 13th.

Here is my information, which regards only the technical side of the question whether *To travel or to wait?* Your mother will have to decide for herself—this after mature consideration and taking into account advice from various sources! Your mother will surely reach the correct decision on this, and then she will *cable* you, as you suggest.

Thus it may suffice if I repeat, from my last letter of August 31, that after the completion of certain formalities, we will need a

—*Period of two to three weeks* in order to get your mother ready for the voyage. The

—Visa for the U.S. is only of secondary interest to us; as opposed to my last report, *Cuba-Berlin* is again functioning—at least for now—so that your mother need fear no difficulties here, all the less because we have *finally* received from you a photo-copy of the Cortina telegram[17] that completely replaces the particulars of the Cuban requirements. You must understand me, dear Fritz, we here are accustomed to having only 100% sure things in hand, in order to compensate for the very uncertain times!

But now I think that the question of

—*Visa for Cuba* is in order! As for the question of ships, I hear that the *Compagnia-Transatlantica* bookings for September and October are guaranteed by the Madrid office—for a guaranteed reliable

17. Cortina was the Cuban Minister of State; the contents of his telegram are not known.

passage I consider only the Bilbao-Cuba route on the two ships *Conte de Camillas* and *Magellanes,* as supposedly all the other lines are either very primitive, or unreliable as to booking of berths![18]

Land transport was good, then bad, now it's supposed to be better again. That is the least risk, we must do everything to prepare your mother as well as possible for this journey; the main thing would be if you could arrange care for your mother from the Spanish border onwards. Can this still be done, since you too must first get permission from there, etc.?

That your mother would feel well in *Havana* I fully believe but am convinced that you could then shorten her stay in Cuba! They say here, however, that the obstacles are very large now and will probably get even larger, as the U.S. maintains a very rigid policy in this matter!

—*USA documents,* should they arrive here, we will destroy, as we mentioned; but I rather suppose that they will be delivered to you via Washington! There is no embassy in Vienna—therefore we cannot bring about a return from here, or forwarding to Cuba!

So I repeat:

—*Cuba visa* is totally—according to today's situation—in order, so only the matter of the ship has to be solved, and you will receive elucidation about that in your mother's letter, or in her cable, if she should decide on the question—to travel or to wait—.

Ernst Skutsch

September 2

My dear, dear children,

I have no typewriter and must see how I can get along without it; but I just want to say right away that we are entirely satisfied in our little room. It is very cozy, and above all we have really very nice landlords, brother and sister, about Lene's age. We have bought a two-burner stove and a gas pipe, and in front of me on the table stands a splendid wartime-*Linzertorte;* converted to peacetime stan-

18. Ernst probably means the *Marques de Camillac* and the *Magallanes.* Early in September, the Spanish liner *Navemar* arrived in New York with five dead and with twelve hundred passengers crowded into facilities meant for fifteen. Tickets had been sold for $400 to $1,500 per person.

dards, one could even set it on your table. If they would only leave us alone here, we would be quite content.

Now to your letters, my dear boy. I received your No. 26 a few days ago, and yesterday No. 27 with the photocopy, which is very valuable. As for taking a journey, that is a difficult dilemma: on the one hand, the thought of leaving Lene here alone in order to bring myself into safety; on the other hand, the prospect of being with you again, with the reservation of perhaps having to stay alone in Havana for a long time and costing you a heap of money. Then, the thing that weighs most heavily is my fear of the hardships of the trip, which would not have frightened me just a year ago. I am, as I have often written you, so thin that there is not much left of me; whether I should risk something that may turn out to be an adventure I really don't know.

I hope that Harry has arrived in Havana; I just heard today that a cable arrived from Mrs. Ekstein announcing her arrival. I think the two ladies traveled together, and they could tell you what obstacles such a journey involves. Mrs. E. was the luckier; so far as I know, everything worked out for her; but that's the exception: the rule is that it doesn't work. Please ask Harry when you write to her whether she, who knows my physical condition, thinks that I could travel. Above all, dear Friedrich, you could find out from her how one can and cannot do various things here. The Community Center, which is the big power in these things here, does most things wrong and doesn't always have accurate information. Harry can tell you a tale about that.

At any rate, I could be ready within six weeks, or even earlier, since, as I have written you, I have the estate portfolio all ready, as has Lene. The house we will have to turn over to an executor; the Community Center takes care of that, and it would not be much trouble. I could even, as someone told me today, take along the big luggage, if the fees are reasonable, and if you, dear Friedrich, pay the 100 Swiss Francs and some dollars for the freight; here one can no longer do that.

Please ask the two new arrivals about the whole journey, and then decide yourself whether I should go. I know that I would risk spending my last penny and then possibly not getting away; that has always been the case, and it doesn't frighten me. This way or that,

I would come to you poor as a church-mouse. What frightens me is the thought of arriving a miserable wreck and being a burden to you, rather than a help. One thing you must promise me: Liesel must keep her maid, who has helped her gain 11 pounds (she doesn't mention how much she lost). I couldn't bear the thought that I might have to live for months in Cuba at your expense, while you economize on yourselves and Liesel drudges on by herself.

A thousand kisses to all of you,
Mamina

September 5

My dearest boy,

Today Ernst found out at the Community Center that, contrary to yesterday's information, it is quite uncertain how long the Cubans will continue to have an office in Berlin, and then the visa would have to be changed around completely, and nobody knows from where. Such new difficulties turn up daily, and my fear of the journey grows daily. But that is connected with my nerves, which have not been improved by all these difficulties.

In the past few days I have begun to recover physically, since we have found peace in our little room. Perhaps I will soon be ready to pull myself together for a decision. If I had the prospect of coming to you in a short time, it would be much easier to decide, but the way it looks now I would probably have to sit for weeks or months alone in Havana. My longing for you there, and for here, would be very strong. Why are your new countrymen so dreadful and make the lives of poor creatures like us so difficult?[19] It is a great wrong. Of course winter stands before the door, and one cannot think about it too long, or else I would have to wait until spring. I will cable you if I decide to travel; otherwise the letters are enough.

A thousand kisses,
Your Mamina

19. Mamina may or may not have known that the proviso that no American visas be issued to immigrants with close relatives in Nazi-occupied territory had been relaxed somewhat. Nevertheless, by then most of the Czechoslovakian quota had been reassigned to Czech nationals living in Cuba or Portugal.

September 11

My dearest ones,

I would never have thought it possible that we could ever forget our Hansl's birthday; you can see from that fact what insane times we have gone through in the past month. First the excitement of the eviction and then the hunt for a room, Lene daily and often twice a day at the Community Center, I alone with the cooking and packing. When we finally found this little room three days before the deadline, we were both so broken down that we could think of nothing but rest. Suddenly the thought hit me that our darling boy had had his birthday in the meantime—what a feast that used to be! I hope he won't think ill of me if I send his birthday wishes so late.

I have thought and thought, this way and that way, about the project of taking a trip, have consulted with Lene and our friends, and have come to the decision not to go now, as hard as that is for me. The journey in itself becomes harder every day, and not a soul can predict what will happen tomorrow. Another factor for me is that even if I were to get to Havana, I would still not be at my goal. My goal is not to get myself to safety, but to be able to be with you, help you out so long as I am still able to; the thought of living for months alone, idle in Havana and costing you a pile of money which you could use better for yourselves, is unbearable to me, beautiful though it may be there.

Likewise intolerable is the thought of leaving Lene here alone; she would get a stranger to share the room and thus lose the last little bit of comfort—she who has tried all through these difficult times to make everything easier for me. Now I must hold out with her and all the others until the happy end that we all hope for. We know that it will still be a hard time, but we want not to and must not lose hope, and in spring, God willing, I will come; by then it will be easier to get in, and I will be able to get to you by a quicker route.

Now winter is upon us, and Ernst is seeing to our fuel supply; we feel very well in our little home. Lene cooks and keeps house, while I loaf most of the time, which does me good; moreover, on the recommendation of our landlord, I am taking dextrose; I've also got Lene to take it, and for the first time in three years I am gaining weight.

Just at this moment the mailman brought your and Liesel's letter No. 28; it makes me very happy, but now you, my dear boy, will surely be disappointed by what I am just writing. But please be assured, it is better for me, don't worry about us, and don't give yourselves more troubles about the trip—you have plagued yourself enough with it already. I have such a nameless fear of this trip that it is actually a relief to me to have decided to stay here for now. The Berlin consulate no longer exists, and your other questions no longer apply; everything changes from day to day, and nobody knows anything for certain.

Stay well and write often. Lene is out but will be very happy about your news of Eugen—she hasn't had mail from all of them in a long time.

You mustn't consider me a coward; it is because of my nerves that I no longer expect very much of myself; and these things cannot be forced.

Stay well, my most heartfelt kisses,
Your Mamina

My dear, good Hans,

Your Mamina must have become very old and stupid, or else she could not have forgotten your birthday. I hope you are not angry; we have just moved out of our apartment and had terribly much work to do, or else that would not have happened.

So, somewhat belatedly, I wish you everything that is good and beautiful, and for me I hope that I can be present at your next birthday and give you something fabulous. It is too sad for a grandma not to be able to give a grandson anything—nothing at all.

I was very happy about your letters and that you had such a nice time in camp. Now you know how to ride horseback and cook bacon, and you have surely become a great big boy. I will hardly recognize you when I come to you in the spring. I don't want to travel in the winter, at that time of year a trip is very exhausting for old people, but in spring I will definitely come, and I am already tremendously eager to see you all again. I think we will have to tell each other stories all day and all night or we will never get finished.

Now Harriet has already become a lady, and I will have her

teach me how to bake the pretzel-shaped cookies—Mummy writes that she already makes such beautiful ones all by herself. It will be wonderful when I am with you, but now I must close; Tante Lene wants to add a few lines.

I kiss you and Harriet many times,
Your Mamina

Dearest Hansi,

I'll add my own belated birthday wishes. Mamina has already written you that we have had a lot of dumb work. You too will soon be moving, then you will see how much work that is. We have moved into a little tiny room, and so there was a lot of cogitation about the right things to take along. But now that, too, has been taken care of, and we have time to think about all of you once more.

I hope you and Renate will write again soon. We are always so happy with your letters.

Once more, happy, happy birthday and many kisses for you and little Renate,

Your Tante

September 26

My dear ones,

I have no new mail from you, but want to send a few lines anyway so that you won't be without news of me for too long. We are all well; we don't take things too much to heart, and always think of the nice saying that Liesel saw on a cottage in Arosa: "Everything passes." The most important thing is to stay healthy and not to lose courage, and in that, as I already wrote you, Lene is an example to us; our friends come to refresh themselves with her. So I hope that we will last through the winter, and in spring I will get ready to travel.

Yesterday Erich was here; he makes such an odd impression on us that we sometimes think that his whole trip is not to be taken seriously. At the moment he wants to go to Uruguay, even though every child here knows that is totally impossible. Furthermore, I can't for the life of me imagine what those two would do over there.

Tante Tonscha got a very nice letter from her son today. He reports of Mimi's new night job and of his own various prospects; he is always in good spirits and writes to my great joy that he saw you and that you look very rested and well, and the children too. Just stay healthy now, and Liesel, be good and don't plague yourself again now; you've seen that it isn't worthwhile. I too now feel the good effects of the small living quarters; Lene of course also has less to do. I don't want to say that I would not want to work at all—I wouldn't be able to stand that—but everything in moderation, especially in these times that put such a trial on our nerves.

Sometimes we see, like a fata morgana, the time when we will go shopping in the mornings, wallowing in beautiful fresh vegetables and fruits, searching out the choicest ones; then to the butcher where all splendors await the shopper, to the baker and confectioner, the masters of culinary taste—but I had better stop with this fantasy, or I shall have to drink a glass of brandy. That I have not yet broken myself of, even though it appears quite infrequently; one has to be sparing of one's little supply.

How have the children adjusted after the freedom of camp; and how do they like school? Does Harriet still like to wear things pinned to her dress? She could do that here—it is very chic.

Ernst comes more seldom now that we have no travel plans to discuss; instead he has other worries, since he too is now changing apartments, a problem that becomes harder day by day. Our dear neighbors from our former apartment too are at that point, and we must keep on being glad that we had such success.

That's all for now; it is late and time to go to sleep. Good night, my dear good ones, a thousand kisses to you and the children.

Mamina

If a letter should sometime come with a different name on the return address, it means nothing; the post office is far from here, and I sometimes have the letters taken care of by a niece who lives near the post office.

▶ Mamina's fears of the obstacles lying in the way of departure and of the uncertainties of travel were well-founded. As mentioned earlier, only five hundred thirty-five Jews from the "Protectorate" of Bohemia-Moravia succeeded in emigrating during 1941.

Ironically, on September 23, Frederick submitted a new application for a license to engage in foreign exchange: he requested again to be permitted to pay Simmons Tours the sum of $730 for a ship ticket to bring Mamina to Cuba, since his earlier license, issued in August, had become invalid because booking had not been possible.

On September 30, he applied for yet another license in order to provide Mamina with an $80 landing fee extension; $16 and 103 Swiss Francs for transportation of "a few belongings"; and $50 to cover expenses of up to a week in Bilbao, Spain.

Several items in the preceding letter refer indirectly to new regulations affecting Jews: in August, Jews were forbidden to patronize confectioners; on September 15, they were required to wear a yellow Star of David pinned to the left front of their clothing. Only one post office was open to use by Jews, and then only from 1 to 5 P.M. (later the hours were expanded to 12 to 5).

The "niece" was probably Marta Stein, former governess at the Fürths. A Gentile married to a Jew, she was able to keep her husband safe and also to help the Pollatschek-Fürth family. She kept many of Lene's possessions after Lene's deportation and returned them to Peter Fürth after the war.

Hotel Harding Crespo,
Habana
September 29

Dear Doctor,

Please do not take it amiss that I did not immediately comply with your request to report my impression of my trip. The reason is unfortunately familiar to you: I was so totally unprepared for such shattering news,[20] and even today I still cannot grasp this dreadful stroke of fate.

Now above all, I looked up your dear mother shortly before my departure from Prague. She was enjoying the best of health and looks really marvelous for her age. Your mother, as well as I, was very sorry that we could not set forth on this long road to our beloved sons together. I would most gladly have looked out for your

20. Her husband's death in Theresienstadt concentration camp

mother; many old ladies were on the trip, and I helped a good many of them through difficult times.

The trip from Prague to Berlin is wonderful; I left Prague at 10 in the morning, arrived in Berlin at 5 in the afternoon. The cars are all new, and the trip passes really wonderfully. In Berlin I was taken over by an old gentleman from the *Hilfsverein;* all of this would be arranged for your mother by Mrs. Hanna Steiner. I myself stayed in the organization's building, but for your mother a boarding house would be the only thing to consider, and this too Mrs. Steiner could arrange by telephone. The gentlemen from the organization are very kind; they have much work to do, since most of the people have been taken away to forced labor, and only a very few gentlemen remain to take care of the service.

Actually the most difficult days in our journey were the trip from Berlin to San Sebastian. Above all, as little hand luggage as possible, I myself was not allowed to take a hat box but was very happy about that during the journey and now own only a rain-spotted travel hat, having recently lost my beloved beret. Just a lightweight, cheap travel blanket; my travel blanket was stolen from me in Bilbao as we boarded the ship, as was my thermos bottle. The provisions have to be prepared as "ready-to-eat" as possible, since there is so little room in the train that one cannot move. We were eight persons in a compartment; but now it is no longer so hot—when we arrived at the border we had very badly swollen feet. I can tolerate a great deal, but by then I was at the end of my strength and continually had to keep myself going with cognac.

All the documents are taken care of by the Prague Community Center—all of that works well. I myself arrived in Bilbao in the evening, and the ship left on the next day, and there is much running about—the assistance with this is very inadequate.

For the trip a light cotton dress is important, if possible buttoned all the way down, since one arrives very dirty; plenty of cologne, since there is virtually no water for washing. *Very* important: depart from *Bilbao,* not Vigo, because my travel companions had to travel to that place another 28 hours, in overcrowded, very dirty cars (and change trains four times during the night). The Bay of Biscay was somewhat stormy, many were seasick, but the journey on my ship (*Magallanes*), in first class—*very important*—was really good. My cabin was very modest, but the food was outstanding; my cabin boy still stuffed so many marvelous things into my bag that I was able to help many acquaintances in tourist class, which was very poorly provided for.

I myself believe that your dear mother would tolerate the journey very well, since she is fortunately very hale and robust. Many old ladies who traveled with us arrived much fresher than some of the young ones. Of course it depends on many things: whether one is lucky in one's traveling companions, since unfortunately there are many ill-bred and inconsiderate people. But let us hope for the best; I hope that everything will work out now, and I will be able to welcome your mother here, healthy and in good spirits. I wish it for you and your dear wife with all my heart. My heartiest greetings to you, your wife, and your dear children,

Your Olly Ekstein

Very important is a thermos bottle of good coffee and one of tea, since it is only in Frankfurt that a black brew is handed out; in Paris, bread and sausage (by the German travel agency, Mitropa), unfortunately no soup or warm food.

▶ Lucy S. Dawidowicz writes in *The War against the Jews, 1933–1945* (1975) that deportations of Czech Jews to Poland started as early as 1939. Theresienstadt, intended as a "central ghetto for Protectorate Jews," was set up in the fall of 1941. "This ghetto," she writes, "was to serve two functions, that of a 'model' camp to which privileged categories of Reich Jews would be sent and also as a transit camp from which to deport Czech Jews to the death camps in Poland. In 1942 alone, about 55,000 Jews from the Protectorate were sent to Theresienstadt, and most were later deported to Auschwitz and other death camps" (509).

According to Olly Ekstein's son, who had been Frederick's secretary in Havana, his father, Olly's husband, was deported to Theresienstadt before Olly left for Cuba. He must have been one of the earliest.

September 30

Dearest Liesel,

Pepi just sent me your letter of the 15th of this month, No. 18, with Hans's little enclosure. Both made me tremendously happy;

only it hurts me that you are worried about me; it is all too understandable. But I hope, even though you cannot pray, that we will be helped and that we will see you again. When, of course, is very uncertain, but we do not want to lose hope, and we cling to every ray of light.

When I imagine that we, Lene and I, would someday sit with you and shake off this whole ugly dream, play with the children and listen to their tales of heroism—that happiness is hardly to be conceived. We are always terribly amused by everything that you write about the children; they are real Americans already.

Many thanks to Hans for his letter, and tell the children they should start looking around for a job for me; maybe I could do needlework and Renate will sell it. At any rate, I ask to be allowed to use Renate's Bible; I have long wanted to have one too, and so we could read from it together. I no longer go to the beautiful Prague churches; I think it is not well looked upon[21] but am sorry about it. I have not become pious, unfortunately, but it was a source of solace and peace, which I miss.

We continue to be satisfied in our little apartment. Our landlords, the Löfflers, become closer friends to us every day. We share our joys and sorrows with one another more than ever now. Thus also we share the stingily measured coal, and feed our little stove with it. One good thing is that both our cookers in the kitchen use gas, and that makes it agreeably warm, and in the bathroom there is a gas boiler, so that we can have warm water at any time. We would be happy to be able to stay here until we leave for Lisbon.

A thousand kisses to you and the children,

Mama

October 6

Dear Friedrich,

I received your letter No. 29 and shortly afterwards No. 30; a half hour later, your cable,[22] which understandably threw us into

21. Probably because she was required to wear the yellow star.

22. The subject of the cable was probably the new Cuban visa that Frederick had obtained for Mamina.

quite a bit of excitement, since now we have to decide; and I have decided, if it is at all possible, to travel. I also wanted to send you a cable telling you that, but for the moment all work at the Emigration Office has been stopped, so that I haven't been able to find out anything, and Čedok also refused to send the cable because I didn't buy the ship ticket from them.

You know that I have already turned in the portfolio: it is the so-called Estate Portfolio, and its purpose is to determine one's estate and the taxes on it, which I have also already paid. For emigration, however, a supplementary portfolio has to be made, and I now hope that the work for that at the office will soon be resumed. How matters with the house will develop, I still do not know, but I know that the deadline is not too far off.

Yesterday a gentleman from the Community Center told Ernst that the *Magellanes* would sail *not* on the *22d* but on the 11th of November, and today I found out from Irma that she was notified by the director that a passage had been booked for her on the ship *Marques de Comillac,* leaving Bilbao on November 27, and she is to receive confirmation in ten days.

You will surely find out there with which of the ships and when the group—to which I definitely want to attach myself—is to travel, and you could possibly change the booking accordingly, even though it is unlikely that Irma will get away at all, since her house business is still not in order. But perhaps Conrad's relatives will come along. That would after all be something that could make things easier for me, more so than traveling with Erich, who gets on my nerves terribly and wouldn't help me in the least. Above all I must have a confirmation from the steamship company, without which nothing can be done, and a reliable address of a helper in Bilbao, who could allot me the money needed there and other assistance; otherwise I would be like Harry, who didn't even have enough money for a postage stamp.

That I am causing you such a lot of expenses makes me very sad, but I hope that it is really as you, dear boy, write, and that I won't have to sit too long in Havana. However beautiful it might be, it wouldn't make me happy; it's not as if I had some occupation there. I wonder whether it might not be possible for me to live in a little boarding house run by emigrants and to help them with the household and cooking instead of paying; that would give me much pleasure, more than simply going for walks in Havana. The drone's life that we used to live is something that we have got quite out of the habit of.

Altogether I am aching to get away to you; I won't think of the problems of the journey. Enough people have survived it, and I hope it will be somehow bearable. What bothers me with this and in general is my hearing, which has become much worse; you must prepare yourselves for finding me much changed; you will enfold a shriveled up little old woman in your arms, my dear boy.

Thousands of kisses to Liesel and the children, also from Lene, who is fussing about in the kitchen; she now regrets very much, unfortunately too late, that she can't travel with me. What would I give for it, if she had insisted less stubbornly on her viewpoint. She helped no one with it.

Your Mamina

October 13

Dearest Friedrich,

I have asked Onkel Fritz to let you know, when he sees you,[23] that you should if at all possible push forward my emigration, for my longing for you has just recently risen immeasurably. Not only that, but Lene too has now come to the conviction that her staying here would do nobody any good, and she would be happy if it were possible to get a visa for her; Ernst and his wife feel the same way. I don't know, of course, if all of this can be brought about; but at any rate, our situation, as you know, is none too cheerful. Tomorrow the first transport leaves; we don't know if and when our turn will come, but at any rate if this should happen, a trip to you would no longer be conceivable.

Lene would like to buy her ship passage here; she can do this through Čedok without any difficulties. For the moment the Emigration Office is not functioning, but we hope it will begin again soon;

23. Since Onkel Fritz Heller lived in Switzerland, this obviously means "when he writes to you." Why Mamina found the use of code necessary at this time is not clear; later, after the United States had entered the war and she could no longer write to the Pollatscheks, the reasons are more evident.

and then we would have to put everything into getting ready. Even our worry about becoming a burden to you in Havana must now be put aside; we are sure that some possibility of working will turn up, and then when we arrive in the USA, Lene will look for a job, and with her talents should be able to find one. We are quite aware of the size of the sacrifice that you are both making for us, but there is no other way. The date of the journey doesn't matter at all, I am not worried about company for the trip, nor am I frightened of the strain, if only I can come to you and not leave Lene here to an uncertain fate.

Now just one more thing: you can imagine in what circumstances Tante Tonscha lives here. Fritz, understandably, has not yet thought of bringing his mother over to him, and she has waited patiently until it could come to pass. Now the situation for her too is—now or perhaps never. Certainly Fritz is not in a position to support his mother, but she could certainly keep house for them and give Mimi the chance of finding a job and earning money. Fritz mustn't forget that his mother made the greatest of sacrifices in order to make their emigration possible. Through her help they have laid by some money for a rainy day, even if not much, with which they would have to keep Tonscha above water in Havana for a time. She can buy the ticket and take care of the other travel expenses here.

The most difficult thing of course remains the obtaining of landing money. My understanding doesn't reach so far as to solve this, but at any rate it is not thinkable that you should provide this. I just thought whether there might not be some friend and well-wisher among your acquaintances who would do a good work for love of me, and in these dreadful times, might once more do that which he has already done in the greatest measure, in order to heal one of the countless wounds that are apportioned us. Never was willingness to help more in order, and never were people more thankful for help than now.

Even if nothing more were accomplished than getting the necessary documents for emigration in hand, much would be achieved with that, a position which you, my dear boy, took care of long ago, just as you always judged our situation correctly. What a pity for the time lost, especially for Lene. When I see how hard she works, how she shuns no kind of work, does everything with such skill, and how everyone loves her; then I can confidently say that she would easily have been able to accomplish something for her family over there, much more than she has by staying here and guarding their things, which, if she leaves here unwillingly, will anyhow all be lost. Please think all this over, and let us know what you think of it; whatever you do will be the right thing. We are all well and are taking care to remain that way, for the moment that's the only thing we can do.

Many thousands of kisses,
Your Mamina

Does the wife of your friend still have anyone in her homeland?[24] That place might be our destination if the other idea doesn't work out. Addresses of any friends there would be very helpful to us.

Dearest Friedrich,

As you see from Mother's letter, you are going to have more work with us again, and I can only assure you that I feel sorry about it. I for one do not really believe that the matter can be taken care of so *a tempo,* but above all it would put Mother at ease if something were to be done. As for me, I am not so easily excited, but anyway it may be the best thing to make the attempt. Today I was together with our friend Dr. Fritz K., who will probably soon leave us.

A thousand greeting to all of you,
Your Lene

▸ The longing for emigration was spurred by various events of the time. On October 1, the Jewish Religious Congregation was ordered to register a thousand Jews daily. The first transports "to the east" left on October 16. Beginning on November 16, transports began leaving from Prague for Theresienstadt.

Food restrictions and the compulsory wearing of the yellow star have already been mentioned. A summary of other restrictions put into effect during the second half of 1941 is as follows:

Jews were not allowed to visit the woods in greater Prague.

Jews were not allowed to enter public libraries.

24. Franz Petschek's wife was Polish.

Jews' use of post offices was restricted to certain hours.

Buses and trolleys were forbidden to Jews.

Telephones were taken out of Jews' homes, and Jews were forbidden to talk to Gentiles on public phones; later, all use of public phones was prohibited to Jews.

On October 23, Jews were forbidden to buy (or receive as gifts) fruits, nuts, jams, cheese, sweets, poultry, or game. On November 11th, the prohibition was extended to include onions and garlic; and on December 2, wine and spirits were added to the list.

On October 25, 1,938 typewriters, as well as ski outfits, phonographs, records, cameras, film projectors, binoculars, and adding machines were taken from Jews to furnish Gestapo offices.

The replacement of Konstantin von Neurath by Reinhard Heydrich as *Reichsprotektor* of Bohemia and Moravia on September 27 caused matters to become rapidly worse. *Aufbau* reports on October 24 that "storms of telegrams" were arriving in the United States, asking for passage to Cuba, which was the only way out. In some cases it was possible to pay for passage from Prague. On October 31, *Aufbau* reported that Jews were now being deported "to the east" weekly. All legal emigration from the Reich was forbidden by the fall of 1941. Nevertheless, two hundred seventy-three persons managed to leave the Protectorate in 1942, and ninety-three more before July 15, 1943.

[photocopy; original in Spanish]

REPUBLIC OF CUBA

MINISTRY OF FINANCE

DEPARTMENT OF IMMIGRATION

HAVANA

Havana

October 16, 1941

Sr. Manuel Quintana Espinosa
City
Dear Sir:

In reply to your letter of the 13th inst., Incoming Register No. 22323, I wish to inform you that this Department has reached a favorable decision on the request and therefore grants an extension of a further six months to the authorization issued on March 29 of this year to Mrs. HENRIETTE POLLATSCHEK to disembark in the National Territory as a tourist, said extension expiring March 29, 1942.

This communication, together with the original permit, may be shown to any shipping line for the issuance of the proper ticket.

Very truly yours
/s/ Dr. Aurelio Ituarte
Director General of Immigration

[carbon copy; original in English]

October 18, 1941

The Federal Reserve Bank
70 Pine Street
New York City
Sirs:

Reference is made to License No. NY 211000, renewed under No. NY254849.

Under this license I paid to Simmons Tours, Inc. a deposit of $500.00. As said firm could not produce any results in behalf of the ticket of my mother, I saw myself obliged to cancel said order and request the refund of my deposit.

I intend to order a ticket for my mother through the firm Paul Tausig and Son, Inc. 29 West 46 Street, New York City and I, therefore, request to change the above license to said firm and extend same for an additional term of 30 days.[25]

Very respectfully yours,
Frederick H. Pollatschek

FHP: HEE

October 20

My dearest boy,

I have just received your dear letter No. 31. It is full of love and wisdom, as is everything from you; only unfortunately much has

25. Frederick marked his new Application for a License to Engage in a Foreign Exchange Transaction, etc., "URGENT" and stated in it that his mother was "threatened with deportation to Poland if she does not emigrate immediately."

changed that will influence my and now also Lene's travel plans unfavorably.

You certainly judged our SOS call correctly, and will, I hope, believe that we have not become totally insane; but it is now most probable that we will have to take a different route,[26] and our reunion will be postponed into the distant future. Everything that you write of the hardships of a trip to Havana would be child's play now, and none of our former considerations are valid any more, so great is our yearning to see you again. Lene too is totally of this mind, but it happens that these great hindrances have come up.

We have notified the Jewish Community Center that we have visas and ship tickets; whether this circumstance will make a postponement possible to the time when the interrupted work at the Emigration Office is resumed, is something no one knows. At any rate we are making our preparations for the other journey, getting together all the warm things that we own, in which Lene's ski clothing is useful to us; it will be difficult for us to part from this little room, but we will withstand that too with God's help. Lene will find work, and I will continue to hope and not despair.

Otto and his sister left us today, also Fritz K. and our dear nice neighbors from our former apartment; Tonscha's turn would come together with ours, and we hope that we will meet again somewhere out there. If it should be at all possible to resume our journey to you from there, we will naturally do everything possible; but we still do not know anything about that. At any rate you need not worry about the shipping of my large luggage; that is completely out of the question—perhaps at some later time. We can take along 50 kilos, and with that one naturally takes the most important things and nothing superfluous.

What you and Liesel write about her tonsillectomy made us very sad, even though it is, thank heaven, over; but now it would be time for you all to stay well. Pity that you cannot already spend the winter in California; that would do you all good—and we with you in that heavenly land—I don't even dare to think of that. Now if only Liesel

26. "To the east," i.e., Poland. The delusions Mamina and the others had about their fates there are demonstrated later in this letter, as well as in their belief, expressed in the postscript to the October 13 letter, that personal contacts in Poland could be of help.

could run around as a phoenix, and the two little scamps as archangels, that would be a complete paradise. How I long for them and for you two; how eternally long are these three years of our separation.

I am quite tired today, we have had much running around, many errands, then still the dentist; I am sewing sleeping bags out of our various blankets, Lene is baking zwieback and cookies, and in between, our true old friends come to see us.

Now farewell; I will write again soon, a thousand greetings and kisses to you all, from Lene too.

Your Mamina

What you write about the visa for Cuba is not valid at the moment, but Harry will confirm for you that a so-called pre-visa (the statement of the foreign minister), which I already have in hand, is sufficient; the visa is stamped into the passport just before the departure in Berlin. Walter, whom I met today, asks you to assure Conrad that with his various skills—cooking, photography, and flower-making—he could support himself, that is, never become a burden to anyone. Now really everyone who can help, must help.

Next time write to Mrs. Marta Stein, Prague, Vršovice Sámová 28.

October 30

My dearest children,

Our old true friend on which I used to type has left us for good now,[27] and it may be that I will soon not be able to write regularly either; in that case, please don't worry; it will surely just be a passing thing until the mail functions smoothly again.

For the moment we don't yet know if, when, and where the journey will take us. Your cable, dear boy, came from Hapag[28] on the 26th and will probably be useful to us to this extent, that we will be put on the list for emigration—I am already on it and Lene has

27. As mentioned earlier, typewriters, as well as ski outfits, phonographs, records, cameras, film projectors, etc., were confiscated from Jews on October 25. The letter is handwritten.

28. Hamburg-America Line, a steamship company. Probably the cable informed Mamina of a booking.

hopes; then if the business is taken up again, we could still perhaps come to you. May God grant it.

We are in good health though nervous; uncertainty is the worst thing. Please write from now on to Marta Stein, Prague-Vršovice, Sámová 28. She would keep mail from you until she gets an address from us; she could also read the letters and carry out your wishes reliably.

I received Liesel's dear letter and read it with great pleasure, like everything that comes from you. Stay in good health, and pray that we stay so too and that we can see each other again. Unfortunately, I was not able to give Liesel's lines to Otto, since he left the day before with his sister, as did Dr. Fritz K. and Willi P., very dear friends, and also a lot of acquaintances. I hope we will see them once more in our lifetimes. Perhaps Conrad's wife can find out from her homeland whether Mamina eventually arrived there.

Tante Tonscha was here this afternoon and had a very nice letter from her son and one from Tante Ella. Bobbo has also left, with his wife and mother-in-law. We will of course continue to send you news of how things go with us.

Once more, don't worry, we are calm and prepared; so long as I have Lene with me, I am not unhappy, and I hold myself together so as not to make things hard for her. You must know the saying, "Even at the grave he sows hope," and that's the way we'll continue.

A thousand thanks, my dear children, for all your efforts and love; my poor boy, what a lot of work you have had with us. I embrace you all,

Your Mamina

Your letter No. 32 just came; many thanks for all your kind and good advice, but unfortunately I won't be able to use it for the moment. Just one thing I must explain to you: technically, my emigration was really never possible, since I never had confirmation of a ship ticket in my hands—this was due to Gestorum's swindle[29]—and therefore I was never able to begin with other preparations.

The consideration of becoming a burden to you for months in Havana was just a secondary one, although determined by the quite

29. What the swindle was isn't clear.

mistaken optimism that kept us prisoners here (I for my part believed in it the least). And life here was always bearable up to now. Now, to my great sorrow, there probably won't be much we can do; but as I said, I won't lose hope.

▶ *Aufbau* reported on October 31 that two thousand Jews had already been deported from Prague, and another six thousand had received notice of imminent deportation. On November 7, the newspaper printed a report from Prague stating that forty-two thousand persons had already been "transported" and recounting the rumor that they were being sent to demolished parts of Russia, not to Poland.

November 11

My dearest children,

Cables whirl around us here,[30] and everything would be beautifully arranged by you, my dear good boy, if only our departure were possible.

We have let a few days pass in order to make inquiries everywhere before answering the question of whether we could reach the ship by the end of December. But neither at the Community Center, at Hapag, nor at Čedok does anyone know when the work at the Emigration Office will be resumed. So today we sent you a cable via Hapag saying that for the moment the travel opportunities are uncertain but that we will cable again if there is any change. That you are risking the tickets and everything else is a dreadful pity, but there is nothing else to be done.

Now Lene and I have been notified through you that our visas are in Berlin, and we will probably soon be notified by Berlin too; the bookings are ready too, so we must just wait and hope that all your efforts will be rewarded and that we sooner or later reach our yearned-for goal.

Supposedly the other journeys[31] have been halted, and we are taking a breath; we would give a lot to know where and how all our

30. On November 8, Cuba issued a visa for Lene; on the 10th, Frederick applied to Paul Tausig & Sons travel agency for steamship tickets for Lene and Mamina. The cables relate to these activities and to others. See Frederick's letter dated December 3.

31. i.e., the deportations

friends—Otto, Fritz K., and many others—are. Up to now no news of them has arrived, and we think of them every hour—if only we could help them somehow!

We are well; I have been suffering for nearly two weeks from a bad toothache; today the tooth was pulled, and now it's better. It was a so-called "bridge-pile" tooth, and that is why I allowed myself to be plagued by it for so long. May God grant that the pile on which you, my boy, are laying the bridge for a better future for us be as solid as the root of my old tooth was, and may God greatly reward you for what you are doing for us; you have no idea what it means to us.

Tonscha is happy too that Onkel Fritz has taken her matter in hand and will finance her; she is not quite as far as we, but on the way. I hope that Fritz has got in touch with you regarding the ship, etc.; it would be nice if we could travel together. I wrote to Tante Ella today; you know that her husband died shortly after an operation. I am in constant postal communication with Pepi—she is an angel, and full of worry about us, the dear. Is Liesel all right again? And the good children?

I must close; I miss the machine very much.

A thousand greetings,
Your Mamina

November 12

Dear Fritz,

Since we do not know now for when the tickets should be ordered, since the travel possibilities are so uncertain, I would recommend putting the money for the tickets at the disposal of the Čedok agency here—in dollars—and doing this via Čedok's Portuguese agency:

Chester Merill Ramos & Co.,
33 Rua da Misericordia, Lisbon, Portugal
Cable address: Hustler Lisbon

with the condition that Čedok can use the money when an opportunity for emigration arises—that is, when your mother and Lene are ready to travel, and only then should they obtain the necessary ship passage. I spoke with Čedok yesterday about this matter; of course no binding agreement is possible here; you would have to obtain that when you remit the money to them. Whether all this is possible is something I cannot judge from here, but it seems to me that for the moment it's the only way of somehow reaching the goal.

Just to be sure: A possibility may naturally present itself by which you may find a different combination there; as I have said, I must leave that to you—emigration may be permitted again within the next days or weeks, so that I can just recommend to you that you get the whole matter in order as soon as possible, so that your mother and Lene then, as soon as they are ready to travel, can have disposition over ship's passage.

A similar combination might also be possible through a different travel agency, including ones that are not located in Prague, possibly in Switzerland, and this could then best be accomplished by Onkel Fritz.

Let us hear from you soon, and good things: we think of you often, and continue to wish Mr. and Mrs. Konrad[32] and you all the best!

Your Skutsch

November 19

My dearest boy,

A weak glimmer of hope has arisen: yesterday I was with Tonscha at Mrs. Hanna Steiner's, who said, perhaps I can tell you more in a week, come again and ask; today Lene went with Aunt to a gentleman whom Onkel Fritz recommended, a very important person, and this person stated that it all depends on how the negotiations in Berlin[33] work out. So something does seem to be stirring; and the thing that is very important for us is that the newly resumed transports were suspended today. What that signifies, we do not know, except for one thing—that it means time won for us. We have been very nervous again in the last few days.

Meanwhile an inquiry recently came from the post office asking

32. Franz Petschek (Konrad) was attempting to arrange emigration for some other friends.

33. What negotiations this refers to is not known—probably it was only another rumor.

whether we had received your cable of November 7; I can imagine that you must have been quite impatient having to wait so long for our answer, but we kept thinking that we would find out something, and it was always in vain. At any rate, it was wise of you, as you say in your last cable, to make a definite booking on the *Nyassa*[34] for January 4; there is simply no other way but to take this risk, because once the departures have been assured there will be a wilder rush for tickets than you can imagine. Countless people already have visas now, and all have the same wish that we do. Aside from that, we are fine. Today Lene received a very nice letter from Harry, who complains that she is without news of us; but we wrote her two letters some time ago. It would be too lovely to see her, too, again soon, and to sit in the warm sun.

Today Erna, the widow of Conrad's uncle, was here; she also has a ticket for January 4, and hopes for fulfillment.

Many thousands of greetings,
Mama

▶ *Aufbau* reported on November 21 that the deportations had begun again. On November 28 word came that the Berlin-Lisbon train was no longer running. On December 5 the flood of cables had let up, but more than eight hundred telegrams with emigration permits had left Cuba the week before.

December 1

My dear ones,

Though rich in cables, I yet hear little from you. We received your cable No. 5529 of November 22, regarding the Cuban visa, and No. 9658 of November 27 about the confirmation of the Wagonlits reservation and informing the Portuguese Consulate in Berlin. Lene also has the visa confirmation now, but I do not; I assume that I will not receive a new one, since the visa was extended. So everything would be ready except, unfortunately, for the Emigration Office.

This morning Toncha and I went to see Mrs. Hanna Steiner to

34. The *Nyassa* and the *Serpa Pinto,* Portuguese vessels, were the only ships that continued to carry refugees to the United States and Canada after July 1942. The booking on the *Nyassa* was apparently the outcome of Frederick's November 10 application to Paul Tausig & Sons.

ask her what the outlook was, and whether we should postpone the December–January date, to which she answered, "Unquestionably." It is impossible to make this deadline, but she still hopes that the work will be resumed, and she is going to try to help us as much as she can; she knows Tonscha very well and is very nice to us.

So today, with heavy hearts, we sent a cable to you asking you to postpone the deadline; how and for how long, we must leave to you, since unfortunately we know nothing at all, and can let you know only when something happens. I hope we will continue to stay here; the departures are being resumed, and not to such a distant point, for the moment to the vicinity of Kulhaneks' home; we must be content that this is the case.[35] Our other plans would suffer thereby, but we could still remain in contact. Mrs. Steiner advises that, in case we have to leave, we should notify the consulate in Berlin to direct everything to the Community Center here c/o Mrs. Hanna Steiner; and you, dear boy, must do the same in case you get a cable from us saying "Departed."

I received a letter from Onkel Fritz, in which he laments that you have not answered his three letters and the same number of cables; he wanted to work together with you in Tonscha's matter. That would have been quite complicated. Do write him a few lines when you can. Tonscha has everything ready. Walter has a promise of aid on the journey from some Monsignor in Boston, so you needn't worry about him, at least. You have enough other worries; I wish it were all over and that a normal life could begin again, for you too.

Lene had a very sweet letter from Harry, who is enchanted with Havana and sorry that she will soon have to leave there; why she doesn't spend the winter there, I don't know. It would have been beautiful still to meet her there, but there can't be any hope of that now.

From Otto and the others we have still heard nothing, but they are said not to be doing well; Lene once sent Otto money and we

35. Kulhanek, a Fürth family friend, was from Leitmeritz, near Theresienstadt (Terezín). Mamina hoped that Theresienstadt, rather than Poland, was the destination of the new transports. Theresienstadt, known as the "old people's ghetto," was not an extermination camp, although, of course, many died there. What went on "to the east" was a mystery. Also, Theresienstadt was in Czechoslovakia and therefore closer to home.

also sent some to Bobbo, but now that is no longer permitted: what a pity. We think of them constantly.

Now it will soon be Christmas, the fourth in exile; how will things be next year? One mustn't think and mustn't remember, or one can't stand it.

In order to distract myself for the time being, I have begun studying Spanish on my own; it goes into my old head with difficulty, but a few crumbs do stick. I've stopped taking English lessons and just read now so that I don't forget everything; sometimes I review something too. Hansl and Harriet will have to take me on as a pupil. I hope that all their Christmas wishes will be fulfilled and that they will have a happy holiday; children are really the only ones who have any joy left.

And you, my good children, be of good spirits; we will see each other again. Until then, a thousand thanks for everything that you are doing for me; celebrate Christmas as well as you can, our thoughts will always be with you.

Hasta la vista and a thousand kisses,
Your Mamina

Lene sends her greetings.

▶ The following letter, the only one from Frederick that we have, must have been returned to him at the outbreak of war with Germany, December 11th.

On December 19, *Aufbau* reported that the *Nyassa's* departure was uncertain, and that other ships' departures had been "postponed." Cuban visas had been invalidated by the lack of transportation, and American residents who had made deposits in Cuba ($2,650 per refugee) were advised to try to get refunds.

December 3

Dearest Mother and Lene,

Unfortunately we haven't heard from you for the longest time now, and if I am not mistaken, your letter No. 7 was the last one that reached us. But in the meantime we have had an animated exchange of cables, and even though this is not fully satisfying, we must not lose courage, nor will we, and that includes you. For now we have made a big step: you both have the visas for Cuba and the tickets, and now everything depends on when you can reach the ship in Lisbon. In order to fill every loophole in our correspondence, I will once more repeat all the cables and the circumstances as they appear according to the latest developments:

To begin with, I am sending you a photocopy of Cable No. 8948, according to which the Cuban visa for Lene is granted. It follows from this that all the legal requirements have been fulfilled. Therefore the Cuban Consulate in Berlin can make no objection of any kind. Now there is another photocopy containing the landing permit for Lene. The content is the usual and requires no explanation. Now there is a photocopy of the extension of the landing permit for Mother, valid until March 29, 1942. I have already sent Mother the cable in which it is confirmed that Mother, that is, that all legal, i.e., financial requirements have been fulfilled for Mother.

As a result, I cabled Hapag on November 21:

> Henriette Cubavisa 1802 further cable 9902 acknowledging fulfillment Cubalegation Berlin financial requirements furthermore Cubavisa Lene 8948 with same confirmation arrived. Cable earliest if *Nyassa* reachable.

Thereupon I received a cable from Hapag on November 25:

> Attempting everything necessary Pollatschek, firm confirmation currently impossible. Will cable if postponement necessary. Ernst and Walter request travel assistance.

I was very happy over this news, all the more so since I had meanwhile heard that Erna and Irma are to travel to Lisbon on December 20. To my greatest disappointment, the following cable came yesterday from Hapag:

> Departure Pollatschek, Fuerth Schneider not possible now. Postpone date. Will cable when necessary.

There was nothing else to do but, with a heavy heart, to postpone the tickets for January 4 on the *Nyassa;* that is, I cabled Lisbon and requested that they transfer the passage for you two and for

Erich and Grete to the next departure of the *Nyassa.* I assume that this will be about four to five weeks later and that you will then definitely be able to reach this ship. I will still find out the exact date of departure and will then of course immediately cable you.

What the reason is that some can reach the ship, but you cannot, is unfortunately not known to me, and we are all the more disappointed, since we had thought since you had the portfolio all ready and, as I once heard from Ernst, that the departure could follow within two to three weeks, if necessary even earlier, you could certainly reach the ship.

But we must not let ourselves become discouraged, since unfortunately the journeys, as we well know, never go quite according to plan; but on the other hand we also know that everyone who earnestly wanted it and worked on it, finally did get out. So we will hope that you will simply arrive in Havana in February instead of in January, and the joy will be that much the greater, if that is possible.

Please notify Erich of the above, so that I don't have to write to him directly. He should excuse my choosing this abridged route, but I have so much to write that I couldn't manage, much as I would like to. I don't have any help anymore either, since Dr. Ekstein, who used to work for me, has taken a position with a transport company, and I have to take care of all the running around and writing by myself.

Fritz B. received a letter from Onkel Fritz with the wildest scolding, how badly we have managed everything here regarding Tante Tonscha; however, the dear old boy has no notion how difficult it is to do such things and how we have hounded ourselves to get everything ready quickly, not to mention the raising of the necessary means. Fritz and I have literally done our utmost, and our dear uncle's reproaches are downright laughable. But we—Fritz and I—have borne them smilingly.

It's a long time since I have heard anything from Eugen and unfortunately nothing from Peter either. I recently met a gentleman who saw him in his school[36] and who told me that he is very well.

To write of our own little events among all these complications really seems to me out of place. But, since you will unfortunately

36. Either officers' training school, or simply code for army

still have to rely on our written reports for a short time, I assume that you will derive some pleasure if I report something to you about the children and ourselves.

We are having the proverbially gorgeous New York autumn, and even though it is already December, the sun shines almost all the time and it is mostly mild and warm. Meanwhile I am still using the car, and I often drive with the top down, it is so warm. The children have become enthusiastic car riders and can't get enough.

Last Sunday we went to see Hans and Stella, who send their greetings. They have a very nice place; they have rented a place on the Hudson River, about an hour by car from the city, in the middle of a large estate. Ernst Mayer and his wife were there too, and Köppl,[37] and all of us with Hans's children took a walk in the nearby park belonging to the Rockefellers, which is not less than 18,000 acres in size—an acre being about as large as half of our beloved garden. But Mr. Rockefeller took no notice of us, and furthermore anyone can go walking there.

Our Hans is still delighted with his Spanish lessons. Twice a week he goes into the city on the subway, and he already takes all this quite in stride.

Best greetings to you all,
Your Friedrich

37. Hans and Stella Weinmann (later Wyman), friends from Aussig. The others mentioned were other Aussig friends.

1942

January 5

[to Fritz Heller]

My dear ones,

Tonscha has just brought me your letter, dear Fritz, and Lene and I are especially happy about it; so little mail comes for us now that we greet every word all the more thankfully. Thank you for your good wishes for the New Year and your encouragement not to lose hope; it is often very hard, but we will pull ourselves together and continue to hope for a reunion with all our loved ones.

That you had such a lovely holiday made me very happy; here it was quite still and sad this time—no tree, no presents, no Christmas carp, and unfortunately no Christmas matins either. Tonscha was not able to spend the evening with us either, since there is no room for her to spend the night here in our tiny little room. So we were alone with our thoughts and memories of our loved ones. On Christmas Day, Wednesday, Tonscha was with us; we had quite a decent meal, as good as possible, and now these days too are over.

I hope we will still be here for a while, and you can soon send us greetings from Friedrich's family again. I am so happy that they are all well; tell them the same from us. I had a letter from them from the 7th of November, still full of travel plans and hopes for a reunion. The good boy—what trouble and agitation all of that has brought him, and still the goal is not reached. What else can we poor people do but have patience and continue to wait.

Lene is now very impatient since no news comes from her family, neither father nor son. On Christmas Eve she kept talking about whether Peter had yet laid his little boy under the Christmas tree. It could have been a girl too of course, but expectant grandmothers always think of a boy.

I wonder what Hans and Renate did; they were surely happy as always on Christmas Eve, with their tree and their presents; I just hope that their wishes were fulfilled and that their parents were happy too with their happiness. Friedrich always says, the only use of memories now is to forget them, they distract one too much from the future. He is of course right, but it is so difficult, when the present is without joy and the future dark. We will try to find a little star that will light our way into this darkness. Your confidence, dear Fritz, will help us; and so we wish you too a good, blessed year.

Many greetings to you, kiss Liesel, Friedrich, and
my sweet little rascals a thousand times,
Your Jettla

▶ After the outbreak of war with the United States, direct correspondence between Czechoslovakia and the United States became impossible (with the exception of the letter of January 21, which somehow got through); thus the letters sent to Fritz Heller (Onkel Fritz) in neutral Switzerland were meant largely for the Pollatscheks. Mamina tried in her letters to disguise the Pollatscheks' place of residence and their relationship to her; thus phrases such as "when you talk to them" must be interpreted as "when you write to them." "My friends" in other letters means "my family."

Mamina signed letters to her brother *Jettla* (pronounced "Yettla"), the nickname for Jindřiška, the Czech form of her first name, Henriette, which was the name she was known by to most of the family.

January 21

My dearest ones,

I received your letters 34 and 35 on the same day; both of them, though much delayed, made us very happy.

It was with melancholy that I read all your good advice about traveling; how beautiful everything would have been if fate had granted it, and how little the strains of the journey would have mattered to us; we will surely have to bear quite different things before we see each other again. When that will be only God knows, but we continue to trust in a happy end and reunion with all of you, my dear ones.

That you want to move to a milder climate[1] and that I should someday meet you in this paradise surpasses my keenest wishes; the preparations that you have already made for it are also a pleasant surprise. You will surely feel very well there, and especially your health will profit enormously.

We note your Christmas and New Year's wishes with the conviction that they will be fulfilled. We would just like to know how you spent the holidays, whether Santa Claus granted the wishes (if possible), and whether the young ones were content. Liesel's desire to bake a Christmas stollen next year—I would for all my life love to see that wish transformed into reality, especially if Lene could help; she cooks excellently, even with today's meager ingredients—what a field day she would have if everything were again available.

This week she had an especially happy day with the news that she has become a grandmother, and I bask in the honor of being a great-grandmother. I wonder whether I will ever get to see little Patricia. If only I at least had wool to knit something for the baby, but unfortunately there is none of that now, and I must tame my longing. We don't know many details yet but that Peter is very happy with his wife and child, we found out from Otto's mother; Emil wrote one of his beautiful letters to Lene in which he gave us this news.

We are in good health and have even filled out a little recently. That is probably because of the holidays. Lene gave free rein to her emotions and some carefully hoarded eggs, and that did us good. I only hope now that I can hear from you again soon and that you are all well too. Don't worry too much about us; the dear Lord will continue to help us.

A thousand kisses,
Your Mamina

1. The Pollatscheks planned to move to California, but because of wartime restrictions, they postponed the move until 1947.

February 28

[to Fritz Heller]

My dear ones,

I thank you, dear Fritz, most heartily for your letter, which made me especially glad, as does everything that you report of my friends. I sent a part of your letter to Liesel's mother; she is always delighted to hear about the young people and the children. If it's possible, have them enclose a greeting themselves the next time. I am very happy that the boy is so talented in languages; I already marveled at the two little rascals' Swiss-German when I spent three weeks with them in Lucerne—unfortunately I understood little of it. They are both very bright and especially well brought-up children; may God keep them in good health.

Recently I celebrated my 72d birthday—that isn't the right word—for one cannot celebrate now; the times are too serious for it, and my thoughts were always with all of you—what would I give to see you again.

Three years ago I was in Lucerne, and it was such a warm, lovely day of early spring; the little ones made flower pots of wet clay in the garden, stuck the first mosses, snowdrops, and primroses into them, and set them on the breakfast table. There, too, fine Swiss chocolate shone, and a jar of Masox meat extract which I still keep today in my rucksack as an untouchable reserve. Liesel's mother was there at the same time as I; in the afternoon we had jelly roll—it was a fine celebration! When one becomes so old, one's memories of such festive hours become doubly valuable, and I live on them.

The daily routine of which you, dear little brother, write is very delightful; you still have your work, your stimulation, and your lovely, friendly family life. I wonder if I will ever get to see that. Sometimes I am quite despondent; my allotted time is not very long any more, and I cannot wait long. It is probably because of these times that I feel much older than I am; especially my hearing has suffered a great deal, and that disturbs me terribly and also causes me to draw away from others and more and more into myself. It isn't too difficult for me; our few good old friends have almost all left us; those who remain neither stimulate nor excite me. People just keep talking about the same thing, and they don't interest me.

Tonscha is the one person I see as often as possible. She is much more sociable than I, has masses of friends, and, thank God, she still has her lovely, warm and cozy apartment. Ours is quite cramped and not always warm either, but we must praise each day that we still have this. Tell our friends there they shouldn't worry about us; it is probable that we will continue to live here peacefully.

By now Liesel and her family will probably have moved to the country[2] and feel very well there; how gladly I would have helped them; with moving I am certainly experienced. If it were granted me to visit them there, with a detour via Gombach,[3] that would be the apex of all the wishes that I still have. Perhaps I will revive there as much as it is still possible and, with rehabilitated nerves, find a renewed joy in living. I had always intended to remain robust and agile for a long time, and so will I try to be if circumstances become more favorable.

My greetings to you all,
Jettla

March 12

[to Fritz Heller]

My dear ones,

I read your letter at Tonscha's, dear Fritz, and was happy to hear of your well-being. I'm only very sorry that you haven't been able to speak to Liesel and her family recently; they must be taken up with their move. I hope they will now finally have found a home; they have moved around so much already. The children will probably get used to the new place the most quickly, at least it has always been so before; they love change and travel above all. The main thing, of course, is for Friedrich to find some satisfying work that will provide for them without straining him too much, but I hope he has made preparations for that before burning his bridges; he is careful enough for that.

April 2 is Liesel's birthday; I can't even send her my wishes be-

2. The Pollatscheks were to spend the coming summer in Schroon Lake, New York, and then move to Lake Placid, New York. That move was still several months off, but Mamina's confusion is understandable, as the Pollatscheks had been planning the move before the mails stopped.

3. The Hellers' residence in Switzerland

cause I don't know where they will be; but if you have the chance to see her, please tell her that all my love and all my thoughts, together with my best wishes, will be with her. Her children will cover her with surprises, and I hope there will be a birthday cake too. If fate is kind to me, I will get a piece next year.

I try so far as possible to take care of my health—I've never had much to do with doctors—in order to be able once more to see the beautiful land in which you live and to press you all to my heart again. I would also love to be able to read your new book; a pity that you have so much else to do and have had to put aside this dear child of your muse. Now it would be time for spring to come and to draw you from your desk into the fresh air. We, too, long for the sun and warmth. The winter was long and hard; it's decades since I have been so cold. Still we are happy that we can still spend this time in our little room—how much longer? We do not know.

We had a happy day when Lene received a letter from her son, the happy *pater familias;* I can hardly imagine him. I last saw him when I went to Lucerne and he took me to the train here, a real boy, full of pranks in his child's head, but already halfway a man, worrying about the problems of the future. When I came back three weeks later, he had left. Now I hope he will write again soon; he can hardly imagine what joy it gives us—we have so little of that.

Tine must slowly be starting to think about her garden; does she sow flower seeds, or does she buy seedlings? How I used to love this occupation! The garden and the outdoors altogether: from our one window here we see a high, dirty fire wall and an equally dirty court; if we squint sideways we catch a glimpse of the next building—which contains a Methodist church—and of a small lawn with a mighty plane tree: at any rate something that will bear buds and leaves. If we are still here by then, we want to put a couple of flower pots out on the windowsill and simulate a garden, since, despite the fire wall, the sun shines in a few hours a day. I will seem to myself like old Ekdal in *The Wild Duck* when he went hunting in the attic.

Please, when you speak to Liesel, ask her how they are planning to live—whether outside the city, and if they have a garden and a balcony, how many rooms, etc. Her mother would like so much to know everything possible about their lives. She writes me often and is happy to be able to speak to me, even through this route; will they have a maid or will they take their present help with them, and will they be living near her childhood friend, Otto W.?

From Madeleine and sister-in-law Luise from Th.[4] we had short, inconsequential cards, but still a sign of life; they are in good health, and so far they are all right.

That's all for today; my warmest greetings for all of you who are dear to us and all our loved ones, large and small. Let us hear from you again soon.

Your Jettla

▶ The apartment that the Pollatscheks were to rent in Lake Placid was a third-floor walkup on Main Street. It had two bedrooms. A garden bordering Mirror Lake was at the back of the building, the ground floor of which housed a furniture store. They did not have a maid.

Otto W. is Otto Wittenberg, who had settled in California; evidently Mamina believed that the Pollatscheks had moved there.

Theresienstadt, a former garrison town in northern Bohemia, was set up as a ghetto in late 1941 (see note following the letter of October 13, 1941). It was referred to as the "old people's ghetto" and was to be a transit station before liquidation, as well as a repository for European Jews who, for whatever reason, were not to be liquidated immediately. Believing it to be an alternative to death, the *Judenräte* (Jewish Councils) cooperated in planning for the deportations. But not everyone was fooled, as is revealed by the tone of Mamina's letters. By April, ten thousand Jews from Bohemia-Moravia were already living in Theresienstadt, according to *Aufbau*.

Mamina's brother Fritz Heller—"Onkel Fritz"—was a retired engineer who wrote scholarly works on poet Rainer Maria Rilke. His wife's name was Tine.

April 15

[from Tonscha to Fritz Heller]

My dearest ones,

By the time my letter arrives, you will be home from beautiful Pellerin, I hope all three well rested.

Recently I had occasion to speak to Lene; she is really a splendid person. She makes her way magnificently wherever she is, is always

4. Theresienstadt. Luise was the wife of Mamina's brother Eugen.

in good humor, and looks bravely in the face of any hardship. She sends regards to you and all our other dear ones. She is healthy as a horse and working hard, so she has little chance to write. So I have promised her to report everything worth knowing. Of course she misses Mother and all the rest of her loved ones, but as I said, she feels well and content everywhere.

Thus too her mother, as I have heard, is calmer now and more confident. The breathing-spaces are unfortunately very short, so despite everything, we cannot find rest; we have become shriveled up bundles of nerves, tired old women with no pleasure in life—everything about us is so inconsolably sad and desolate.

My dear Sunday guest no longer comes any more either; I miss her very much, since she took care of all of my affairs. Karl has begun his summer vacation, but his wife is not too delighted with it. Of other acquaintances I see and hear very little; aside from Jettla, I see no one—they all have their sorrows, and one doesn't want to disturb them.

Have you spoken with Leopold[5] and Friedrich again? Please give them our regards, Ella and her family too of course. I regularly send Bobbo a trifle, but hardly ever hear from him; I hope they all continue well.

I will close for now; I hope I can still write to you often and receive news from you as often. Best and heartiest greetings,

Your Tonscha

▸ Lene was not "transported" until May 7, but before that she spent six weeks in a "sanitarium," read: prison. Tonscha's "speaking" to her probably means that she had received a letter from her. That Lene was "healthy as a horse" must be taken with a grain of salt; that she was "working hard" less so.

The Sunday guest is Karli; she and her children met Karl, her husband (from whom she was divorced), at Tonscha's or at Mamina's every Sunday for as long as she was able to. What Karl's "summer vacation" was is not clear: He was "transported" on June 3, 1942, supposedly to Theresienstadt. The entire train containing seven hundred persons, however, was never unloaded in Theresienstadt,

5. i.e., Fritz Bischitzky, who had changed his name to Leo Birch.

where it stood for four days. Thereafter it disappeared with no survivors—presumably as a revenge measure for the assassination of Reichsprotektor Reinhard Heydrich on May 27.

The State Jewish Museum of Prague writes: "Helena Fürthová [Helene Fürth] [was deported] May 7 1942 to Terezín [Terezín is the Czech form of Theresienstadt] the transport 'At' and the number 123. This transport stayed in Terezín 2 days, the designation was changed in 'ax', but the deportationsnumbers remained unchanged. The particular place of deportation is not known. The destination of the transport were probably the concentrationscamps Sobibór and Ossowa."

Other sources state that transport "ax" from Theresienstadt probably went to Ossov, near Sobibór. No deportees from this transport returned or survived. Sobibór was one of three killing centers (the others were Belzec and Maidanek, near Lublin) built in the spring of 1942.

As we find out from the May 16 letter, Lene was sent to Siedliszcze, a work camp about twenty-five miles east of Lublin and twelve miles west of Chelm (Mamina writes *Cholm,* but obviously Chelm is meant). Sobibór was some sixty miles northeast of Lublin. It is possible that Lene was taken first to Siedliszcze and then to the death camp; at any rate it is not clear whether she died in the work camp or in the death camp.

May 6

[to Fritz Heller]

My dear ones,

It is easily possible that these will be the last lines from me for a long time. Lene leaves tomorrow, without my having been able to see her again; we said farewell to each other in writing, for I will surely soon follow her. My suitcase stands packed with the most necessary things, and my state of mind is deeply sorrowful, all the more so since my health leaves much to be desired.

I hope that someone of our friends will still remain here in order to, as far as possible, continue giving you news of us, and us a sign of life from our friends over there. Until further notice write to our address here; our landlords will know what to do. They have been particularly touchingly kind in these difficult days, as was Toncha, who took care of everything, for I have been totally useless.

I would like to know Clärly's last name, possibly also the address of one of your friends. Please notify Lene's family and Friedrich's that they should no longer count on direct news of her and that they shouldn't worry if my letters too will be missing. We are in God's hands and hope for His and for your gracious help, that He maintains us in good health and that we see one another again in the not too distant future.

Good-bye, as long as I can I will continue to write. Thank you for your last letter, dear little brother, and the charming pictures; I didn't know that there still was a springtime.

A thousand kisses,
Your Jettla

May 16

[to Fritz Heller]

My dear ones,

I am answering your welcome letter by return mail. Your dear, warm words did me good, even though it is impossible to quiet my sorrow. Yesterday I received the first card from Lene; she writes from the journey onward "into the blue." Where the journey leads she does not know, and I will probably wait without hearing anything about it for months; there is no contact and no mail.

And so my last hope of seeing my good child again is gone, and I keep asking myself how I will continue to bear this life. It has gone on too long; the nerves no longer hold out. I don't want to continue to belabor you with my miseries; I only ask you, dear Fritz, to let Lene's family know somehow, and also Friedrich's, that they should not count on news of her nor soon of me either. I will let you hear from me as long as I can, but that cannot last very much longer.

I am still occupied with healing my foot. The doctor is doing his best to cure the painful suppuration of the cuticle of the big toe. It is somewhat better, but I can walk only with great pain. In the afternoons I lie on the couch while Tonscha, the Samaritan, always ready to help, sits beside me, and takes care of everything, for I haven't been outside in weeks. The open window and, in the courtyard next door, a tree that is beginning to get leaves have to take the place of spring for me, the saddest one of my life.

If only I would receive a line from the children; nobody who doesn't live here can imagine what we suffer. But there I go again complaining. I simply know no other song.

Thank you for your love, and a thousand greetings,

Your Jettla

I have just received news from Lene, thank God I at least know where she is at the moment. She writes that they are living very primitively in a little nest, but she is well and in good spirits. The furnishings consist of a heap of straw and a poorly heated oven, for which she hunts up the wood; but the people with her are nice, and she hopes that they will receive their luggage, which so far hasn't been the case. She seems to have only her rucksack and her bag of food, from which she has been living up to now. The trip lasted two days and two nights, during which they had to provide their own food. Her address is: Siedliszcze/near Cholm, district Lublin—*Generalgouvernement,* A.T. 123.[6]

Do you by any chance have an acquaintance near there who might take an interest in her? She would be thankful for any help. Poor thing! Let Eugen and Friedrich know the address too; maybe they know of someone in the area.

May 16

[from Tonscha to Fritz Heller]

My dear ones,

Unfortunately we can report only sad things. Jettla's condition, physically and emotionally, cannot be imagined; I have never seen the poor thing so hopeless and inconsolable as now. It is a gruesome fate that awaits us. Lene was our support, and now that she is gone there is no happy hour for either of us. We live always in fear and anxiety; now there seems to be a little breathing space, but we will hardly be allowed to stay much longer within our four walls; then we will have to say farewell to everything that has been dear and precious, for it is as good as impossible that we old people will be able to carry on.

6. The *Generalgouvernement* was the eastern part of Germany's portion of Poland, intended as the destination for all deported Jews.

Deepest thanks for your dear letter and your prayers for us; perhaps the bitter chalice will pass us by for a while longer. The next time you see Leopold give them our warmest greetings and kisses; other than that, there is nothing cheerful that I can relate to them. I am happy to be able to assume from the last reports that they are well; that is my only consolation. Bobbo wrote recently, just a few lines; he received our message, and we immediately sent another.[7]

Here I had to interrupt my letter in order to hurry to Jettla. Her landlords—unbelievably fine people—came to me with the message that yesterday evening, after the treatment of the foot, she got such terrible pains that she took countless pills and has slept for hours since then. We immediately notified the doctor who is treating her, and he reassured us completely. Jettla was also quite conscious again, only somewhat weak. I stayed as long as I could in order to get home in time; the landlady is an angel, since I after all cannot stay there, as much as I would like to. Tomorrow I will take up my post with her in the morning, will send off the letter from there in the afternoon, and will still add a few lines about her condition.

Jettla is again more or less all right, only the sorrow about Lene lies heavy on our hearts. Sincerest greetings to you all,

Tonscha

May 24

[to Fritz Heller]

My dear Fritz,

You gave me a great joy with the lovely photos, the first after long, dreary weeks, and I am all the more thankful to you and the others involved. Please tell them when you see them how happy I was and that I shed tears of emotion on seeing these sweet childish faces; when I last saw them they were almost babies, and now they have become handsome big young persons; I can hardly realize how they have grown and how good-looking they have become. I wonder if they have sent some pictures to the grandma in Aussig too; if not, they should do it as soon as possible; in the meantime I'll send her these to look at, but I must get them back.

7. i.e., package or money

I thank you too for your dear letter and everything that you report. Do Friedrich's family want to leave the city or just move to a different apartment? At any rate, I wish them and you happy days of vacation and a good rest.

If and when I will leave here I don't know; every day brings new rumors, and one's nerves barely hold out. My thoughts now are always with Lene, and as long as I am here I will do everything possible to make her lot easier, sending her money, small packages and also bigger ones so far as it is allowed; until now I have received no acknowledgment of receipt. Since the first news of her, I have had none.

An acquaintance recently said that it is possible to send food to people there through a committee in Sweden, but the person didn't know anything more specific, and I am doubtful about the possibility. But it occurs to me that Emil and Eugen have good friends in Sweden—Turre, for example—who, along with one of his friends, once stayed in Nestersitz as a guest at Eugen's for quite a long time. Please, if you see someone from the family, ask them about it; they could at any rate make inquiries, and I would have to send them Lene's address: Siedliszcze/near Cholm, district Lublin, *Generalgouvernement* A.T. 123. I am sure that the people there who were close friends of Peter's would do everything possible to help her.

My foot has recovered to such an extent that I was able today, for the first time in weeks, to go outside. I was quite wobbly and very tired, but it nonetheless did me good. How nice it would be to have a little balcony or some little place where one could sit in the sun, but that no longer exists, and I think longingly of our beautiful garden, where the lilacs must now be in bloom. All that is gone now, and I can only hope that I will live to see a better spring.

Today is Whitsunday, and on one such on May 24, Friedrich was born; that was a lovely holiday, and today I am with him in spirit—he and his family are probably in the country in celebration of the day. Tell him that I beg all the blessings of heaven for him, he is the best son that a mother could wish for; I hope his son will take after him.

Now all the best to you, give my warmest greetings to all our loved ones, and be embraced by

Your Jettla

June 21

[to Eugen]

My dear Putz, dear little brother and Tine,

My heartiest thanks for your dear letters, which as always made me very happy; how happy Liesel[8] would be if I could send her Eugen's letter. But unfortunately my mail to her now functions so badly that she receives neither letters nor money and packages from me, while her letters arrive quite regularly. So I had to limit myself to sending her a copy of the letter to Henriette;[9] as an experiment I am writing a registered letter this time. She always writes with concern about her mother, the good child, and bears her heavy lot with admirable courage.

Everything would naturally be much easier if Turre and Kjell,[10] those good friends, could do something for her, because, since everything that her mother has tried so far has come to naught, she has literally nothing but the clothes on her back. Her money will soon be used up, since everything is very expensive; her work so far has not been paid, so that they can't think of buying even the most necessary things. When it begins to get cold, she will be exposed to all the rigors of the weather. You can imagine the concern of her mother when she thinks of all this—no warm clothing or underclothing, no blanket, no sturdy shoes, nothing. May God grant a way out, and that Lene stays well.

I hear that you have all become quite slim; I hope Emil and Sopherl have recovered in the warm sun. We all could use peace and a few other things to restore some of the once-taboo fat. It made me very happy to hear that Peter and his family are well, that he has success and recognition in his career. Lene will be particularly happy about that. I have sent her that news and your love and greetings and pray now that everything finds its way to her.

If you, dear Putz, see Friedrich, please give him and his family my greetings; he should ask Hans and Franz P. sometime if they or rather their wives still have some connections that might be of use to Helen; one must try everything. Of course it would have to be an

8. i.e., Lene. The letter is full of coded names.

9. i.e., herself

10. Friends in Sweden. In a later letter, Eugen writes that Turre's father had sent money to Lene.

A. relation. I probably won't see Salypol until I get there, which is possible; one can't reach them by letter. Madeleine, Pepsch, and Martha are at an unknown place, as is Walter Sk.; I haven't heard from him in weeks.[11]

My sister thanks you for your greetings, which she returns in kind; I embrace you in old, true friendship, as well as all your family, to whom I wish health and all good things.

Your friend,
Henriette

For little brother and Tine there is not much room left today, I only hope that you all enjoyed your beautiful vacations, and that all three of you, Clärly included, have returned to your duties at home with new strength. Heartiest greetings, and I will write more fully next time.

Your Jettla

▶ On May 25, 1942, Paul Tausig & Son, Inc., travel agency refunded the balance of Frederick's deposit of $1,230 for ship passage for Mamina and Lene (an earlier partial refund had been made January 2), minus various handling and other charges.

Of the Polish labor camps, Raul Hilberg writes in *The Destruction of the European Jews* (1961): "The cost of the labor camps was very low. All camps were primitive. No comforts were allowed. No clothes were issued. Food was supplied in some camps by the nearest *Judenrat* [Jewish council] and in the camps by the civil administration, but the chief ingredients of the workers' diet were only bread, watery soup, potatoes, margarine, and meat leftovers. Working from dawn to dusk, seven days a week, the Jews were driven to collapse. A survivor reports that even small camps, with no more than 400 to 500 inmates, had approximately twelve dead every day" (166).

The publication of this ground-breaking book was made possible by financial aid from Franz Petschek and his wife.

11. Helen = Lene; Helene. The wives of Hans and Franz Petschek were from Poland. "A" means Aryan. "There" is Theresienstadt. Salypol, Pepsch, and Martha were friends of whom nothing further is known.

Emil and Sopherl, Eugen's parents, died natural deaths. Eugen was deported and, after having been seen once in a camp near Paris in the summer of 1944, disappeared without a trace—although Peter found evidence after the war that Eugen survived until 1945 and was shot by the Germans as they were retreating. Peter, who fought with the Czech forces, eventually took part in the invasion of Europe.

July 1

[to Fritz Heller]

My dear ones,

Tonscha is just going to the post office, and I will make use of the opportunity of sending all my sincerest greetings with her. It is always possible that I will soon be leaving, and then the letter-writing, and unfortunately the letter-getting too, will be over. That would be a heavy blow for me, because your and Lene's letters are my only happiness.

I was happy to see from Tine's and your, dear brother's, letters that you recovered and rested very well on your vacation; now you are at home again, and the two hard-working ladies are, as always, at their chores. How I would once more like to water flowers, like Tine, in God's early morning and in my nightgown! The Prague summer, always between walls and sooty houses, is very joyless. I hope it will be the last one of these.

Where are our friends, Liesel with her husband and children,[12] spending their vacation? Is school out where you are, and how were the report cards? Surely marvelous, as always. I had a letter from their grandma; she looks forward to the promised photos, which will have arrived by now. I am very excited to know where the family will settle, and I hope I will find it out; at any rate, if you see them, tell them that my deepest wishes accompany them everywhere, and I haven't given up the hope of once more seeing the beautiful land of Switzerland and all of you.

Lene writes often, always cheerful and satisfied, despite the fact that her life is as primitive as can be; for a long time she had no letters from me, but now, with great happiness, she acknowledged a let-

12. i.e., Pollatscheks. As usual, the letter is really intended for them, but because of censorship problems, Mamina disguised their whereabouts and their relationship to her.

ter, a telegram, and a package. It was one of countless others, which may perhaps still get there, and she was overjoyed about every little morsel. She always writes that she is totally well, that a worker's life agrees with her; it is truly lucky that she has such an adaptive nature and nothing can get her down. She was especially thankful for the news of her husband and hopes that he and the rest of the family remain well. It would be nice if Lene would receive some of your gifts and those of her other friends; but the mail does take quite long.

For today, just all my hearty greetings to you and all of our friends,

Your Jettla

▶ The above was Mamina's last letter. The Jewish Religious Communities in Bohemia wrote to Frederick in a letter dated February 15, 1963: "We wish to inform you that Mrs. Jindriska Pollatschek, born on 2/26/70, last residing at Stepanská 10, Praha II, was deported to Terezín in transport No. Aaq-635 on 7/13/1942, and from there to Treblinka in Poland on transport No. Bw-1020 on 10/19/1942. The said person did not return."

Those to be deported were usually summoned at night. The summons, with day and time to report, were sent out by the Jewish Religious Congregation. Social worker Hanna Steiner had organized young people to help the old and infirm prepare and carry their luggage.

The deportees were told to bring their luggage, including blankets and provisions for five days (the total not to exceed 50 kilograms), and their Estate Declaration together with any cash, bonds, jewelry, or other valuables. The deportees, in groups of a thousand, assembled at the Prague trade fair, where they slept in old wooden barracks and used open-air latrines. Each group stayed for three or four days while filling out forms, handing over their valuables, etc.

The transport that carried Mamina to Theresienstadt was one of fifty-seven that arrived that month from Bohemia-Moravia, Germany, and Austria. Only two transports left Theresienstadt that month. On July 1, the population of Theresienstadt was 21,304; on July 31 it was 43,403. In transport Aaq on July 13, 1942, were a thousand deportees; of these, forty-five were still alive on July 11, 1944. Transport Bw from Theresienstadt to Treblinka contained 1,984 deportees. None of these are known to have survived.

The voyage to Treblinka, northeast of Warsaw near the village of Malkinia on the River Bug, was a long one. Had Mamina been taken to Auschwitz, as most Theresienstadt inmates were, she would have had a shorter voyage. In Treblinka's thirteen gas chambers, ten to twelve thousand persons were gassed daily.

In an account titled "A Year in Treblinka Horror Camp," Yankel Wiernik writes:

> The Treblinka camp was divided into two sections. In Camp One there was a railroad spur and a debarkation platform for unloading human cargo. Next was a large area where the belongings of the newcomers would be laid out. . . . Nearby was an infirmary. . . . Two men worked there, wearing white smocks and Red-Cross brassards, and passing as physicians. From the arrivals they chose the aged and ill, and seated them on a long bench facing a trench. Behind them stood Germans and Ukrainians. They killed the victims by shooting them in the back, so the bodies fell at once into the mass grave. When they had assembled a large number of cadavers, they gathered them together and set them on fire. (178)

It is well known that the Nazis dictated the contents of cards and letters written by their prisoners. One may thus guess at the authenticity of Lene's sentiments.

Fribourg,
July 14

[from Fritz Heller to the Pollatscheks]

Dear Fritz, dear Liesel,

I hope you are in possession of my letter of June 15, as well as the enclosed letter from Jettla, which I sent to you via Eugen Fürth.

Today another such came, along with a few lines that Lene addressed to her mother.[13] To my joy I saw from these that the poor one had received two packages and one shipment of money from Switzerland—a real miracle. I immediately sent her another ten Francs via the Red Cross and will continue to do this monthly.

It is astonishing how brave the poor thing is. She has to do hard labor, hours daily at a river flood-control, without pay, like a slave. Her little suitcase, the only thing she was allowed to take along, was taken away from her, so she has literally nothing but the clothes on her back. She sleeps with 20 fellow sufferers in a miserable lean-to

13. All of these letters are missing.

on a small heap of straw! What will happen when winter comes? At the least she would need a pair of sturdy, warm boots. Unfortunately I cannot send her these through the Geneva Red Cross, since the exportation of shoes and clothing from Switzerland is forbidden. I beg you, in Jettla's and Lene's name, do everything humanly possible to send, via the *American Red Cross,* some shoes and a warm jacket, and now and then some money.

Jettla and Tonscha are "still in our possession"—that means that they have *not yet* had to "travel."[14] I am making all possible efforts to save them from the dreadful fate that has already met almost all of those people there. Up to now I have succeeded—but how much longer? I tremble for them every day.[15]

And what is happening with you? Consider that you are the only ones who still give Jettla the strength to endure; she yearns so dreadfully for a line from you—but you write either letters that I cannot send on to her, or not at all. You must at all events, so long as the poor thing is still alive, send a letter with *every* Clipper, written in German with no place names, without mentioning the country that you live in. From Liesel's mother she received a letter with photos of the children, which made her very happy.

Many hearty greetings from all of us to all of you.

Your Onkel Fritz

July 26

[from Lene to Marta Stein]

Dearest Marta,

I have no idea whether this letter will reach you, I just want to thank you with all my heart for your very great efforts and thank you for all the good things that you are doing for my mother and now for me. I don't know what I would have done without you, right from the start. On the 17th after a few days I received your greeting; I also received the green dress and the vest with great pleasure. I don't know whether anyone has told you that Pat's grandmother is

14. Actually, Mamina had to "travel" the day before this was written.

15. What Fritz's "efforts to save them" were, one may only speculate. Most likely they were imaginary.

now in contact with Wladyslaw Nazaruk, so one can get in touch with her easily. She is well in other ways too, satisfied with her work, since she is now given a prescribed amount to do each day; when that is finished, she can lie in a beautiful meadow for the rest of the day, which is very comforting. She often thinks of her mother and just hopes that she has become a little acclimatized and doesn't miss everything too much.

She also recently had a nice letter from her Onkel Fritz; maybe Ernst could thank him sometime and tell him he should write again soon. She would very much like to have a little Zacherlin against fleas, an old brassiere from her friend Marta or Maňka, and maybe a little piece of used soap. Her friends shouldn't be angry that she bothers them so.

Please send news more frequently; cards and registered letters arrive well. Many thanks to Maňka for her dear card and for everything that she is doing for me. She should also thank Dr. Sch. for his greetings, which arrived. Turre Korch's father (Peter's friend) also wrote me a very nice letter. So you see, I have not been forgotten, which is very comforting.

To you, my dear, good one, and to your husband, all the best and a thousand thankful greetings from

Your old friend

The sisters after whom Maňka asks are not here, only a young girl with the same first name, Lise.

▶ Lene's last letter (above) was sent to Marta Stein. It is full of coded messages: *Pat's grandmother* is Lene. Wladyslaw Nazaruk was a Pole who traveled between Poland and Prague and was able to deliver packages to Lene. *Nice* and *very nice* imply that money was sent. Dr. Sch. was Václav Šebek, who had contacts with the Prague police force and aided many people in escaping. He was the contact man with a Prague police officer who obtained and forged passports, while the British Consul issued false visas. Šebek also arranged with some of the sleeping-car conductors to hide people in the cars. In this fashion he had supposedly had a passport, visa, and train arrangement ready for Lene, when she was somehow found out and immediately deported. Šebek had some of the Pollatscheks' porcelain and glass buried in his garden; after the war he gave this to Patricia Fürth, Peter's daughter.

Lene is reported to have been seen by an acquaintance, shoveling coal, barefooted.

December 28

[to Frederick Pollatschek]

Dear Fritz,

During the Christmas season I had to work a great deal of overtime, on the average 12 hours a day, so that I did not get a chance to write to you.

First of all I wanted to let you know that about ten days ago I had a letter from Tante Ella, who writes that Onkel Fritz wrote that your mother, as well as mine, are in Theresienstadt. By the end of October they were certainly there. That is in a way a ray of light—but from the other relatives one has received no news. Lene is said to have left the place where she was—nobody knows where to. All the news, both positive and negative, comes from the Swiss Red Cross.

Now poor Eugen too must be in immediate danger. Did I write you that Onkel Fritz has, for a change, applied for an American visa again?

How are you, and what are you doing? How are the children, and how is Liesel's health? We are both in our old jobs, and so far we are well. Let us hear from you. All the best for the New Year—a better one, let us hope.

Your Fritz Bischitzky

Postscript

The fates of Mamina, Lene, Toscha, Eugen, and many other family members and friends have been indicated in the notes or in the glossary.

Those who survived the war were, of course, the Pollatschek family; Peter Fürth and his family; Onkel Fritz Heller and family; and Tonscha's son Fritz Bischitzky and his wife Mimi. Here is what became of them:

Fritz and Mimi changed their surname to Birch, and Fritz became Leo. They remained in New York, where they both worked until their retirement. Both died in the 1980s.

Fritz Heller and his wife remained in Switzerland, where they died in the 1960s. Their adopted daughter Clärly still lives there.

Peter and his British wife Elsie Annie (nicknamed Eky) and their daughter Patricia returned to Czechoslovakia after the war. A son, Stephan, was born in 1953. The family left Czechoslovakia in 1967. Peter and Eky eventually moved to France, where Peter died in 1988. Eky, Stephan, and Patricia and her husband, Richard Millward, now live in England. Patricia's daughter, Lene, by an earlier marriage, lives in Germany.

The Pollatscheks moved from Lake Placid to Florida, and from there, after the war, to California. By then they had changed their surname to Polt. Frederick (Friedrich) died in 1967. Elizabeth (Liesel) lives in Oakland, as do John (Hans) and his wife. They have three grown children. John is a retired professor of Spanish, the language he began to study during the family's stay in Havana. Renata (Renate, changed to Harriet, then changed back to Renata) lives in Berkeley with her husband, Frederick Schmitt, a professor of computer science. She is a writer and retired college instructor.

Glossary

of Names, Places, and Institutions

This glossary includes only those names and terms that appear more than once and that have some significance in the letters. Some names of people are listed by their first name, as the name most often appears in the letters

Aufbau. An American Jewish newspaper, published in New York. It gave information on emigration problems and conditions in Europe to Jews already living in the United States, such as the Pollatscheks.

Aussig. Industrial city in northern Bohemia, home of the Pollatscheks. Known in Czech as Ústí.

Belvedere. A park near the Prague castle (Hradčany) where Mamina and Lene used to walk, until parks were closed to Jews

Bischitzky, Fritz. Only son of Mamina's sister Antonie (Tonscha). Married to Mimi. Immigrated to the United States, changed his name to Leo Birch, and died in New York in 1982.

Bobbo (Robert Bischitzky). Son of Mamina's sister Ella and her husband Emil Bischitzky. He and his wife Lotte died in a concentration camp. His sister Liesl immigrated to England before the war.

Čedok. Czechoslovakian travel agency

Chobo (Erwin Chobocky). A cousin of Mamina, who with his wife Margit, immigrated to Palestine in 1939. After the war, they returned to Vienna, where Erwin died in 1956 or 1957.

Clärly (Heller). An adopted daughter of Mamina's brother, Fritz Heller, who lived with him and his wife in Fribourg, Switzerland

Clipper. A transatlantic plane. Mamina often sent her letters "via the Clipper," i.e., airmail.

Cohorn. Neighbors of Mamina's at the Horní Stromka apartment, 1940–41. Deported (to Theresienstadt?) October 1941.

Conrad. *See* Petschek, Franz

Daisy (Heller; Schmidt). An adopted daughter of Fritz Heller, married to a Gentile lawyer named Lolly Schmidt. Lolly was Tonscha's sponsor at her confirmation.

Ekstein (Heinz, later Henry). Ekstein was Friedrich's secretary in Havana. He later changed his name to Eastman. His mother met Mamina in Prague and later wrote to Friedrich about her own experiences traveling to Cuba. Henry, his wife, and their son live in the United States.

Ella (Heller; Bischitzky). A sister of Mamina, married to Emil Bischitzky (a cousin of Adolf and Victor Bischitzky, who married other Heller sisters).

Mother of Bobbo. Born January 2, 1875. Ella with Emil went to England early in 1939 to visit their daughter Liesl and her husband, who had emigrated. They survived the war in England. Ella died in 1962, Emil in 1960(?).

Else (Bischitzky). Wife of Franz Bischitzky, the son of Mamina's sister Olga and her husband Victor (brother of Adolf, cousin of Emil). Franz and Else survived the war in Sweden.

Emil. *See* Ella

Emma (Heller; Grünberger). A sister of Mamina, married to Max Grünberger. The latter died before the war. Emma died in a concentration camp. Their children were Juscha (Goldmann) and Willi. Juscha and probably her husband, as well as their daughter Marianne (Mädi) and Marianne's baby, all died in the camps. Two other daughters survived in England. Willi Grünberger joined the Czech forces, immigrated after the war to the United States where his wife and sons were already living, and died there about 1960.

Erich (Schneider). Family friend and physician. His father was the Pollatscheks' family doctor. Probably died in the camps.

Ernst (Skutsch). A cousin of Mamina and also a cousin of Walter Skutsch. Married to Mimi. Ernst, Walter, and Mimi all died in the camps.

Eugen (Fürth; nicknamed Putz). Husband of Lene. Spent several years in France looking after his parents; died in 1944 or 1945, either in Auschwitz or shot by German troops.

F. C. *See* Petschek, Franz

František. Mamina's lawyer, probably a Czech Gentile

Franz B. and Else. *See* Else

Friedländer, Mrs. Former neighbor of the Pollatscheks in Aussig. Two of her sons, Willi and Paul, survived the war in England; another survived in Paris. Mrs. Friedländer probably died in the camps.

Friedrich (Pollatschek; Frederick; Fritz). Mamina's son and the recipient of most of Mamina's letters. His wife was Liesel, their children Hans (John) and Renate (Harriet/Renata). *See also the Postscript.*

Fritz K. (Kettner; Dr. Fritz K.). Friend of the family; died in the camps

Fritz O. (Osthoff). A cousin of Liesel Pollatschek, from Aussig. A half-Jewish lawyer, he survived the war.

Fürth, Lene (Helene; Helen; Tante Lene). Mamina's daughter and Friedrich Pollatschek's sister, married to Eugen Fürth, mother of Peter. She was born April 24, 1893, deported to a work camp in Poland in 1942, and presumably died there or in an extermination camp.

Fürth, Peter. Son of Lene and Eugen Fürth. Survived the war in England, where he married Elsie Annie (Eky). He returned to Czechoslovakia after the war, left there in 1967, and died in France in 1988. Wife Eky, daughter Patricia, and son Stephan live in England.

***Generalgouvernement* (General Government).** An area in the interior of Poland, including Lublin and Warsaw, under a civil administration; established by Hitler in 1939

Goldmann, Hilde. Young woman friend of Mamina who attempted to reach Cuba but apparently failed. Her brother had immigrated to Cuba and was in contact with the Pollatscheks there. Her fate is unknown.

Grünberger, Willi. Son of Emma and Max; married to Gerda. Gerda, who retained her maiden name, Subak, and the couple's two sons fled to America during the war. Willi joined them after the war.

Grüner, Otto. Cousin of Eugen and was a family friend; died in the camps

Hanne, Hanka. Daughter of Juscha Goldmann, granddaughter of Emma and Max Grünberger; married an Englishman and immigrated to England

Hans (Hansl; Hansi). Son of Friedrich and Liesel Pollatschek, born August 20, 1929. Anglicized his name to John; the family changed their surname to Polt. He lives in California with his wife Beverley. Three children.

Harry (Lentner). Cousin of Eugen and widow of Friedrich Pollatschek's former tailor. Immigrated to Cuba, later to the United States

Heller, Fritz (Onkel Fritz). Mamina's youngest brother, born June 16, 1879. With his wife Leontine (Tine) and adopted daughter Clärly he immigrated to Switzerland in 1939 and lived there until his death in 1960. Tine died in 1963.

Heller, Robert. Son of Mamina's brother Eugen and his wife Luise. Deported to Theresienstadt (Terezín) and later to another camp but survived.

Henriette (Heller) Pollatschek (Mamina; Jettla). The writer of most of the letters in this book. Born in 1870 and married to Hermann Pollatschek in 1890; mother of Lene, Friedrich, and two other sons who died during World War I. She was deported to Terezín on July 13, 1942, and from there to Treblinka in Poland on October 19, 1942. She did not survive.

Herbert. Son of Mamina's brother Karl and his wife Ida. Married to Hilde. Both survived the war, and Herbert died in 1973. Their descendants live in Czechoslovakia.

Hilde. Wife of Herbert

***Hilfsverein (Hilfsverein der deutscher Juden;* Welfare Organization of German Jews).** An agency specializing in assistance for emigrants

Ilse (Krebs). A friend of Lene who lived in their building on Svehlová Street. Her husband and son got to safety in England, but she died in the camps.

J. Abbreviation for "Jewish"

Jettla. *See* Henriette

***Jüdisches Kultusgemeinde* (Jewish Community Center).** An organization that attempted to supply aid and news to would-be emigrants

Jüdisches Nachrichtenblatt (*Jewish Newslettery*). The only semi-reliable source of news that Czech Jews had access to after the German invasion.

Karl (Bischitzky). Son of Mamina's sister Olga and her husband Victor. Karl's wife, Karla (Karli), divorced him in 1940, partly to escape persecution. Their two children, Karel and Vera, survived the war; Karli died in Prague in the 1960s. Karel lives in southern France with his wife; Vera divides her time between Germany, Prague, and Israel. Karl died in the camps.

Karli (Bischitzky). Wife of Karl Bischitzky

Konrad. *See* Petschek, Franz

***Kroitzschgasse* (Kroitzsch Street).** The street in Aussig where the Pollatscheks and Mamina lived

Lederer, Josefine. Elisabeth (Liesel) Pollatschek's mother, born October 15, 1874. A Gentile, she survived the war in Czechoslovakia. After the war, she moved with her son Willi and his family to Germany, where she died in 1967. Also called Pepi.

Lene. *See* Fürth, Lene

Lentner, Harry. *See* Harry

Libitzky, Dr., and Mrs. Libitzky was an eye specialist from Aussig; his wife was a friend of Mamina's. He died before the war. His son survived the war in England. Mrs. Libitzky's fate is not known.

Liesel (Lederer; Pollatschek). Wife of Friedrich/Frederick Pollatschek

Lisa. Wife of Willi Lederer, Liesel Pollatschek's brother

Lolly. Husband of Daisy

M., Dr. (Dr. Josef Morák). A Czech lawyer engaged by Mamina

Madeleine (Schick). A cousin of Mamina. She worked as a maid, first for some other cousins, then for Franz Petschek's aunt and uncle, Erna and Johann Bloch. Died in the camps.

Mädi (Marianne Goldmann). Daughter of Juscha, granddaughter of Mamina's sister Emma and her husband Max Grünberger. Died in the camps.

Mahler, Eugen. Former law partner of Friedrich Pollatschek. Was in a "sanitarium" (probably a prison or concentration camp) for a time. His later fate is not known.

Mamina. *See* Henriette

Maňka (Maňka Ruž; Maňka Ružičká). A Czech friend of Mamina and Lene. Mamina's sponsor at her confirmation.

Max (Grünberger). Husband of Mamina's sister Emma. Died before the war.

Mimi (Bischitzky). Wife of Fritz Bischitzky. Ernst Skutsch's wife was also named Mimi.

Nestersitz. Small town in northern Bohemia, home of Lene Fürth and her family

Onkel Fritz. *See* Heller, Fritz

Otto. *See* Grüner, Otto

Paula. Sister of Otto Grüner; died in the camps

Pepi. *See* Lederer, Josefine

Peter. Son of Lene and Eugen Fürth. Went to France in 1938 or 1939; joined the Czech forces in France in October 1939. In June 1940, went to England and participated in the European invasion. Married Elsie Annie (Eky), who, with their daughter Patricia, joined him in Czechoslovakia after the war. Son, Stephan, born early 50s. Peter left Czechoslovakia in 1967. Died in France, 1988.

Petschek, Franz. Often referred to in the letters as "your friend and well-wisher," "F. C.," "F. K.," "Konrad," or "Franz Conrad." A second cousin of Friedrich's, head of the I. Petschek coal works in Aussig, and son of the employer of

Mamina's husband. With his wife Janina and their daughters, immigrated to Switzerland and later to the U.S. Helped many others emigrate. Died around 1960.

Pollatschek, Henriette. *See* Henriette

Protectorate. The Germans established the Protectorate of Bohemia and Moravia on March 15, 1939, following the notorious Munich Agreement, in which France and England ceded those sections of Czechoslovakia to Hitler. Slovakia became an independent state.

Putz. *See* Eugen

Reichsprotektor Reinhard Heydrich. "Protector" or ruler over the "Protectorate" of Bohemia and Moravia from 1941 until his assassination in 1942. Ordered all Czech Jews over sixty-five to be sent to concentration camp Theresienstadt.

Renate (Renatchen). Daughter of Friedrich and Liesel Pollatschek, born June 4, 1932. Changed her name to Harriet, and the family changed its name to Polt. Later changed name back to Renata. Married to Frederick G. Schmitt; lives in California.

St. Emmanus (Cloister of Emmanus). Prague church where Mamina and Tonscha were confirmed

St. Vitus Cathedral. Prague's cathedral, visible from all over the city

Schneider, Erich. *See* Erich

Šebek, Václav. A Czech who attempted to help Mamina and Lene during their last days in Prague. He hid some of the women's belongings by burying them in his garden, and returned them to Peter and Eky Fürth, Lene's son and daughter-in-law, after the war. He did not fare well under Communism after the war.

Skutsch, Ernst, Walter, and Mimi. Cousins of Mamina. *See* Ernst

Sophie (Sopherl). Mother of Eugen Fürth; lived in France. Her husband's name was Emil. They died natural deaths during the war.

Stein, Marta. Former governess in the Fürth household. A Gentile, she was married to a Jew. Helped Mamina and Lene during the war.

Steiner, Hanna. A leader in Zionist women's work, who for years helped Jews to emigrate. Died in the camps.

Sudeten German Party. A pro-Nazi political party in pre-war Czechoslovakia

Sudetenland. The northern part of Bohemia near the German border. The area, with its largely German-speaking population, was coveted by the Germans, who invaded it in 1938.

Tante Ella. *See* Ella

Theresienstadt. Czech concentration camp to which Mamina and Tonscha were "transported" in 1942

Tine. Wife of Mamina's youngest brother, Fritz (Onkel Fritz). They moved to Switzerland before the war and survived the war there.

Tonscha (Tante Tonscha). Mamina's sister Antonie, born January 10, 1876; wife of Adolf Bischitzky, mother of Fritz. Transported to Theresienstadt July 16,

1942, with transport number Ar93; then on October 22, 1942, to Treblinka with transport number Ex1698. She died in or en route to Treblinka.

Treblinka. Death camp in Poland where Mamina died

Vera. Daughter of Karl and Karli, granddaughter of Mamina's sister Olga and her husband Victor Bischitzky. She stayed with Mamina and Lene for a time in 1940 and now lives in Germany, Prague, and Israel.

Walter. Cousin of Ernst Skutsch; died in a camp

***Weinberge* (*Vinohradý* in Czech).** District in Prague, location of Mamina and Lene's apartment, August 1940–August 1941

Willi. Son of Josefine Lederer and brother of Liesel Pollatschek. A half-Jew, he survived the war, moved with his family to Germany after the war, and died in Munich in 1971. Married to Lisa and was father of Franz and Richard, all of whom currently live in Germany.

Bibliography

Adler, H[ans] G[ünther]. *Theresienstadt, 1941–1945: Das Antlitz einer Zwangsgemeinschaft* [Theresienstadt, 1941–1945: The face of a prison community], 2d ed. Tübingen: J. C. B. Mohr (Paul Siebeck), 1960.

———. *Die Verheimlichte Wahrheit: Theresienstädter Dokumente* [The concealed truth: Theresienstadt documents]. Tübingen: J. C. B. Mohr (Paul Siebeck), 1958.

Agar, Herbert. *The Saving Remnant: An Account of Jewish Survival.* New York: Viking Press, 1960.

American Council on Public Affairs. *Czechoslovakia Fights Back.* A document of the Czechoslovak Ministry of Public Affairs. Introduction by Jan Masaryk. Washington, D.C., 1943.

von Arent, Benno. *Ein Sudetendeutsches Tagebuch 13. August bis 19 Oktober 1938* [A Sudeten German diary, August 13 to October 19, 1938]. Berlin: W. Limpert, 1939.

Aufbau (New York), weekly, 1940–42.

Benes, Eduard. *Memoirs of Dr. Eduard Benes.* Boston: Houghton Mifflin Co., 1954.

———. *Nazi Barbarism in Czechoslovakia.* London: G. Allen & Unwin, 1940.

Benes, Vojta, and R. A. Ginsburg. *Ten Million Prisoners.* Chicago: Czech-American National Alliance, 1940.

Berger, Natalia, ed. *Where Cultures Meet: The Story of the Jews of Czechoslovakia.* Tel Aviv: Beth Hatefutsoth, Nahum Goldmann Museum of the Jewish Diaspora, 1990.

Bodensieck, Heinrich. "Das Dritte Reich und die Lage der Juden in der Tschecho-Slowakei nach München" [The Third Reich and the position of the Jews in Czechoslovakia after Munich]. *Vierteljahrshefte fur Zeitgeschichte* [Quarterly of contemporary history] 9 (1961).

Bradley, J. F. N. *Czechoslovakia: A Short History.* Edinburgh: University Press, 1971.

Brandes, Detlef. *Die Tschechen unter deutschem Protektorat* [The Czechs in the German Protectorate]. Vol. 1. Munich: R. Oldenbourg, 1969.

Council of Jewish Communities in the Czech Lands. *Terezín.* Prague, 1965.

The Czechoslovak Ministry of Foreign Affairs (Department of Information). *Four Fighting Years.* London: Hutchinson & Co., 1943.

Dagan, Avigdor, ed. *The Jews of Czechoslovakia: Historical Studies and Surveys.* 3 vols. Philadelphia: Jewish Publication Society of America, 1968–84.

———. *Two Years of German Oppression in Czechoslovakia.* London: Czechoslovak Ministry of Foreign Affairs, Dept. of Information, 1941.

Dawidowicz, Lucy S. *The War Against the Jews,* 1933–1945. Bantam Books Edition. New York: Holt, Rinehart and Winston, 1975.

Erdely, Eugene V. *Germany's First European Protectorate: The Fate of the Czechs and Slovaks.* London: Robert Hale, 1942.

——. *Prague Braves the Hangman.* London: Czechoslovak, 1942.

Feingold, Henry L. *The Politics of Rescue: The Roosevelt Administration and the Holocaust,* 1938–1945. New Brunswick: Rutgers University Press, 1970.

Friedman, Saul S. *No Haven for the Oppressed: United States Policy toward Jewish Refugees, 1938–1945.* Detroit: Wayne State University Press, 1973.

Goldhagen, Daniel Jonah. *Hitler's Willing Executioners: Ordinary Germans and the Holocaust.* New York: Alfred A. Knopf, 1996.

Grant Duff, S[hiela]. *Europe and the Czechs.* Harmondsworth, England: Penguin Books, 1938.

Grossmann, Kurt R. *Emigration: Geschichte der Hitler-Flüchtlinge, 1933–1945* [Emigration: The history of refugees from Hitler]. Frankfurt am Main: Europäische Verlagsanstalt, 1969.

Hilberg, Raul. *The Destruction of the European Jews.* Chicago: Quadrangle Books, 1961.

——. *Documents of Destruction: Germany and Jewry, 1933–1945.* Chicago: Quadrangle Books, 1971.

——. *Perpetrators Victims Bystanders: The Jewish Catastrophe 1933–1945.* New York: HarperCollins, 1992.

Iggers, Wilma Abeles. *The Jews of Bohemia and Moravia: A Historical Reader.* Detroit: Wayne State University Press, 1992.

Institute of Jewish Affairs. *Hitler's Ten-Year War on the Jews.* New York: Institute of Jewish Affairs of the American Jewish Congress and the World Jewish Congress, 1943.

Jacoby, Gerhard. *Racial State: The German Nationalities Policy in the Protectorate of Bohemia-Moravia.* New York: Institute of Jewish Affairs of the American Jewish Congress and the World Jewish Congress, 1944.

Janowsky, Oscar Isaiah. *People at Bay: The Jewish-Problem in East-Central Europe.* London: Victor Gollancz, 1938.

The Jewish Black Book Committee. *The Black Book: The Nazi Crime against the Jewish People.* New York: Duell, Sloan and Pearce, 1946.

Kennan, George F. *From Prague after Munich: Diplomatic Papers 1939–1940.* Princeton: Princeton University Press, 1968.

Korbel, Josef. *Twentieth Century Czechoslovakia: The Meanings of its History.* New York: Columbia University Press, 1977.

Král, Václav. *Lesson from History: Documents Concerning Nazi Policies for Germanization and Extermination in Czechoslovakia.* Prague: Orbis, 1961.

Lederer, Zdenek. *Ghetto Theresienstadt.* Translated by K. Weisskopf. London: E. Goldston, 1953.

"Letters from Berlin, 1942: From the Last Days of the Reichsvertretung." *Leo Baeck Yearbook.* Vol. 2. London: Published for the Leo Baeck Institute of Jews from Germany by Seeker & Warburg, 1957.

Lewy, Guenter. *The Catholic Church and Nazi Germany.* New York: McGraw Hill, 1964.

Luza, Radomír. *The Transfer of the Sudeten Germans: A Study of Czech-German Relations, 1933–1962*. New York: New York University Press, 1964.

Mackworth, Cecily. *Czechoslovakia Fights Back*. Europe Under the Nazis Series. London: Lindsay Drummond, 1942.

Mackworth, Cecily, and Jan Stransky. *Czechoslovakia*. Preface by Jan Masaryk. London: Macdonald & Co., 1943.

Mendelsohn, Ezra. *The Jews of East Central Europe Between the World Wars*. Bloomington: Indiana University Press, 1983.

Miroslav, J. M. J. *Ruthless Neighbor: A Czech Looks at Germany*. London: Blackie & Son, 1940.

Morse, Arthur D. *While Six Million Died: A Chronicle of American Apathy*. New York: Random House, 1968.

Moskowitz, Moses. "The Jewish Situation in the Protectorate of Bohemia-Moravia." *Jewish Social Studies* 4, no. 1 (January 1942).

Der Neue Tag [The new day] (Prague), daily, 1939–41.

New York Times, late city edition, daily, 1939–42.

Pilch, Judah. *The Jewish Catastrophe in Europe*. New York: American Association for Jewish Education, 1968.

Reitlinger, Gerald. *The Final Solution: The Attempt to Exterminate the Jews of Europe, 1939–1945*. London: Vallentine, Mitchell, 1953.

Schoenberner, Gerhard. *Der Gelbe Stern: Die Judenverfolgung in Europa, 1933 bis 1945* [The yellow star: The persecution of the Jews in Europe, 1933 to 1945]. Gütersloh: Bertelsmann Sachbuchverlag, 1968.

Shabtai, K. *As Sheep to the Slaughter? The Myth of Cowardice*. Foreword by Gideon Hausner. Bet Dagan, Israel: Keshev Press, 1962.

Tartakower, Arieh, and Kurt R. Grossmann. *The Jewish Refugee*. New York: Institute of Jewish Affairs of the American Jewish Congress and the World Jewish Congress, 1944.

Tenebaum, Joseph. *Race and Reich: The Story of an Epoch*. New York: Twayne Publishers, 1956.

Vrba, Rudolf, and Alan Bestic. *I Cannot Forgive*. New York: Grove Press, 1964.

Wechsberg, Joseph. *Visum für Amerika: Ein Buch für Auswanderer nach den Vereinigten Staaten und Kanada* [Visa for America: Book for immigrants to the United States and Canada]. Mährisch-Ostrau, Czechoslovakia: Verlag Julius Kittls Nachfolger, 1939.

Weisskopf, Kurt. *The Agony of Czechoslovakia, 1938–1968*. London: Elek Books, 1968.

White, Lyman Dromwell. *300,000 New Americans: The Epic of a Modern Immigrant-Aid Service*. New York: Harper & Brothers, 1957.

The Wiener Library. *Persecution and Resistance under the Nazis*. The Wiener Library, Catalogue Series No. 1. 2d ed. London: Vallentine, Mitchell, 1960.

Wiernik, Yankel. "A Year in Treblinka Horror Camp." Translated by Moshe Spiegel. In *Anthology of Holocaust Literature*. Edited by Jacob Glatstein, Israel Knox, and Samuel Margoshes. Philadelphia: Jewish Publication Society of America, 1969.

Wiskemann, Elizabeth. *Czechs & Germans: A Study of the Struggle in the Historic Provinces of Bohemia and Moravia.* 2d ed. London: Macmillan, and New York: St. Martin's Press, 1967.

Wlaschek, Rudolf M. *Juden in Böhmen: Beitrage zur Geschichte des europäischen Judentums im 19. und 20. Jahrhundert* [Jews in Bohemia: Contributions to the history of European Jewry in the 19th and 20th centuries]. Munich: R. Oldenbourg Verlag, 1990.

Wodak, Ernst. *Prag von Gestern und Vorgestern* [Prague yesterday and the day before]. Tel Aviv: Edition Olympia, 1948.

Wyman, David S. *Paper Walls: America and the Refugee Crisis, 1938–1941.* Amherst: University of Massachusetts Press, 1968.

Zilliacus, Konni ["Diplomaticus" Pseud.]. *The Czechs and their Minorities.* London: T. Butterworth, 1938.

Meine geliebten Kinder!

Gestern bekam ich von Mutter
des Hauses so anschaulich! ge
Euer Leben und Treiben vorste
Küchenzettel, der ja recht schmie
bis sein dass es kleine Suppe
und theuere Fische bekommt
sehr; das kann wohl nur an
liegen. Hier giebt es jetzt masse
schöne Erdbeeren und Kirschen
wenn auch noch nicht billig, es
theuerer geworden, besonders Wo
zum Wohnen gehört. Lene un
Plan, vorausgesetzt dass wir,
hier sesshaft bleiben werden.
unsere Wohnungen, bleiben abe
ich muss vorerst bissel Ruhe
nung wenigstens drei- Monate
oll. dann werde ich trachten